MAXIMISING LEARNING IN PHYSICAL EDUCATION

Maximising Learning in Physical Education identifies some key challenges in physical education that impact pupils' learning, looking at how they manifest over time and suggesting possible ways teachers can address them.

Each chapter features a real-life case study or a scenario to illustrate a specific challenge and identify some possible causes. It then draws on theory, research and evidence that might explain what is happening. This book highlights how teachers use theory and research evidence to help address the challenges and maximise pupil learning. The challenges include:

- reflection/reflective practice
- the process of learning
- progression and continuity in the curriculum
- assessment
- use of feedback
- motivation
- behaviour for learning
- learning in the physical, cognitive and affective domains
- inclusion, special education needs and disabilities
- trauma-informed pupils
- participation in physical activity outside lessons.

Many chapters are co-written by practising teachers and teacher educators and all include key takeaways and reflections, making this essential reading for all secondary physical education teachers.

Susan Capel is a Professor Emerita at Brunel University, London, where she was the Head of the School of Sport and Education.

Joanne Cliffe is a freelance researcher. Her background is in teaching secondary physical education and then higher education as an Associate Professor at the University of Birmingham.

Julia Lawrence is an Assistant Professor at Northumbria University, Secondary Lead Mentor for Scarborough Teaching Alliance and Subject Lead for Physical Education with Exchange Teacher Training.

MAXIMISING LEARNING IN PHYSICAL EDUCATION

A Practice to Theory Approach

Edited by Susan Capel, Joanne Cliffe and Julia Lawrence

LONDON AND NEW YORK

Designed cover image: Getty Images

First edition published 2026
by Routledge
4 Park Square, Milton Park, Abingdon, Oxon, OX14 4RN

and by Routledge
605 Third Avenue, New York, NY 10158

Routledge is an imprint of the Taylor & Francis Group, an informa business

© 2026 selection and editorial matter, Susan Capel, Joanne Cliffe and Julia Lawrence; individual chapters, the contributors

The right of Susan Capel, Joanne Cliffe and Julia Lawrence to be identified as the authors of the editorial material, and of the authors for their individual chapters, has been asserted in accordance with sections 77 and 78 of the Copyright, Designs and Patents Act 1988.

All rights reserved. No part of this book may be reprinted or reproduced or utilised in any form or by any electronic, mechanical, or other means, now known or hereafter invented, including photocopying and recording, or in any information storage or retrieval system, without permission in writing from the publishers.

Trademark notice: Product or corporate names may be trademarks or registered trademarks, and are used only for identification and explanation without intent to infringe.

British Library Cataloguing-in-Publication Data
A catalogue record for this book is available from the British Library

ISBN: 978-1-032-66295-4 (hbk)
ISBN: 978-1-032-66294-7 (pbk)
ISBN: 978-1-032-66297-8 (ebk)

DOI: 10.4324/9781032662978

Typeset in Interstate
by codeMantra

CONTENTS

List of Illustrations   vii
List of Biographies   ix

Introduction   1

Chapter 1   **Challenges related to reflective practice: helping teachers to reflect**   5
Paul McFlynn

Chapter 2   **Challenges related to pupil learning: helping pupils to learn effectively**   16
Julia Lawrence

Chapter 3   **Challenges related to progression and continuity in the curriculum: curriculum development to support pupil progress**   27
Susan Capel and Julia Lawrence

Chapter 4   **Challenges related to assessment: developing effective assessment in lessons**   42
Joanne Cliffe and Katie Potter

Chapter 5   **Challenges related to use of feedback: using feedback for effective learning in lessons**   61
Joanne Cliffe and Katie Potter

Chapter 6   **Challenges related to motivation: enhancing the motivational climate for year 10 girls**   73
Victoria Clements and Kevin Morgan

Chapter 7   **Challenges related to managing behaviour: using behaviour for learning in lessons**   84
Joanne Cliffe and Chris Ewing

Chapter 8   Challenges related to promoting learning in the physical domain: developing physical competence – curriculum, pedagogy and assessment   100
Richard Blair and Neve Blair

Chapter 9   Challenges related to promoting learning in the cognitive domain: developing pupils' declarative knowledge and thinking   117
Julia Lawrence

Chapter 10 Challenges related to promoting learning in the affective domain: meeting the emotional needs of pupils   130
Kate Bancroft and George Kinkead

Chapter 11 Challenges related to inclusion, special educational needs and disabilities: supporting hard-of-hearing pupils in a mainstream specifically resourced provision in their physical education lessons   141
Rebecca Foster and Alice Smyth

Chapter 12 Challenges related to enacting trauma-informed practice: supporting trauma-affected pupils   153
Oliver Hooper, Vincent Coleman, Rachel Sandford, Thomas Quarmby and Shirley Gray

Chapter 13 Challenges related to pupil participation in physical activity and sport outside lessons: what can be done in physical education that might increase young people's participation in physical activity and sport beyond school   164
Ken Green, Daragh O'Hare, Suzy Twist and Hannah Vecchione

Chapter 14 Challenges related to my own context: identifying and addressing challenges in my own teaching   179
Julia Lawrence

Author Index   191
Subject Index   197

ILLUSTRATIONS

Figures

4.1	Case study part 1 - example of a component (the head) in an ineffective assessment policy for key stage 3 physical education with annotations (Figure 4.1 was devised by the case study school and is reproduced here with permission)	44
4.2	Lesson criterion shared with the class (based on English Schools Gymnastics, 2019-2020)	45
4.3	Example of assessment for a trampolining front-drop lesson (Figure 4.3 was devised by the case study school and is reproduced here with permission)	51
5.1	Badminton backhand serve 'figure of 8' warm-up relays (reproduced with permission from the case study school)	62
7.1	Relationships in the behaviour for learning model (taken from Garner, 2019). Source: After Tod and Powell (2004)	94

Tables

3.1	A simple guide to progression in the NCPE in England (adapted from AfPE, 2018)	33
3.2	Movement forms	34
4.1	Year 7 gymnastics unit of work assessment (based on English Schools Gymnastics, 2019-2020) (Figure 4.4 was devised by the chapter authors and the case study school and is reproduced here with permission)	54
6.1	School eFSM data for 2022-2023	74
6.2	TARGET structures (Ames, 1993; Morgan, 2017)	76
9.1	Types of knowledge	118
9.2	Activating hard thinking in physical education	122
11.1	Interventions that might be considered when teaching HoH pupils	145
14.1	Challenges identified by staff	183

BIOGRAPHIES

Kate Bancroft is a research fellow within the Social Sciences division at the University of Oxford. Prior to this, she was a researcher in the Faculty of Social Sciences and Public Policy at King's College London, where she also served as deputy director of the PhD Applied Public Policy programme. Kate was a secondary school physical education teacher in Leeds for seven years. Her research interests centre on the intersections of gender and sport, with a particular emphasis on gender equality, which has been a driving force throughout her career.

Neve Blair is in year 13. She is studying A-level History, Psychology and Philosophy. She is a competitive rower in a Skiff, single scull, double and coxed quad; she has represented her region in a coxed quad at the National Championships 2023. Neve also rows Cornish Pilot Gigs; she was a member of the 2023 Girls National Championship winning crew and represented her county in 2022 and 2023 at the county championships.

Richard Blair is a senior lecturer in Physical Education and Sports Coaching at the University of Gloucestershire. His teaching is focussed on policy and pedagogy in education, physical education and youth sport. He has two main areas of research and scholarly interest, how teachers, coaches and other adults understand the contexts of physical education, youth sports and physical activity and their role within each of the different settings, and children's rights in physical education and youth sport. Richard is an active volunteer coach who also spends some of his spare time helping to launch and retrieve wooden rowing boats.

Susan Capel is a Professor Emerita at Brunel University London, where she was a Professor and Head of the School of Sport and Education. Susan has worked in physical education for over 50 years. After qualifying as a teacher, she taught in Cardiff and Hong Kong. She then completed her PhD at the University of Oregon. On returning to the UK, Susan took a post at Bedford College of Higher Education (now the University of Bedfordshire), where she was in charge of the physical education part of the BEd degree and then led the PGCE course. She then became director of the Academic Standards Unit at Canterbury Christ Church University College (now University), before moving to Brunel University London. Susan's research and writing has focused largely on learning to teach physical education. She has edited/co-edited several books on learning to teach, most of which are continuing to be published in new editions, as well as some designed for newly qualified teachers as well as more experienced teachers.

Victoria Clements is an experienced educator with a passion for teaching and learning who has taught physical education for 20+ years in Wales. Having trained at the University of Wales Institute Cardiff, first in Sport and Physical Education, and later completing a PGCE in Secondary Physical Education, she has a wealth of experience in the sector. As a former Head of Department, she is experienced in leadership of the design and implementation of curriculums at key stages 3 and 4. More recently, as a deputy head of faculty, the focus has shifted towards teaching and learning and the implementation of evidence-based teaching practice across departments. As a teacher of health and well-being, and with a research interest in physical literacy and pedagogical approaches, she actively looks to collaborate with a wide range of stakeholders to help inform and shape policy.

Joanne Cliffe is a freelance researcher. Her background is in physical education. She taught in secondary schools before moving to higher education, where she was an Associate Professor at the University of Birmingham. She led the Physical Education Post Graduate Diploma in Education (QTS) and the Master's in Teaching Studies. She also supervised to completion doctoral students in education and leadership. Joanne is a Principal Fellow of the Higher Education Academy. She holds numerous appointments on educational committees both nationally and internationally. Joanne's research interests cover the areas of physical education, school leadership, emotions, emotional labour and emotional intelligence, where she has widely published and presented. She is co-author of *Primary PE: Unlocking the Potential* and has co-edited physical education subject books in the Learning to Teach series, namely *Learning to Teach Physical Education in the Secondary School* and *A Practical Guide to Teaching Physical Education in the Secondary School*.

Vincent Coleman is a PhD candidate in the Moray House School of Education and Sport, University of Edinburgh. Currently, his research focuses on trauma-aware pedagogies in physical education and how teachers learn about and respond to trauma. Before moving into academia, Vincent taught physical education for six years in secondary schools in Scotland and abroad.

Chris Ewing is currently Assistant Headteacher for Behaviour and Attendance at Ridgewood High School in Stourbridge, West Midlands. Having graduated from Staffordshire University with a BA (Hons) in Sport and Recreation Studies, Chris completed a PGCE in Physical Education at Loughborough University. Chris has over 25 years' experience teaching physical education, including roles as Head of Physical Education and Faculty Leader for Performance Studies. In addition, Chris was a contributor and mentor to the PGDipEd (QTS) course at the University of Birmingham.

Rebecca Foster MBE is a Principal Lecturer of Adapted Sport at the University of Worcester. Rebecca advises trainee physical education teachers and sports coaches how to become aware of disability as they develop their teaching/coaching philosophy. Rebecca's research focus is based around D/deaf sport and inclusive, high-quality physical education. Rebecca has co-edited a book on how to better include young people with disabilities in physical education titled *Physical Education for Young People with Disabilities*.

Shirley Gray is a Senior Lecturer in Physical Education at the University of Edinburgh. Her research explores how teachers understand and enact curriculum policy, and how they might be supported in their learning to provide their pupils with positive and socially just learning experiences in physical education. More specifically, her research focuses on issues relating to health and well-being, social and emotional learning, gender, digital health, pupil motivation and the professional learning of teachers. Shirley has published and edited in peer-reviewed journals and books broadly in the areas of physical education curriculum, pedagogy and professional learning.

Ken Green is Emeritus Professor of Sociology of Physical Education and Youth Sport at the University of Chester as well as a Visiting Professor at Inland University of Applied Sciences, Norway. He is editor-in-chief of the *European Physical Education Review*, and his books include *Understanding Physical Education* (2008), *Key Themes in Youth Sport* (2010), *The Routledge Handbook of Youth Sport* (2016) (co-edited with Andy Smith), and *Sport in Scandinavia and the Nordic Countries* (2019) (co-edited with Thorsteinn Sigurjónsson & Eivind Skille). His main research interests revolve around physical education and youth sport.

Oliver Hooper is a Senior Lecturer in Physical Education and Youth Sport in the School of Sport, Exercise and Health Sciences at Loughborough University. Oliver's research explores young people's experiences within physical education and youth sport contexts, with a particular focus on the experiences of marginalised youth. Within his research, Oliver utilises participatory methods to facilitate youth voice and to promote young people's meaningful involvement in research. Oliver has published various peer-reviewed research papers and books, including *Critical Pedagogies in Physical Education, Physical Activity and Health* and *Research with Children and Young People in Physical Education and Youth Sport*.

George Kinkead is a doctoral researcher at the Policy Institute, King's College London, exploring how social networks in educational institutions shape social capital. His research applies evidence-based approaches from education, psychology and behavioural science to improve educational systems. He studied politics, philosophy and economics at the University of Manchester before training as a teacher with Teach First. He later worked as the Head of Department and Deputy Head of Sixth Form in London and the Southwest. George holds an MSc in Education and Leadership from the University of Bristol and an MRes in Sustainable Futures from the University of Bath. He also works part-time as a parliamentary researcher in the House of Lords.

Julia Lawrence is an Assistant Professor at Northumbria University, secondary lead mentor for Scarborough Teaching Alliance, and subject lead for physical education with Exchange Teacher Training. She has over 20 years' experience in teacher education, focusing on primary and secondary physical education and mentoring. Julia is co-editor of *Learning to Teach in the Secondary School*, *Learning to Teach Physical Education in the Secondary School* and *A Practical Guide to Teaching Physical Education* and is Series Editor for *Mentoring in Secondary Schools*.

Paul McFlynn is a Senior Lecturer in Education and course director for the PGCE in Physical Education at Ulster University. He is also the postgraduate research tutor for PhD students in the School of Education. Paul's research to date has concentrated on the role of critical reflection in initial teacher education and on the role of mentoring in initial teacher education. His other main research interests lie in the areas of special educational needs and social justice.

Kevin Morgan trained as a physical education teacher at South Glamorgan Institute of Higher Education from 1984 to 1987 and began his career teaching in secondary schools. In 1993, he moved into higher education as a teacher trainer at De Montfort University (DMU), Bedford, and in 2000, he joined Cardiff Metropolitan University (formerly, UWIC) as a Senior Lecturer in Sport and Physical Education. From 2006 to 2016, he was programme leader for the MSc Sport Coaching and Pedagogy programme at Cardiff Met. He was then appointed programme director for the newly developed Taught Doctorate from 2016 until his retirement as a full-time academic in January 2024. His research interests are in pedagogy and physical literacy, with a particular emphasis on motivational climate and teaching and learning methods. Kevin gained an MPhil in 2000 at DMU and a PhD from UWIC in 2006, focusing on the teaching approaches that promote an effective motivational climate in physical education lessons. In 2023, he became Professor of Sport Pedagogy at Cardiff Met and is currently Emeritus Professor.

Daragh O'Hare is currently the Head of Physical Education at Neston High School, Cheshire, UK. Since graduating from the University of Chester in 2006 with a BSc (Hons) in Sport and Exercise Sciences, she has held a number of posts of responsibility at two secondary schools, including Head of Year 11 and Head of House as well as wider school roles such as gifted and talented coordinator and tutor for the Aim Higher programme.

Katie Potter is the Head of Physical Education at new school in Birmingham. Moving into her eighth year of teaching, Katie graduated from the University of Worcester in 2016 and later earned a PGDipEd (QTS) in Physical Education, followed by a Master's degree in Teaching Studies from the University of Birmingham. At Christ Church Secondary Academy, she has had the unique opportunity to devise and develop the curriculum for physical education. Katie coordinates 'Learning Outside the Classroom' and also leads the Duke of Edinburgh Award programme. Passionate about teaching and learning, she has completed her NPQML in leading teaching. Additionally, Katie mentors physical education students in undergraduate and PGCE programmes and has mentored early career teachers (ECTs) in physical education.

Thomas Quarmby is a Reader in Physical Education and Sport Pedagogy in the Carnegie School of Sport at Leeds Beckett University. His research broadly explores the role and value of physical education, physical activity and sport for children and young people from socially vulnerable backgrounds – particularly care-experienced youth. In addition, Thomas has published numerous peer-reviewed research papers and book chapters on trauma-aware pedagogies for physical education and sport contexts.

Rachel Sandford is a Reader in Physical Education, Youth and Social Justice in the School of Sport, Exercise and Health Sciences at Loughborough University. She has over 20 years' experience of undertaking research on young people's engagements with/development through physical education, physical activity and youth sport. More specifically, her research has centred on youth development, embodied identity, values-based education, trauma-informed approaches and the sport/physical activity experiences of marginalised youth. Rachel has published widely in academic journals on these topics and has authored various book chapters and edited books, including *Research with Children and Young People in Physical Education and Youth Sport*.

Alice Smyth gained a BA (Hons) degree at Leeds Beckett University. She has been teaching for 15 years with roles including Director of Sport and Director Learning. She is Trust Wide Subject Lead for the David Ross Education Trust. This role involves overseeing the intent, implementation and impact of a trust wide physical education curriculum. She still teaches in a secondary academy delivering core, GCSE, A-level physical education and BTEC sport. She was designated Specialist Leader for Education in 2019. Alice is motivated to raise aspirations and improve well-being among young people, enabling achievement at school and equipping pupils with the tools needed to live healthy and active lives.

Suzy Twist is joint programme leader for the BSc in Physical Education and Sports Coaching at the University of Chester. She has a BSc (Hons) and PGCE from Leeds Metropolitan University and an MRes in Physical Education. Suzy taught for 20 years in a range of secondary schools as Head of Department, Head of Girls' PE and School Sport Coordinator. In addition, Suzy has taught in primary schools, acting as physical education mentor to generalist teachers. Her current research interests revolve around the transition from primary to secondary school physical education.

Hannah Vecchione has taught for over 30 years across five key stages in mainstream and special schools across the city of Manchester. In addition, she has worked as both school sport coordinator and partnership development manager in the Wythenshawe and South Manchester School Sport Partnership as well as strategic director of professional learning. Hannah has been awarded Advanced Skills Teacher and Lead Practitioner Status for her work at the nationally recognised St John's RC Primary School in Manchester. Under her guidance, the school has been awarded the School Games Gold Mark seven times and the new Platinum award, as well as the Youth Sport Trust's Quality Gold Mark award twice. In addition, Hannah has served as a member of the national Physical Education Expert Subject Advisory Group, Greater Manchester's Physical Education Strategy Group, Manchester's PE School Sport and Physical Activity Strategy Group and the North Western Counties Physical Education Association.

Introduction

The core mission of education is to ensure that all pupils learn. It therefore follows that the core mission of physical education is to ensure that all pupils learn in the subject. Thus, the responsibility of physical education teachers is to facilitate the learning of each and every pupil. This sounds both obvious and easy, but it is far from it.

Although there are basic teaching skills and underpinning theory, research and evidence which inform teaching, there is no one right way to teach, no one specific set of skills, techniques and procedures that teachers must master and apply mechanically and no one set of learning activities, teaching strategies and approaches they must use in order to provide the right conditions to facilitate pupil learning. Teaching is a complex activity. Classes, groups and individual pupils are different and unique and, in order to facilitate learning, each day brings a new challenge for teachers in relation to each class, group and individual pupil. Further, as we know, teachers are also different and unique. They have different personalities and characteristics and hence develop their own unique teaching style. Thus, in order to teach effectively to facilitate learning, teachers need to blend the art (or craft) and science of teaching in ways which they feel is appropriate for a particular class, group and/or individual pupil. To achieve this, they must use their own professional judgement, to take account of the needs and abilities of a class as a whole, groups of pupils and individual pupils to identify underpinning theory, research and evidence in order to decide the content, which learning activity(ies), teaching strategies and approach(es) to use with a specific class, groups of pupils and individual pupils at a specific moment in time in a specific context.

Although many teachers blend the art and science of teaching effectively for many aspects of teaching, there may be one or more aspects which they recognise need further work in order to effectively facilitate learning. For example, assessment of learning data may be inaccurate as pupils are not always assessed in relation to what they have been taught; teachers may not engage in meaningful feedback so pupils are not given the opportunity to correct or improve their practice or the extra-curricular activities programme does not provide opportunities for all pupils to participate outside curricular physical education lessons. Where the art and science of teaching are not blended effectively and/or one or more aspects of teaching are not utilised effectively, the learning of a class, group or individual pupils is going to be sub-optimal. For example, pupils may not be fully motivated or their behaviour is such that they are not effectively engaged in learning.

DOI: 10.4324/9781032662978-1

Thus, in order to maximise learning opportunities for all pupils, teaching must not become routine. Rather, it is important to reflect critically on an ongoing basis, on the progress of a class, group and individual pupils and what factors are likely to be impacting their learning. Theory, research and evidence, along with professional judgement, then need to be used to adjust teaching to facilitate pupils' learning. Indeed, in education generally and physical education specifically, there is much talk about evidence-based practice and/or about applying theory, research and evidence to practice. However, in our experience, this is not always achieved effectively to facilitate learning. For example, many teacher education courses claim to be research-informed, as student teachers carry out research for their assignments. However, student teachers do not always apply this research in their teaching, or a teacher may consider that they are up to date with research on assessment for learning, but they do not consider the research to be sufficiently in depth to change their practice to promote pupil learning.

Although there is a considerable body of literature on much of the theory, research and evidence underpinning learning in physical education, not all of the literature applies the theory, research and evidence to practice. Further, even where applied to practice, the context in which it is applied may be different to the context in which an individual teacher is engaged (for example, the type and location of the school, the age of pupils, the curriculum, etc.). As a result, teachers may find it difficult to apply theory, research and evidence to their own practice or may have trouble transferring theory, research and evidence from a general context to their own specific context. This may be exacerbated by a number of factors; for example, early in their career, teachers may focus on the science of teaching, that is, they may focus on basic teaching skills against which they are likely to be 'judged' with regard to qualifying as a teacher or passing an induction period. Indeed, they may copy what a mentor or other teacher does without thinking about it. One reason for this is that they may not have enough experience and/or confidence to apply theory, research and evidence to their developing practice. Later in their career, a teacher may be teaching as they have always taught without thinking too much about its effectiveness in facilitating pupil learning. The pupils are busy in lessons, and if the teacher cannot see that they could do more to facilitate pupil learning, they may not prioritise the application of theory, research and evidence to their practice.

As a result, in our experience, theory, research and evidence is not used effectively to underpin practice by all teachers in all situations. Even where teachers attempt to apply theory, research and evidence to their practice – despite their best efforts, teaching does not always go according to plan and sometimes a class, group and individual pupils do not learn (either they do not learn at all or they learn less than anticipated) in a lesson or over a period of time.

The aim of this book is to support teachers to use theory, research and evidence to support teaching to facilitate pupil learning.

About this book

To achieve this, this book highlights some issues which pose challenges for teachers and which do not maximise the learning for all pupils in physical education. It then identifies relevant theory, research and evidence to help address each of the issues/challenges before considering how this was (or can be) applied in practice.

This book contains 14 chapters, 13 of which cover a different issue/challenge which we identify as fairly common in physical education. These cover an issue/challenge for an individual teacher to address an issue/challenge for a department to consider. The issues/challenges are: reflection/reflective practice; the process of learning; progression and continuity in the curriculum; assessment; use of feedback; motivation; behaviour for learning; learning in the physical, cognitive and affective domains; inclusion, special education needs and disabilities; trauma-informed pupils; and participation in physical activity outside lessons.

In order to achieve our aim of teachers being able to apply theory, research and/or evidence to their own practice to facilitate pupil learning, each chapter presents a fairly common issue/challenge which is likely to be familiar to many physical educators, either in:

a) a case study of actual practice in one school or
b) a scenario which comprises a composite of practice in a number of schools identified by the authors of the chapter.

Each chapter then identifies some theory, research and evidence which could be used to help address the issue/challenge to adapt teaching to facilitate pupils' learning. Finally, the chapter looks at how some of the theory, research and evidence was, or can be, used in practice to address the issue/challenge.

a) for a case study, this looks at what the teacher and/or the department as a whole did in response to the issue/challenge and the impact this had on pupil learning or
b) for a scenario, this looks at what action a teacher and/or a department could take to address the issue/challenge in order to facilitate pupil learning.

Thus, unlike many other publications which focus on theory, research and evidence and apply that to practice, in this book, we start by highlighting an aspect of practice and/or situation which is likely to be recognisable by many physical education teachers in many schools as impacting on pupil learning and then consider and apply theory, research and/or evidence to address that specific aspect of practice or that situation.

The last (14th) chapter is designed to support teachers by providing a structure which they might find useful in addressing an issue/challenge in their own context.

About you

We recognise that you, as readers, have different amounts and types of experience, different beliefs and values about physical education and are working in different contexts. For example, you may be in the early stages of your teaching career, trying to link your practice in different schools to the theory, research and/or evidence you have been learning in your initial teacher education programme. You might be an experienced teacher who identifies an issue/challenge which needs to be addressed in order to better facilitate pupils' learning. This issue/challenge may be in your lessons, in the physical education department or across the school. You might be a mentor or teacher educator who is supporting a beginning teacher to develop their practice, and you need to work with them to enable them to consider carefully how they are planning to meet the needs of all pupils. You might be a researcher either focusing on one or more of the issues/challenges in the book or trying to apply the research to practice.

We also recognise that in whatever context you are working, you are busy. There are many things which command your attention on a day-to-day basis. You therefore have to juggle myriad things. However, in our view, what can be more important than facilitating the learning of all pupils you teach? We hope that the content and approach taken in this book are relevant to whatever context you are working in. Although you may be able to use the examples for specific issues/challenges in your own context, we also hope that the book inspires you to look at other ways in which you can apply theory, research and evidence to address issues/challenges in your own context. We also hope that the book inspires you to critically reflect on other aspects of teaching to better facilitate pupil learning.

You, as readers can, of course, use the book as you see fit; there is no one best way for the book to be used. The book is designed to dip in and out rather than read it from cover to cover. However, as you read relevant chapter(s), we encourage you to reflect on, constructively critique and actively engage with the material in the book to consider its relevance in the context in which you work and, most importantly, how it can be used to facilitate the learning of each and every pupil in physical education in schools.

About the authors

The authors hail from a range of backgrounds. Many chapters have more than one author, although some chapters have a single author. Most co-authored chapters include a school-based person and a person working in teacher education, although the authors of a couple of co-authored chapters both work in higher education. Most school-based contributors are teachers; however, one is a pupil. In some single-authored chapters, the author has worked with a particular teacher and/or department to develop the case study which the author has then written up. In other co- or single-authored chapters, the author(s) have drawn on information about the issue/challenge gathered from a range of schools from which they have developed a scenario. Together, we hope the variety of authors and their wide experience provide information on a range of issues/challenges which are common in physical education in many schools.

And finally

We hope you find this book useful in exploring key issues and challenges, and in considering how the learning of each and every pupil in physical education can be effectively facilitated within your own context.

Susan Capel
Joanne Cliffe
Julia Lawrence
July 2025

Chapter 1 Challenges related to reflective practice
Helping teachers to reflect
Paul McFlynn

Introduction

This chapter focuses on how one physical education department in a Northern Ireland co-educational post-primary school faced difficulties in ensuring all pupils were appropriately challenged during physical education lessons. The prioritisation of extra-curricular sport over physical education curriculum experiences was resulting in learning experiences that were sport-orientated as opposed to learning-orientated. In addition, and what eventually became the catalyst for change, was the change in pupil intake, particularly in relation to the increasing intake of pupils with special educational needs (SENs). When pupil numbers began to fall, the school had to be proactive in keeping enrolments at an acceptable level. The school began to promote itself as a school that could cater for a wide range of SENs, and as a result, enrolment of pupils with SENs began to increase. The head of department (HOD) became increasingly aware of the challenges that this was presenting in physical education and, by their own admission, should have addressed the issue earlier. The lead author began working with the HOD and teachers in the department via the implementation of reflective practice approaches. The aim was for the physical education teachers individually, and as a department, to engage with reflective practice in relation to both their current provision and future planning for and implementation of physical education for all pupils (including pupils with SENs), including in relation to curriculum provision, pedagogical approaches and utilisation of classroom assistants.

Case study (part 1)

This case study focuses on a co-educational secondary school in Northern Ireland. Traditionally, the school placed major emphasis on extra-curricular sport, particularly in Gaelic football, hurling, camogie and soccer. As a result, physical education lessons tended to focus on these invasion games, meaning that other statutory areas, such as gymnastics, athletics and swimming, were often neglected. Pupil intake was high, with the school generally over-subscribed. However, from 2008 onwards, pupil enrolments began to fall, and in an attempt to ensure the school was sustainable, the school focused on ways that it could increase pupil numbers. One such way was their focus on admitting pupils with SENs. The school began to specialise in SEN provision, and as the years progressed, the number of pupils with SENs increased; SEN intake now stands at 56%. This became the catalyst for traditional team-based sports to become less of a priority in physical education lessons.

The increasing numbers of pupils with SENs in physical education lessons meant that physical education teachers were encountering many challenges. Unlike other subjects within the school, physical education classes were not streamed in relation to ability levels, so the range of ability within classes was extremely wide. Continuing with established practices and routines resulted in many unsatisfactory experiences for both teachers and pupils. It was clear that significant change was required and that the situation had been allowed to run for too long. The admission by teachers that there was a problem and that change was required, particularly in relation to pedagogical practices across the department, was significant, but how could the teachers individually, and as a department, go about enacting meaningful and sustainable change? Providing time and space for teachers, individually and as a department, to begin reflecting on their practice was a critical component. Engagement with pupils and parents would also be needed in order to attain feedback on current physical education experiences and learning of all pupils. The feedback, in conjunction with teacher reflections, would then allow the department to audit their current provision and create a curriculum map that could potentially cater for the needs of all pupils. In order to make changes, subject-specific continued professional development (CPD) was needed, along with investment in equipment and resources. The following section considers how the issue might be addressed.

Possible ways of addressing the issue

There are a number of ways that this issue can be addressed, and this section outlines such possibilities. Identification and admission of the problem by physical education teachers individually and as a department is important, but identifying effective solutions is needed in order to create teacher buy-in. The first and most important aspect to be considered is getting teachers to engage with meaningful reflective practice. If teachers can begin to reflect on their practice and identify areas for improvement, then these insights can become the starting point for improvement of their pedagogical practices and thus improve pupil learning. Seeking feedback from pupils and their parents also helps identify issues for improvement, and using this information in conjunction with teacher reflections will help identify pedagogical issues and thus areas that require CPD. Reflections, pupil and parental feedback and identification of CPD requirements will undoubtedly have implications for curriculum planning, and a critical component of this will be how teachers cater for the diverse range of needs via appropriate inclusive design principles. Considering the specific context that teachers find themselves in with the high number of pupils with SENs, many of whom have a classroom assistant, gathering feedback from classroom assistants and looking at ways of utilising them more effectively in lessons is an issue that also requires attention.

Reflective practice

Providing the time and space to engage with reflective practice should be the first priority for these teachers. They may be reluctant to engage with such practices (Hobbs, 2007), so providing a range of approaches might be the best option, so that teachers do not think that there is only one way to reflect (Shoffner, 2008). Starting off with individual teacher reflection, the completion of a post-lesson reflection template may be an option, as this will allow teachers to respond to particular questions such as *what went well in this lesson and why?, what did not go well in this lesson and why?, if you were teaching this lesson again, what aspects would you change and why?* Alternatively, teachers could engage with reflections in an unstructured way via the use of journal writing.

Central to reflective practice though is getting individual teachers to utilise their reflections and put the learning into practice, something which can be difficult. Teachers could engage with the process of peer review as a means of developing/facilitating their reflective practice. This would involve a teacher being observed by other teachers in the department and engaging in post-lesson feedback discussions. Pairing teachers up would mean that each teacher would experience the roles of both reviewer and reviewee. Lamb, Lane and Aldous (2012) found that peer review created a safe, relaxed, equal and pedagogic space to reflect without the fear of being judged. Convincing teachers to engage with peer review may be difficult, as teachers may fear being judged and hence it may take some time to trust colleagues.

Finlay (2008) highlighted the importance of providing adequate support for individual teachers when they begin to engage with reflection and the need for them to feel safe and have support from others considered to be 'effective reflectors'. She argued that teachers must also have the opportunity to experiment with a wide range of reflective strategies in a variety of contexts, such as "formal, informal, written, verbal" (p.17). As a result of engaging in a wide variety of reflective forms, individual teachers can begin to understand what approaches suit them in particular situations and what methods suit specific contexts. Therefore, if the teachers in the department are going to engage with reflective practice, they must explore various approaches so that they can decide which approach suits them best.

Pupil voice

The role of pupil voice in helping teachers to reflect on, shape and inform their practice has gained increasing importance, particularly within the last decade (Morgan, 2011). Warwick *et al.* (2019) noted that the catalyst for this change was the United Nations Convention on the Rights of the Child (1989), which asserts that young people should have some say on the issues that impact their lives, including "the right to express a view and the right to have the view given due weight" (Lundy, 2007, p.931). Coates and Vickerman (2010) noted that very little importance is given to hearing the views of pupils with SENs, particularly in relation to their perceptions and experiences of physical education. This view is supported by Allen *et al.* (2024), who noted that the voices of pupils with SENs are often trivialised, reformulated or, in most cases, not investigated at all. In the case study school, physical education teachers could engage with all pupils in order to gain access to their views in relation to their physical education experiences and learning and use the feedback to inform evaluations and reflections. Utilising this feedback in conjunction with teacher reflections is important. Flutter and Rudduck (2005, p.536) noted, however, that "voices are nothing without hearers". Therefore, there is an onus on teachers to take these views seriously and analyse the feedback to identify the key issues that can be used to help shape and amend curriculum plans. Allowing pupils to express their views via a survey, along with possible follow-up focus group interviews, would be a logical approach.

Parental engagement

Accessing the views of parents/guardians in relation to their child's physical education experiences and learning would also be useful as children are likely to have shared their views on physical education with their parents/guardians. The school could engage with parents/guardians via a survey that contains open questions that permit parents/guardians to elaborate and explain ratings. Considering the high number of pupils with SENs in the school, gaining the views of parents/guardians of pupils with SENs would be important. Paseka and Schwab (2020) stated that the parents'/guardians' views are necessary in order to gain an external perspective on inclusive practice. Access to this information in conjunction with teacher reflections and pupil voice data would enable the physical education department to reflect and make fully informed decisions regarding curriculum planning and, subsequently, pedagogical decisions.

Curriculum review/audit

Reflecting upon current curriculum provision is an aspect that the department must consider. Whilst it may be expected that teachers will do this during their reflections on lessons taught and lessons observed, an explicit reflection on this by all teachers within the department, where curriculum content and pedagogical approaches are examined, will permit a thorough review and subsequent holistic reflection. Utilising ongoing teacher reflections, pupil and parental/guardian feedback would help this process and allow the department to design a curriculum that meets the needs and expectations of all pupils, whilst at the same time satisfying statutory curricular demands. It is important to note that reviewing the curriculum in terms of activity provision must also involve a review of pedagogical approaches. Making use of unit plan reviews and teacher reflections on what worked and what did not work is important in helping to refine/amend curriculum provision, which can lead to enhanced pupil learning experiences (Zhang and Zhang, 2023). It is possible that such a review will identify the curriculum/activity areas that teachers may need CPD.

Utilising classroom assistants

Engaging with classroom assistants, particularly for pupils who have a statement of SENs, would seem to be an obvious strategy. Regular communication with the special educational needs coordinator (SENCO) and familiarisation with pupils' personal learning plans (PLPs) to develop an understanding of the specific needs of all pupils with SENs would allow teachers to make fully informed planning decisions. Central to aiding this planning will be developing a good relationship with relevant classroom assistants as they are the individuals who work most closely with the pupil and often know their needs best (Coates and Vickerman, 2010). Using the unique insights that classroom assistants have in terms of how particular pupils react/behave in certain situations, combined with the subject expertise of the physical education teacher and the use of CPD courses for both teachers and classroom assistants, has the potential to create a much more cohesive and inclusive physical education setting (Maher and Macbeth, 2013). Whilst physical education is a unique learning environment, it is often neglected in much of the research that analyses educational inclusion. Maher (2016) noted the important role that SENCOs and classroom assistants have to play in relation to inclusion in schools. He noted that SENCOs hold key decision-making positions within the organisational and operational structure of schools, which means that "they can influence, to degrees, the extent to which school policy and pedagogical practice is inclusive" (Maher, 2016, p.150). Whilst they do not hold key decision-making decisions within schools, classroom assistants can play an active role in shaping cultural norms and values related to inclusive physical education. Therefore, it is clear that active engagement with the SENCOs and classroom assistants is crucial if physical education lessons are to be made more inclusive.

Continued professional development

Access to and engagement with relevant CPD specific to the issues, along with reflection on these, would help teachers, individually and as a department, to address the issues. Continuing with established practices is unlikely to create the learning environment required to match the needs of all pupils in lessons. Engagement with Disability Sport Northern Ireland (DSNI) could be part of this CPD, considering their pedagogical expertise in relation to adapting content to suit the needs of individual participants. Accessing a DSNI workshop would be beneficial in relation to enhancing teachers' knowledge and understanding. It would be important that all classroom assistants also avail themselves of relevant CPD so that their involvement in assisting pupil learning can be maximised. This view is supported by Maher (2016, p.275), who stated that classroom assistants "who are expected to support pupils with SEN in physical education should be trained to do so". Maher (2016) found that the majority of classroom assistants in his study were "not adequately equipped with the knowledge, skill or experience to include pupils with SEN in PE" (p.275).

Differentiation

In order to include all pupils in learning, differentiating content to meet the learning needs of all pupils is regarded as a basic requirement in all classrooms (Whipp, Taggart and Jackson, 2014). Appropriate differentiation is an expected element of good planning, thus devising units of work and lesson plans that would cater for the needs of all pupils seems an obvious and expected way of catering for the learning needs of all pupils (Heidorn and Mosier, 2019). However, implementing a range of suitable differentiation strategies can be a difficult task for physical education teachers. One difficulty that can arise is that physical education teachers may not possess the level of subject knowledge required that allows them to plan activities that cater for the complex needs of particular pupils, resulting in them planning activities that are not matched to the needs of each pupil (Heidorn and Mosier, 2019). Teachers may also fail to reflect on their teaching, meaning they are unable to recognise instances where planning for differentiation could be better. To cater for an ever-increasing population of pupils with SENs, the school could also invest in a range of appropriate equipment that would allow teachers to modify and adapt activities to the needs of pupils. The purchasing of such equipment is only likely to take place if the aforementioned aspects have been addressed, because it is only after conducting a curriculum and pedagogical review that the necessary equipment investment would be recognised.

It is important to note, however, that the most fundamental issue to be addressed is the need for physical education teachers, as individuals and as a department, to undertake a rigorous and genuine approach to reflective practice. It is likely that some teachers have not engaged with such practice for many years, meaning that they could possibly be reluctant to engage or indeed pay lip service. If they fail to engage with reflective practice in the way that is required, then, all other areas identified above will be under-developed. It is likely to take time to convince some teachers of the need to invest time and effort with reflective practice, and teachers will need support when undertaking such activities.

Case study (part 2) – the school's response

This section provides an overview of the actions taken by the physical education department and individual teachers and the impact that such changes had on the learning of all pupils and on the teachers. It discusses the following areas: reflective practice, pupil voice, curriculum review and classroom assistants.

Reflective practice

Convincing teachers to engage with reflective practice was a difficult task. An initial meeting was held with the department where responses to the current situation were discussed, and an action plan was drawn up. The department was keen to explore many of the areas listed above, but reflective practice was not mentioned. I emphasised that if they were to make the best possible changes, then reflective practice had to be a core strategy for how they moved forward. I could sense a reluctance, but support from the HOD was crucial in convincing the rest of the department that their engagement with reflective practice would be a worthwhile use of time and enable them to address issues in a more effective and informed way. To begin with, teachers agreed to complete post-lesson reflection templates for all lessons they taught. The template contained the following questions:

- What went well in this lesson and why?
- What aspects of this lesson did not go well? Reasons why certain aspects did not go well?
- If teaching this lesson again, what changes would you make?

It was agreed that teachers would take time at the end of each day to go through their reflections, discuss these with a colleague and make note of key issues that emerged. Looking back at the process, the HOD stated,

Initial engagement with reflection after lessons was tough for some department members since they hadn't done anything like this in years. However, as the weeks progressed, I could see that they were getting more into it and some of our discussions after lessons were really good. We were all supportive of each other and I think everyone started to relax more. We then got to the point where we realised that we were discussing each other's lessons but only based on the person's reflections and that it would be better if we watched each other. We then introduced the process of peer review.

Peer review

Engaging with peer review was also a new experience for the teachers, but it appears that the timing of this was right because they were beginning to embrace the reflective approach and starting to trust each other. The HOD stated,

> it was a bit strange at the start because some of us hadn't been observed by a peer in years and I think we all tend to be a bit protective of our own teaching. So letting someone else observe you was a big thing, but it ended up being a really good experience. Using the advice provided by xxxx was helpful in that we followed a clear protocol regarding the completion of the lesson observation template and the post-lesson discussion was really a conversation as opposed to the reviewer just giving their feedback. It really did feel collaborative which is the only way it would work.

Peer review helped teachers become aware of their strengths and areas for development in their own and others' practices, and it was the identification of areas for improvement that allowed teachers to improve their teaching and learning. The HOD stated,

> peer review was great in that it meant that we each had these areas to work on and because we knew that everyone was working on something, it sort of created a real desire to do things better and in a way reinvigorated some staff and the outworking's of this was that we began to see an increase in pupil participation via less non-participants and there was an obvious increase in pupil motivation levels.

It is clear that the peer review process resulted in improved learning experiences for both teachers and pupils.

Pupil voice

The teachers embraced the concept of pupil voice by issuing short surveys to all pupils (years 8-12) on their experiences and learning in physical education. The survey also included some open-ended questions that allowed pupils to provide qualitative responses. Key messages emerging from the feedback were as follows:

1. Across all year groups, many pupils cited their dislike for traditional team games, stating that they participated in these games way too often.
2. Across all year groups, at least 25% of pupils stated that they did not enjoy physical education. There were a range of reasons for this response, but the most frequent response was that they felt they were not good at physical education and found it difficult.

3. Across all year groups, pupils made reference to a lack of learning in physical education.
4. Across all year groups, but mainly years 8-10, pupils noted that there was a need to include a greater variety of activities.
5. A number of pupils with SENs made reference to not having their classroom assistant present or involved in the physical education lessons.

The HOD collated the feedback and shared with other all teachers. Whilst some of them found the feedback difficult to accept, there was a desire and commitment amongst teachers to begin to address the issues raised. The HOD stated,

> The feedback from the pupil surveys was a very worthwhile exercise. Whilst some of it made for uncomfortable reading and there was a lot of soul searching, we could not run away from it. It was clear that too many of our pupils, across all year groups, were not enjoying physical education. It was clear that we needed to change our ways, both in terms of our curriculum offering and how it was taught.

The department created an action plan and shared this with the senior leadership team (SLT). The first action point that they chose to address was curriculum provision, and this became the catalyst for a curriculum audit.

Curriculum review

The first point to be addressed in the action plan was the completion of a curriculum audit which focused on what was being taught across each year group and by individual teachers. Putting this information down for all teachers to see and review was an important first point. The HOD stated,

> Actually getting it all down on paper as to what each staff member was teaching was an interesting exercise and it allowed us to instantly see that we were too games focused and this correlated with what the pupils said. It was at this stage we went back to the curriculum and looked at the statutory and non-statutory elements and it was obvious there were gaps. So, getting agreement on what needed to change in terms of the breadth of our offering was important because we had to get that right before we looked at how the activities should be taught but I suppose we were already working on that with our reflective work.

The changes emerging from this process ensured that the physical education provision was broader and more balanced. The pupils benefitted greatly from this change as was evidenced in pupil survey data at the end of the first term of implementation. The key findings from this survey were as follows:

- majority of pupils welcomed the change in provision, with many citing less focus on games
- in years 8-10, at least 85% of the pupils were now enjoying physical education
- pupils with SENs welcomed the inclusion of their classroom assistant in physical education lessons.

The department continued with their peer review process, and it was during these ongoing observations of their new provision that there became a greater focus on pedagogy. Less focus on extra-curricular provision ran in parallel with a change to the physical education curriculum. Teachers realised that engagement in the traditional sports of Gaelic football, hurling, camogie and soccer during physical education lessons was poor, with many pupils displaying signs of disengagement. The HOD stated,

> in light of the pupil feedback we agreed to continue with the peer observations of each other and rather than base judgments just on what we thought, we needed to ensure that we were hearing the views of pupils on a daily and weekly basis so we began to use ways of getting their feedback during and after lessons via the use of exit slips, review of learning post-its, peer and self-assessment tasks because the main question we had to keep asking, was, how engaged are the pupils and are they learning? I think we had all slipped into a way of teaching physical education whereby keeping them active was our priority as opposed to focusing on their learning.

The HOD also acknowledged that the ongoing observations amongst the department and the ongoing pupil feedback was helping teachers reflect daily on their practice. He stated,

> It's strange because at the start we were all somewhat reluctant to engage with the reflective practice work but suddenly when we became used to observing each other and using pupil feedback, it sort of became second nature and I think the big thing for all of us was that we could see improvements in our practice and the pupil feedback was proof that this was working for staff and pupils.

The peer observations have now become common practice in the department, and the model used by the physical education department has now been adopted across other departments in the school. The HOD stated,

> The big change for me and for the other physical education staff has been our change of mindset regarding reflective practice. I think we all had this view that it was something you did during your PGCE but that once you start teaching you don't have the time but we have come to realise that it should be there every day and that it is actually just part of what good teaching and learning is and that the pupil voice is a critical element in that daily reflective work.

It is clear that engagement with reflective practice and the pupil feedback have had a significant impact upon the teachers and that it has led to improved learning experiences for the pupils. The curriculum review process also helped teachers identify areas where CPD was needed, and this became another point on the action plan for the following academic year.

Using expertise of classroom assistants

As a result of pupil feedback, particularly from pupils with SENs, and ongoing peer feedback, teachers recognised the need to utilise classroom assistants in their lessons. Common practice would have been for classroom assistants to attend lessons, but they were merely observers. This began to change, and teachers were planning for their inclusion in lessons and how they could make best use of them to help improve the learning experience for the pupils involved. This was a new experience for everyone involved, and in the beginning there were many issues to address. Many of the classroom assistants lacked confidence in the physical education environment, and felt out of their comfort zone. The HOD stated,

> Using classroom assistants in our lessons was something we never did[;] they would have been there to bring pupils to the toilet[,] etc.[,] but not involved in the actual lesson, so at the beginning this was challenging for everyone but as lessons progressed we all were starting to find a way to make it work. The best thing we did was just have a conversation before the lesson as to what I wanted them to do and then after the lesson we talked about how it went and it was through his process we learned what worked and what didn't work. Some of the classroom assistants have really embraced the change and have come up with ideas better than mine. The big thing has been that feedback from the pupils with SEN has been really positive and some pupils who are not designated as SEN have also highlighted that they have benefitted from classroom assistant involvement as some classroom assistants just don't work with the pupil they are assigned to but help those who they see need help because there are some pupils with SEN who don't always want the classroom assistant at their back and call.

It is clear that utilising classroom assistants has been a positive move for the department and has had a positive impact on pupils' physical education experiences and learning.

Summary and key points

The case study highlighted in this chapter has identified many important issues for physical education teachers individually and as a department. The catalyst for change in this particular school was the increasing number of pupils with SENs joining the school at a particularly fast rate. Part 1 of the case study described the context that the physical education department found themselves in and identified possible ways that they could begin to address the issues they were facing. Part 2 of the case study outlined the actual steps that the department took to address the issues, and it is clear that the most significant step taken was to engage with meaningful reflective practice. The physical education teachers are still on this journey, and reflective practice is very much at the centre of their daily practice. It took for the department to be in a position of desperation before admitting the need for change, and this case study emphasises the importance of continuous monitoring and evaluation of teaching and learning via the use of ongoing reflective practice. At the time of writing, the physical education department have begun to engage with various CPD courses and have issued surveys to parents. Whilst it has been a difficult and challenging process for the teachers at times, the process has reaped benefits both for the teachers and for the pupils.

We hope that this chapter will encourage teachers to consider the issues raised in relation to their own physical education provision, for example, whether: curriculum and extra-curricular provision is monitored by teachers and pupil voice is heard; there is a clear distinction between physical education and sport; there is breadth and balance in the curriculum; how inclusive provision is and whether there are barriers to being more inclusive; there is effective planning for differentiation; classroom assistants are utilised effectively; and whether teachers engage in effective CPD.

References

Allen, G., Milne, B., Velija, P. and Radley, R. (2024) '"Hearing their voice": the experiences of physical education with pupils diagnosed with severe learning disabilities', *Sport, Education and Society*, 29 (3), 342-357.

Coates, J. and Vickerman, P. (2010) 'Empowering children with special educational needs to speak up: experiences of inclusive physical education', *Disability and Rehabilitation*, 32 (18), 1517-1526.

Finlay, L. (2008) Reflecting on 'Reflective Practice', *PBPL*, paper 52, The Open University.

Flutter, J. and Rudduck, J. (2005) 'Pupil voice: purpose, power and the possibilities for democratic schooling', *British Educational Research Journal*, 31 (4), 533-540.

Heidorn, B. and Mosier, B. (2019) 'Differentiation for student learning in physical education', *Strategies*, 32 (4), 40-44, https://doi.org/10.1080/08924562.2019.1608737.

Hobbs, V. (2007) 'Faking it or hating it: can reflective practice be forced?', *Reflective Practice*, 8 (3), 405-417.

Lamb, P., Lane, K. and Aldous, D. (2012) 'Enhancing the spaces for reflection: A buddy peer- review process within physical education initial teacher education', *European Physical Education Review*, 19 (1), 21-38.

Lundy, L. (2007) '"Voice' is not enough: conceptualising article 12 of the United Nations Convention on the Rights of the Child', *British Educational Research Journal*, 33 (6), 92-942.

Maher, A. (2016) 'Special educational needs in mainstream secondary school physical education: learning support assistants have their say', *Sport, Education and Society*, 21 (2), 262-278.

Maher, A. and Macbeth, J. (2013) 'Physical education, resources and training: the perspective of special educational needs coordinators working in secondary schools in North-West England', *European Physical Education Review*, 20 (1), 90-103.

Morgan, B. (2011) 'Consulting pupils about classroom teaching and learning: policy, practice and response in one school', *Research Papers in Education*, 26 (4), 445-467.

Paseka, A. and Schwab, S. (2020) 'Parents' attitudes towards inclusive education and their perceptions of inclusive teaching practices and resources', *European Journal of Special Needs Education*, 35 (2), 254-272.

Shoffner, M. (2008) 'Informal reflection in pre-service teacher education', *Reflective Practice: International and Multidisciplinary Perspectives*, 9 (2), 123-134.

United Nations (1989) *Convention on the Rights of the Child*, Treaty Series, 1577, 3.

Warwick, P., Vrikki, M., Mette, A., Karlsen, F., Dudley, P. and Vermunt, J.D. (2019) 'The role of pupil voice as a trigger for teacher learning in Lesson Study professional groups', *Cambridge Journal of Education*, 49 (4), 435-455.

Whipp, P., Taggart, A. and Jackson, B. (2014) 'Differentiation in outcome-focused physical education: pedagogical rhetoric and reality', *Physical Education and Sport Pedagogy*, 19 (4), 370-382.

Zhang, J. and Zhang, C. (2023) 'Teaching quality monitoring and evaluation of physical education teaching in ordinary college based on edge computing optimization model', *The Journal of Supercomputing*, 79, 16559-16579, https://doi.org/10.1007/s11227-023-05324-x

Chapter 2 Challenges related to pupil learning
Helping pupils to learn effectively
Julia Lawrence

Introduction

Learning is an active process. It has been described as resulting in a change in behaviour (see, for example, Ambrose *et al*., 2010; Capel, Whitehead and Lawrence, 2025; Gagné, 1985; Heritage, 2008). Within the context of physical education, learning is demonstrated by changes in pupils' knowledge, skills and understanding relative to the activity being taught. Teachers can achieve this by supporting pupils to engage effectively with the learning process.

When looking at learning, careful consideration needs to be given to facilitating changes to pupils' knowledge, skills and understanding. A teacher's understanding of how learning occurs and the learning theories on which this is based will influence the curriculum design, content and the teaching approaches adopted. It will also impact the way pupils are assessed and their learning tracked.

Using a focused case study, this chapter seeks to look at why learning might not be taking place and strategies that might be employed to support changes to facilitate the learning of all pupils. It is important to focus on the learning of all pupils because, as Capel, Whitehead and Lawrence (2025, p. 23) argued, "as learning is undertaken by individual learners and each learner is unique, they progress at different rates". Consequently, it cannot be assumed that all pupils in a lesson will be accessing and demonstrating the same level of learning at the same time.

Case study (part 1) – Seagate school

Seagate is a large secondary school. Within each year group, there are eight classes, each containing up to 28 pupils. Physical education is taught in mixed attaining groups – meaning that pupils of differing abilities are working together. This is a research-informed policy adopted by the school, aimed at raising the aspirations of all pupils (Dweck, 2006) and developing social cohesion (Hallam, Davies and Ireson, 2004).

This is a significant change in pupil grouping from what teachers and pupils have experienced previously. In the past, the department adopted an ability grouping approach based on assessment of achievement at the start of each academic year. As they adopt the new policy, the department are finding that because of the variation in ability levels within a lesson, they are struggling to meet the needs of all pupils. There is growing concern that the learning of some pupils is being disrupted by a lack of challenge, which, for some, is resulting in frustration at having to repeat aspects of learning (for example, repeating the same skills until everyone is at the same level of performance) they feel that are capable of performing. In turn, this impacts their behaviour, resulting in an increase in behavioural incidents. On the other hand, other pupils are finding it difficult to embed and become fluent in the skills they need to effectively take part in aspects of the lesson. As a result, some pupils are becoming frustrated by a lack of success. Further, teachers are finding that they are having to revisit learning that should already have been embedded as they feel that pupils are not able to make connections between what they have previously learned and the activities they are currently learning. For example, whilst they have already followed a unit of work with a focus on badminton, some pupils are not able to transfer their learning in badminton to a unit focusing on tennis.

Teachers are therefore keen to reflect on and identify what effective learning could look like in mixed attaining groups. They acknowledge that they need to consider carefully what they see as effective learning and how this impacts the ways in which they support pupils in the learning process.

They identified two key areas on which to focus:

1. The need to work as a department to better understand how learning takes place and how learning can be supported in relation to the organisation and teaching of lessons.
2. The need for teachers to reflect on the quality of their teaching (including how they present learning activities) so that pupils develop the knowledge, skills and understanding they require to learn effectively in physical education and be able to apply this across different contexts within the physical education curriculum.

The next part of this chapter considers some theory that underpins learning that can be used to inform changes in teaching approaches.

Defining learning

Learning can be defined as "any process that in living organisms leads to permanent capacity change and which is not solely due to biological maturation or ageing" (Illeris, 2007, p.3). For Pritchard (2014, p.1), learning is "knowledge of, or skill in, something through study, teaching, instruction or experience". The Department for Education (DfE) (2024, p.13) argued that "learning involves a lasting change in pupils' capabilities or understanding". Learning is an active process (Kirschner and Hendrick, 2020), meaning that there are specific steps involved for the outcome (change) to be achieved. To be effective, the process must involve exposure to a range of learning experiences which allow the learning to occur and then become embedded. Further, the learner (in the context of schools, the pupils) needs to be engaged in the learning process. As Kirschner and Hendrick (2020) suggested, "you as the teacher can offer everything, but in the end, it's the learner who has the last word" (p.144). So, what can a teacher put in place to support effective learning?

Strategies to support effective learning

Different strategies for supporting effective learning have been proposed. A starting point for looking at strategies for effective learning is to consider the work of Gagné (1985). Gagné proposed that for learning to take place, consideration needs to be given to the learning that is to take place and how best to support that learning. To support this, he identified three core aspects of a lesson. These can be summarised (Bates, 2019) as being:

1. Engagement - specifically how a teacher gains pupils' attention, introduces the focus of learning (or the learning outcomes) and how recall of prior learning is initiated.
2. Delivery - how lesson content is presented, how pupils are supported through their learning and how pupils demonstrate/evidence learning.
3. Assessment - how pupil learning is assessed, how pupils receive feedback and how they are provided opportunities to use this feedback to further enhance their learning.

More recently, Rosenshine (2012, p.12) identified ten core principles of instruction to support effective learning:

1. Begin a lesson with a short review of previous learning.
2. Present new material in small steps with pupil practice after each step.
3. Ask a large number of questions and check the responses of all pupils.
4. Provide models.
5. Guide pupil practice.
6. Check for pupil understanding.
7. Obtain a high success rate.
8. Provide scaffolds for difficult tasks.
9. Require and monitor independent practice.
10. Engage pupils in weekly and monthly review.

Whilst not a checklist for effective learning, such principles provide opportunities for review and reinforcement of learning opportunities. This encourages the teacher to think more deeply about how they are planning and teaching their lessons to ensure that all pupils are able to learn effectively.

In the context of physical education, Capel, Whitehead and Lawrence (2025) suggested that for learning to be effective, teachers need to ensure the following:

- learning builds on what a pupil already knows and can do, so that they can be successful in the learning
- have high expectations of all pupils to participate fully in a lesson and to make the effort required to learn and for pupils to do so
- model expectations clearly, both verbally and physically, highlighting the key points for learning and the success criteria, and providing clear feedback for pupils to improve the quality of their learning
- adapt/differentiate learning activities by giving pupils additional, more complex tasks or providing structured scaffolding and more time to practice as appropriate

- identify the most important knowledge to be learned, giving verbal or visual cues as appropriate for pupils to focus and ensure there are no misconceptions. This allows pupils to maximise the use of their time to practice.

In order to achieve this, Capel, Whitehead and Lawrence (2025, p.28) identified nine principles that teachers should consider to facilitate the learning of all pupils in physical education.

1. Each learner is holistic; the Physical, Cognitive and Affective Domains are all inter-related, therefore all need to be considered.
2. Each learner is unique, therefore needs to be treated as such.
3. Learning is purposive, towards achieving an aim.
4. Learning is an ongoing process that takes time, practice, application and effort.
5. Learning attempts to move the learner on; new learning builds from where the learn is in respect of current learning.
6. Learning is coherent, with a logical order, going step by step.
7. Learning is presented in such a way that it motivates the learner to apply themselves.
8. Learning accommodates opportunities for feedback to the learner.
9. Learning provides opportunities for the learner to take responsibility for their learning.

At this point, it is perhaps important to clarify the domains of learning. Domains of learning refer to areas in which learning can take place. Most commonly referred to are those domains identified by Bloom *et al.* (1956) as:

- cognitive – associated with the acquisition and application of knowledge/intellect – or how we 'think'
- affective – associated with feelings, emotions, behaviours and attitudes – or how we 'feel'
- psychomotor – associated with physical and manual skills moving from copying to becoming an expert (mastery) – or what we can 'do'.

More recently, Gagné (1972) identified five domains in which learning takes place:

1. Intellectual skills (knowing how – also referred to as procedural knowledge).
2. Verbal information (knowing that – also referred to a declarative knowledge).
3. Cognitive strategies (for example thinking skills, analysis skills and problem solving).
4. Motor skills (for example being able to performance-specific actions).
5. Attitudes (an individual's belief and approaches towards something).

Similarities exist between Bloom and Gagné, with Gagné (1972), in some respects, deconstructing Bloom *et al.*'s (1956) domains to a more granular level. However, the domains identified by Bloom *et al.* (1956) are much more prevalent and have been used, for example, to support the development of strategies such as questioning (see Chapter 9 for more information about questioning in relation to learning in the cognitive domain).

Acknowledging that learning takes place within and across the domains of learning is an important concept to understand in order to be specific about what it is that pupils should learn. In turn, this is used to inform a teacher about the teaching approaches they might choose to adopt to facilitate pupils' learning.

The next section looks at the learning process.

The learning process

A starting point for understanding the learning process is to consider the principles of information processing. Established in the 1960s by Atkinson and Shiffrin (1968), the information processing model proposes that information can be taken in (encoded) either visually (what is seen), acoustically (what is heard) or semantically (what is understood) – in essence, both senses (or sensory memory) and existing knowledge are used to process information. If this information is seen as relevant, it is moved to the short-term memory. This has limited capacity so if this information is not rehearsed/practiced/used, the information is not retained. However, if the information is seen as relevant and is rehearsed/practiced/used, it is moved into long-term memory. This has an infinite capacity and allows for information stored there to be retrieved and used to consolidate existing learning or build new learning. When looking at how information is processed, consideration should also be given to:

- the establishment of schema – "a way of organising knowledge; a mental structure of already learnt and available knowledge, skills, and even ideas that is used for organising and perceiving new information" (Kirschner and Hendrick, 2020, p.6)
- the depth of processing – that is, the level of engagement a pupil has with the information being presented to them.

These are discussed in detail below. These draw on some of the principles of instruction (Rosenshine, 2012) and principles for facilitating and enhancing learning in physical education (Capel, Whitehead and Lawrence, 2025) – see above.

The establishment of schema

Central to the process of learning is the pupils' ability to establish schema. Schema are stored in the long-term memory and are used by the pupil as a basis for decisions about new learning. For example, if a pupil sees/experiences an activity that they identify as similar to what they have done before, they can draw on that schema to make decisions as to what to do in this new context. Conversely, if they see an activity as something they have not experienced before, they may struggle to make connections and, as a result, be unable to draw on any prior learning to support them.

Thus, "for optimal learning, new knowledge must be related to the knowledge that students have already acquired" (Kirschner and Hendrick, 2020, p.8). This can occur through assimilation, whereby new learning becomes embedded within an existing schema, or through accommodation, whereby an existing schema is adapted to reflect the new learning that has taken place.

So, if teachers are to support pupils in developing schema, it is important to consider the processes that take place to allow schema to develop. This requires consideration of what is happening before information becomes encoded and stored within the long-term memory.

Sweller's Cognitive Load Theory (1988) links to schema in respect of how information moves to the long-term memory store. The theory focuses on the capacity people have to work with new information. In essence, it argues that the amount of information a person can work with is dependent on what they already know, that is, what is stored in their long-term memory. Therefore, if a person is presented with too much new information, they can become overloaded and limited in their capacity to solve the problem that has been set. Therefore, when thinking about introducing new material, the teacher needs to know what pupils already know about the material or content (their declarative knowledge) and what they can already do (their procedural knowledge).

Depth of processing

How the information presented to pupils is processed relates to the level of engagement or how committed the pupil is to learning that material or content. This is also related to how motivated the pupil is, as this will impact the extent to which they attend to and process the information they are presented with. Thus, as Capel, Whitehead and Lawrence (2025, p.28) identified, learning should be "presented in such a way that it motivates the learner to apply themselves".

There are three identified depths of processing:

1. Shallow: a pupil is focusing on information at a surface level, where they look to describe what they see. Information is therefore not fully attended to and retention is limited.
2. Acoustic: a pupil is attending to learning in more depth. For example, rather than just looking at something, they start to make connections.
3. Deep: a pupil is attending to the meaning (semantic) of what they are processing. As a result, there is increased retention of information, resulting in a greater degree of learning.

Teachers should, therefore, focus on facilitating and stimulating a deep approach to processing. Coe *et al.* (2020) referred to this as stimulating hard thinking. To support this, they suggested that consideration be given to how the lesson is structured, how questioning is used and how pupils are encouraged to explain their understanding (this is explored further in Chapter 9, which looks at supporting development in the cognitive domain).

More recently, Wakefield and Lawrence (2022) identified strategies that can be embedded in lessons to support pupils to become effective pupils. These include:

1. *Developing independent learners*
    As Capel, Whitehead and Lawrence (2025, p.28) suggested, "Learning provides opportunities for the learner to take responsibility for their learning". Independent learners take greater responsibility for their own learning. This requires the development of independent learning behaviours. Such behaviours include, for example:
    Cognitive: "the mental process involved in knowing, understanding and learning" (Quigley, Muijis and Stringer, 2018, p.9). In a physical education context, this might be evidenced in how a pupil deconstructs a skill, identifies specific aspects of their performance of a skill that need refinement and practices these aspects, resulting in an overall improvement in the execution of the skill as a whole.

Social: here, the focus is on behaviours that allow pupils to work effectively with others, for example, how pupils observe their own and others' performances and are able to provide focused feedback that they or their partner uses to make changes, resulting in an improvement in the quality of their performance or how pupils work together in team activities.

Emotional: such behaviours focus on how pupils manage and enact their emotions. For example, when executing a rally in tennis, there is a questionable line call. Pupils able to control their emotions will either question politely or accept the decision. In contrast, pupils less able to regulate their emotion may react by challenging the umpire or becoming aggressive.

Motivation: "willingness to engage" (Quigley, Muijis and Stringer, 2018, p.9). Here, the focus is on pupils' levels of participation and engagement.

To some extent, such behaviours align with the domains of learning identified above with social and emotional behaviour and motivation reflecting learning within the affective domain. They also reflect the concept of self-regulated behaviour, which is "the extent to which learners are aware of their strengths and weaknesses, the strategies they use to learn, can motivate themselves to engage in learning, and can develop strategies and tactics to enhance learning" (Muijs and Bokhove, 2020, p.5). By encouraging the development of independent learning behaviours, pupils are more likely to demonstrate higher levels of self-efficacy, that is their belief that they are able to do so something, or how they feel they will deal with a challenge. This in turn will support their levels of engagement in developing their knowledge, skills and understanding.

2. *Providing opportunities for pupils to use and apply concepts*

   If pupils are to be engaged in deeper levels of processing, careful consideration needs to be given to the activities planned for them to achieve this, to ensure that they are using and applying the concepts they have previously learned.

   Referencing the work of Atkinson and Shiffrin (1968) and Sweller (1988), as introduced above, for information to become encoded and embedded in a pupil's long-term memory, there has to be a period of rehearsal and practice resulting in consolidation. However, there also need to be opportunities for retrieval of existing knowledge to support the accommodation and assimilation processes within schema development. Thus, in requiring pupils to use and apply existing knowledge and concepts, opportunities to strengthen and adapt schema are presented. As a result, it is likely that when exposed to similar concepts in different contexts, they will be better prepared to draw on their prior learning.

3. *Linking to prior learning*

   Ausubel (1968, p.vi) argued that "the most important single factor influencing learning is what the learner already knows". Thus, when providing opportunities for pupils to use and apply concepts, it is important that teachers have a strong understanding of what pupils already know and can do. Without this knowledge, teachers run the risk of planning learning activities that pupils have previously experienced, which may impact on their motivation as they may become bored and/or do not see themselves making progress. Conversely, they may plan learning activities that are either too challenging or assume that pupils already have that knowledge or level of competence. This again has the potential to impact pupil motivation (Chapter 4 focuses on progression and continuity in the physical education curriculum).

4. *Apply knowledge to new contexts*

    Linking existing learning and knowledge to different contexts has been identified above as an important part of developing pupils' ability to apply existing schema to different situations. This might include providing opportunities for pupils to use their existing knowledge in more challenging contexts, allowing them to demonstrate application of their learning.

    In summary, if teachers want pupils to demonstrate deeper levels of processing, they need to establish and build on pupils' prior learning across the domains of learning. They also need to provide increasingly challenging contexts for pupils to work in, contexts that require them to apply their knowledge and understanding in different ways.

    But how should knowledge that teachers want pupils to learn be presented? Returning to the information processing model (Atkinson and Shiffrin, 1968) and Cognitive Load Theory (Sweller, 1988) – information is taken in using the senses. Further, the capacity to process information at this stage is limited, and therefore consideration needs to be given to how information is presented to ensure that pupils do not suffer cognitive overload. Attention, therefore, now turns to how information is presented, specifically in relation to dual coding.

5. *Dual coding*

    Dual coding involves the processing of information both verbally and visually. In a physical education context, this would mean that a skill/practice is modelled/demonstrated whilst verbally explaining it. This is a common approach adopted by physical education teachers for practical activities. However, when teaching theoretical elements of examination physical education, it would be reflected in the use of visual/pictorial representation alongside written or verbal prose. The premise here is that verbal and visual processing is achieved through "cooperating memory systems" (Kirschner and Hendrick, 2020, p.49).

    Having considered how information is presented, processed and some potential strategies around how pupils can be supported to develop and use these processes, consideration also needs to be given to pupils' readiness to learn.

Readiness to learn

Schindler (1948) and Jensen (1969) identified the concept of readiness to learn, that is, "the amount of previous learning that can be transferred to new learning" (Jensen, 1969, p.1). This 'readiness' is not age-specific but is related to the level of maturity (physical, cognitive, emotional, social) of the pupil (see Wakefield and Lawrence, 2022, for more on readiness to learn in physical education). In some respects, readiness to learn can be linked to the independent learning behaviours identified above and reinforces the key concepts that run through this chapter in relation to understanding what a pupil knows and can do already and a teacher's ability to activate/retrieve this prior learning.

Having considered the information presented above, the second part of the case study looks at how some of these points were incorporated by the school so that pupils' learning was more effective.

Case study (part 2) – changes made at Seagate school

Earlier in this chapter, Seagate Secondary School and the challenges they were experiencing in support learning following a change in how physical education was being taught (following the introduction of mixed attaining groups) were introduced. Specifically, the department identified two key areas on which to focus:

1. The need to work as a department to better understand how learning takes place and how learning can be supported in relation to the organisation and teaching of lessons.
2. The need for teachers to reflect on the quality of their teaching (including how they present learning activities) so that pupils develop a deeper understanding of the knowledge, skills and understanding they require to learn effectively in physical education and apply this across different contexts within the physical education curriculum.

Following a period of reflection and focused professional development, the physical education department chose to focus on embedding three non-negotiables within all lessons:

1. In each lesson, learning in each of the three domains of learning (Bloom *et al.*, 1956) would be supported. Learning outcomes would therefore focus on developing pupils' knowledge, skills and understanding in relation to learning not only in the physical domain (psychomotor), but also in the cognitive (what declarative knowledge was to be learned) and affective (how pupils would develop social and emotionally) domains. This gave a clearer purpose for each lesson, with pupils provided with a clearer focus as to what they were expected to know and be able to do by the end of the lesson.
2. At the start of each lesson, the warm-up activity focused on reviewing learning from the previous lesson so that the teacher could identify if there were any aspects of learning that needed to be revisited. Where learning needed to be revisited, activities were structured in such a way as to allow those pupils who had already achieved the learning required to apply this in more challenging contexts, whilst those who needed time to become more fluent were provided with activities that allowed for further practice.
3. Throughout the lesson, regular review of learning against the learning outcomes shared at the start of the lessons was undertaken through the use of questioning and demonstration as a means of checking for understanding and to provide feedback to pupils in relation to the learning that was taking place.

Through lesson observations, pupil and teacher voice surveys, the department were able to review what impact these changes were having on pupil learning.

Whilst initially identifying learning outcomes across the three domains was seen as time-consuming, working collaboratively, the physical education teaching team concluded that it was more effective if they identified objectives that pupils were expected to demonstrate by the end of a unit of work. This meant that during a half-term, all pupils in any one year group were working towards the same three objectives, regardless of the specific activity that might be the focus of lessons. For example, whilst some were focusing on games-based activities and others on aesthetic-based activities, they were all being asked to achieve the same objectives.

In using the changing time and warm-up as a review of prior learning, teachers and pupils identified that they felt the lesson had a more focused start. Activities could be introduced as pupils changed, which meant that they would arrive in the learning space ready to learn. They also felt that establishing this as a routine in all physical education lessons reflected what was happening in other subjects across the school. This meant that pupils already had an understanding of the approaches being adopted.

By embedding regular review of learning within the lesson, pupils reported an increased level of confidence as they knew what they were able to do and what they needed to do to improve further. As a range of strategies to support this review were employed, pupils were able to provide feedback to each other and took increased ownership of reflecting on their own learning. This resulted in a decline in the number of behaviour incidents that had triggered the initial concern of teachers.

As the strategies became more embedded, teachers themselves reported changes in their own behaviours in terms of building more opportunities for pupils to lead their own learning. They also reported an increased willingness of all pupils to work with others during lessons. This was resulting in all pupils making progress in their learning across the three domains.

Summary and key points

The focus of this chapter has been to consider learning, the learning process and the strategies and approaches teachers can use to enhance pupils' learning. To do this, the chapter has not only drawn on the general literature pertaining to learning, but has also referenced the work of Capel, Whitehead and Lawrence (2025), specifically their nine principles for facilitating and enhancing learning in physical education.

From the case study provided, it is clear that by considering and embedding these principles in all lessons, there was an improvement in the quality of instructions given by teachers. This enhanced the learning experience of pupils. Pupils were more engaged in the learning process and able to demonstrate a deeper level of learning. Whilst this chapter serves as an overview of learning, more detail around the domains of learning can be found in Chapters 8 (physical), 9 (cognitive) and 10 (affective), as well as in Capel, Whitehead and Lawrence (2025).

References

Ambrose, S.A., Bridges, M.W., DiPietro, M., Lovett, M.C. and Norman, M.K. (2010) *How Learning Works: Seven Research-based Principles for Smart Teaching*, San Francisco, CA: Jossey-Bass.

Atkinson, R.C. and Shiffrin, R.M. (1968) 'Human memory: a proposed system and its control processes', in K.W. Spence and J.T. Spence (eds) *The Psychology of Learning and Motivation* (Volume 2, New York: Academic Press, pp. 89-195).

Ausubel, D. (1968) *Educational Psychology: A Cognitive View*, New York: Holt, Rinehart and Winston.

Bates, B. (2019) *Learning Theories Simplified* (2nd edition), London: SAGE.

Bloom, B.S., Engelhart, M.D., Furst, E.J., Hill, W.H. and Krathwohl, D.R. (eds) (1956) *Taxonomy of Educational Objectives, Handbook I: Cognitive Domain*, New York: David McKay Co Inc.

Capel, S., Whitehead, M. and Lawrence, J. (2025) *Progression and Progress in Physical Education*, Abingdon: Routledge.
Coe, R., Rauch, C.J., Kime, S. and Singleton, D. (2020) *Great Teaching Toolkit: Evidence Review*, Evidence Based Education, available at: https://www.gov.uk/government/publications/initial-teacher-training-and-early-career-framework (accessed 7 December 2024).
DfE (Department for Education) (2024) *Initial Teacher Training and Early Career Framework*, available at: https://assets.publishing.service.gov.uk/media/661d24ac08c3be25cfbd3e61/Initial_Teacher_Training_and_Early_Career_Framework.pdf (accessed 17 January 2025).
Dweck, C.S. (2006) *Mindset: The New Psychology of Success*, New York: Random House.
Gagné, R.M. (1972) 'Domains of learning', *Interchange*, 3, 1–8.
Gagné, R.M. (1985) *The Conditions of Learning* (4th edition), New York: Holt, Rinehart and Winston.
Hallam, S., Davies, J. and Ireson, J. (2004) 'Grouping practices in the primary school: What influences change?', *British Educational Research Journal*, 30 (1), 117–140.
Heritage, M. (2008) *Learning Progressions: Supporting Instruction and Formative Assessment*, Paper prepared for the Formative Assessment for Teachers and Students (FAST) State Collaborative on Assessment and Student Standards (SCASS) of the Council of Chief State School Officers (CCSSO), Washington, DC: Council of Chief State School Officers.
Illeris, K. (2007) *How We Learn: Learning and Non-Learning in School and Beyond*, London: Routledge.
Jensen, A.R. (1969) 'How much can we boost IQ and scholastic achievement?' *Harvard Educational Review*, 39(1), 1–123.
Kirschner, P.A. and Hendrick, C. (2020) *How Learning Happens: Seminal Works in Educational Psychology and What They Mean in Practice*, Abingdon: A David Fulton Book – Routledge.
Muijs, D. and Bokhove, C. (2020) *Metacognition and Self-regulation: Evidence Review*, London: Education Endowment Foundation, available at: https://files.eric.ed.gov/fulltext/ED612286.pdf (accessed 15 January 2025).
Pritchard, A. (2014) *Ways of Learning: Learning Theories and Learning Styles in the Classroom* (3rd edition), Abingdon: Routledge.
Quigley, A., Muijs, D. and Stringer, E. (2018) *Metacognition and Self-regulated Learning: Guidance Report*, London: Education Endowment Foundation, available at: https://dera.ioe.ac.uk/id/eprint/31617/1/EEF_Metacognition_and_self-regulated_learning.pdf (accessed 15 January 2025).
Rosenshine, B. (2012) 'Principles of instruction: Research-based strategies that all teachers should know', *American Educator*, 36 (1), 12–20.
Schindler, A.W. (1948) 'Readiness for learning', *Childhood Education*, 24(7), 301–304.
Sweller, J. (1988) 'Cognitive load during problem solving: effects on learning', *Cognitive Science*, 12, 257–285.
Wakefield, J. and Lawrence, J. (2022) 'Identifying and developing students' readiness to learn', in S. Capel, J. Lawrence, M. Martens and H.A. Rahman (eds) *CPD for Teaching and Learning in Physical Education; Global Lessons from Singapore* (pp. 64–85), Abingdon: Routledge.

Chapter 3   Challenges related to progression and continuity in the curriculum

Curriculum development to support pupil progress

Susan Capel and Julia Lawrence

Introduction

The main focus of physical education teachers should be to support pupils to make progress in their learning. Thus, through planning, teaching and assessment, it is important to ensure that learning activities enable pupils to learn something new, to embed existing learning and to use existing learning as a base for future learning. In order to achieve this, one important consideration (although not the only one) is progression and continuity in the curriculum. Lack of progression and continuity, reflected in, for example, pupils either repeating what they have already learnt and what they already know, or being challenged at too high or too low a level, may result in pupils becoming demotivated and decreases in the levels of confidence, engagement and participation in physical education. If not addressed, this may result in pupils potentially choosing not to participate in physical activity outside physical education and after they leave school (which is a common aim of many physical education curricula).

The chapter starts by looking at some definitions of curriculum, knowledge and progression and continuity as the terms are used in this chapter. Using a focused scenario, the chapter then looks at how a school identified issues with pupil engagement in physical education as a result of lack of progression and continuity in the curriculum. The chapter then identifies some factors in the design of a curriculum that might impact on progression and continuity. It then looks specifically at the content of a curriculum and how it is taught before considering how continuity in the curriculum may be disrupted, focusing particularly on the transition from primary to secondary school. The chapter then returns to the original scenario to identify actions taken in relation to progression and continuity in the curriculum so that pupils are able to progress in their learning.

Definitions of curriculum, knowledge, progression and continuity

A curriculum can be described as an organisational plan for learning in a subject. More specifically, "the curriculum represents a conscious and systematic selection of knowledge, skills and values: a selection that shapes the way teaching, learning and assessment processes are organized by addressing questions such as what, why, when and how students should learn" (The United Nations, Educational, Scientific and Cultural Organization (UNESCO), 2016, p.5).

In this definition, knowledge refers to declarative knowledge – facts and information about a specific topic, or knowing what or that, for example, 'I know what happens to my body when I exercise', or 'I know that when I exercise my heart rate increases'. The term skills refers to procedural knowledge – knowledge about how to do something, how declarative knowledge is applied in practice or knowing how, as in 'I know how to warm up correctly to avoid injury and can do this in practice'. The term values refers to dispositional knowledge, and includes, for example, attitudes, moral dispositions and motivation, will and commitment or knowledge 'to', as in 'I know to …' (UNESCO, 2016, p.7), for example, 'When warming up I know to work with others to ensure that we share the space and equipment we are using'. In this chapter, the word knowledge is generally used to refer to both declarative and procedural knowledge. In designing the curriculum, careful consideration needs to be given to the selection of declarative and procedural knowledge.

Progression was defined in the first National Curriculum for Physical Education (NCPE) in England as "the sequence built into children's learning through curriculum policies and schemes of work so that later learning builds on knowledge, skills, understandings and attitudes learned previously" (Department of Education and Science and the Welsh Office (DES/WO), 1990, p.13). The terms knowledge and understanding in this quote are what are referred to as declarative knowledge and the term skills is what are referred to as procedural knowledge in this chapter. Thus, progression includes the sequencing of curriculum content so that there are increases in demand/challenge, allowing pupils to progress in their learning.

Benyon (1981) defined continuity as

> the transitions pupils experience from one stage of schooling to another; it can refer to the curricular experiences teachers try to provide for their pupils through a school year; and it can refer to the transitions within a school as children move from class to class.
>
> (p.36)

In the first NCPE, continuity was defined as "the nature of the curriculum experienced by children as they transfer from one setting to another" (DES/WO, 1990, p.13). Thus, in considering continuity, teachers need to focus on whether what is planned, taught and assessed develops continuously or whether progression (and hence pupil progress) is disrupted during any transition in their schooling. Progression in the curriculum, and hence pupil progress, relies on continuity. Indeed, continuity goes hand-in-hand with progression.

To summarise, to support effective learning in physical education, progression and continuity must be considered to ensure that a well-sequenced curriculum is planned that allows pupils to consolidate and build on their existing knowledge, allowing them to be able to apply this in more challenging situations.

Scenario 1 identifies an issue related to progression and continuity in the curriculum in Lawcap School.

Scenario (part 1) - an issue identified at Lawcap School

Lawcap School is a school for boys and girls aged 11-18 years. An issue identified by the physical education department was that many pupils (including able pupils who enjoy physical education, physical activity and sport and take part in extra-curricular activities) were saying things like - 'not this again' or 'we have already done this'. Further, many pupils seemed to be 'switched off' in physical education lessons. On the whole, they were not disruptive, but did not seem to be enjoying physical education, were bored and were largely going through the motions rather than trying hard to learn and progress in the subject.

Physical education in Lawcap School is taught to boys and girls separately. Across years 7-11, the curriculum focuses largely on a range of 'traditional' games - mostly team games such as football, rugby, cricket and basketball for boys and hockey, netball, rounders and, more recently, football for girls. Tennis is the only individual game taught, and this is only offered to girls. Athletics is taught to both boys and girls. Girls are also taught gymnastics and dance in years 7 and 8, but these are not continued in years 9 and above.

Some activities are taught in a number of different years in the school. Frequently, the same (or very similar) content is taught in the same way in the same activity in different years. For example, in netball, pupils are taught the same skills in each year, which they then put into a game situation in the anticipation that the game will be 'better'. This means that there is much repetition of what pupils are learning rather than new learning building on previous learning. However, this is justified by teachers thinking that pupils 'forget' what they learned in a previous unit of work focusing on the same activity.

The activities are taught in a (largely) didactic manner. The teacher explains to the pupils what they are going to be doing, demonstrates (or asks a pupil to demonstrate), then the pupils practice what they have been shown, with feedback given on their progress. Each aspect of knowledge is practised separately and is then put into the appropriate context (for example, a gymnastics or dance sequence, a full game situation or a competition in athletics). Whilst the tasks pupils are asked to do in practice are adapted/differentiated for the abilities of pupils, activity-specific situations, such as games play, are not adapted/differentiated. As a result, the level of challenge may not be appropriate for all pupils, resulting in many of them not being given the opportunity to apply their learning effectively.

Able pupils do not progress because they are repeating work they have already covered and are not being 'pushed' to build on previous learning. On the other hand, less able pupils are not given time to embed knowledge such that it is secure before they are asked to apply it and then move onto the next aspect of learning. As a result, both able and less able pupils are not engaging in learning to the full.

When pupils join Lawcap School in year 7, the physical education department start their learning as a 'fresh start' approach. This means that they teach the knowledge they need at Lawcap without taking account of, and trying to build on, what pupils have learned in their primary schools. The rationale for this is that the pupils attending Lawcap come from a range of primary schools and as such have had different experiences and learned different things in their physical education lessons. Whilst the curriculum in some primary schools has included many of the activities taught in the secondary school, the curriculum in other primary schools has not included these.

In order to address the issues identified in the scenario, the department decided to look closely at their current curriculum. They identified issues with the design of the curriculum and lack of progression and continuity within it. Hence, the department decided to examine the design of the curriculum (including what and how physical education is being taught), with a specific focus on progression as well as identification of areas where lack of continuity occurs.

The next section explores relevant theory, research and evidence on these issues, which the department could draw upon, starting with curriculum design.

Curriculum design

Curriculum design is important because the decisions made can have far-reaching consequences for those being taught. However, curriculum design is not an easy task. In physical education, a subject-centred curriculum is frequently used. In such a curriculum, the focus is commonly on the activities to be taught. However, designing a curriculum is not just a matter of identifying, for example, what content (declarative and procedural knowledge) to include and what content to leave out (for example, what activities will be covered in each year and in each unit of work and what activities will not be taught, as well as what underpinning (declarative) knowledge is needed to support the learning of those activities, for example, knowledge about how to move efficiently and effectively). It requires the conscious and systematic selection of declarative and procedural knowledge, as identified by UNESCO (see above) in the cognitive and physical domains. It also requires consideration of progression in the content (if this is not addressed, pupils will not progress and are likely to be bored – as demonstrated in the scenario). All this needs to be in light of clearly identified aims for the curriculum. Further, consideration needs to be given to a range of other factors, for example, the pupils for whom the curriculum is designed, the facilities available to support the delivery of the curriculum within the school and opportunities within the community to participate in activities outside the taught curriculum.

A curriculum also needs to be flexible to enable adaptations to be made in light of progress by a class, group or individual pupils (such curricula are frequently referred to as problem-centred and learner-centred curriculum designs). In addition, curriculum design and development is never finished; rather, it is important that a curriculum is continually reviewed and renewed; and that the same curriculum is not repeated year-after-year and/or for different classes within a year group without its suitability being questioned.

At present, the predominant type of subject-centred curriculum in many schools is what is commonly called a multi-activity curriculum. A multi-activity curriculum is designed "to promote motor-skill acquisition in traditional and non-traditional sports, games and physical activities" (Brunsdon, 2019, p.29). Research has shown that in a multi-activity curriculum, there are frequently short units of work (or blocks of learning) (for example, half a term) across multiple activities (frequently dominated by large-sided team games). The focus of such curricula is on the activity being taught and when. There tends to be little focus on why an activity is being taught and how it is being taught. Further, progression may not be clear – that is, what pupils should be learning over a period of time, with content building up over the years of schooling to enable pupils to work towards achieving the aims of the curriculum. As a result, pupils may repeat the same content over and over again in different units of work/blocks of learning, focusing on the same activity. Guy (in Kirk, 2010, p.7) called this type of curriculum "a mile wide and an inch deep" and Siedentop (2002, p.372) referred to the same introductory units being taught "again, and again, and again". For example, in athletics, each 'event' is taught in the same way for one lesson (for example, one lesson each on discus, javelin, shot putt, high jump, long jump, etc.) in each year in a secondary school.

So, what is a starting point in redesigning a curriculum which is progressive?

As far back as 1949, Tyler identified four key questions that need to be asked when designing a curriculum:

- What is the educational purpose?
- What educational experiences will best achieve this?
- What is the best way to organise these educational experiences?
- How do you know that the educational purpose has been achieved?

These questions are similar to the "what, why, when and how students should learn", identified by UNESCO (2016, p.5; see above). Since then, various principles that should inform curriculum design have been identified – whether this is a new curriculum or a review and renewal of an existing curriculum, whether it is within a national curriculum or designed independently. These include being: appropriate; coherent; developmental; focused; progressive; relevant; rigorous; vertically integrated; and having breadth, balance and depth (see, for example, Capel, Whitehead and Lawrence, 2025; Green, Cale and Harris, 2018). Further, and of critical importance, no curriculum can be progressive without knowing what pupils are working towards. This is reinforced by the Office for Standards in Education, Children's Services and Skills (Ofsted, 2023), who argued that to ensure effective progression, there needs to be clarity in the aims of the curriculum to be taught.

One common aim of many physical education curricula is for pupils to adopt a physically active lifestyle, both outside physical education lessons and after they leave school. For example, in England, one of the four aims of the current NCPE (Department for Education (DfE), 2013) is for pupils to "lead healthy, active lives" (see DfE, 2013 for the other aims of the NCPE). In Scotland, reference is made to "a programme of activities that aims to provide children and young people with learning experiences that enable them to develop the knowledge, motivation and ability to lead a physically active life" (Education Scotland, 2017). In Singapore, "The purpose of physical education is to enable students to demonstrate individually and with others, the physical skills, practices and values to enjoy a lifetime of active, healthy living" (Ministry of Education, 2016, p.1).

The aims of the curriculum are important because they should direct its design, as highlighted by UNESCO (2016). Ofsted (2018) reinforced this with its focus on the intent (aims, rationale, concepts), implementation (leadership, knowledge, progression, breadth/depth, assessment) and impact (outcomes) of the curriculum.

The content and how it is taught both need to be considered in designing the curriculum in relation to progression. These are considered briefly in the next sections.

The content of the curriculum

As indicated above, in order that pupils work towards achieving the aims of the curriculum, a curriculum should identify declarative and procedural knowledge that pupils should be learning and how this is developed over time. As an example, pupils should acquire and become more secure in a range of general movement patterns both in the early years and early stages of primary education. This should provide the foundation for learning a range of refined movement patterns in the primary school, which can be applied to simplified and/or conditioned forms of recognised activities. In turn, this provides the foundation for learning and progress in a range of specific movement patterns for a range of activities in different movement forms, which becomes more of a focus in the secondary school (for further information about general, refined and specific movement patterns refer to Capel, Whitehead and Lawrence, 2025, pp.186-190).

Attention to progression in content avoids a random approach that can only result in the pupils learning isolated and rather low-level declarative and procedural knowledge or even learning the same declarative and procedural knowledge "again, and again, and again" (Siedentop, 2002, p.372).

Linked to the work on intent, implementation and impact (see above), Ofsted (2023) identified three 'pillars of progress' which underpin how progression within physical education can be supported. These being:

- motor competence - knowledge of the range of movements that become increasingly sport- and physical activity-specific
- rules, strategies and tactics - knowledge of the conventions of participation in different sports and physical activities
- healthy participation - knowledge of safe and effective participation.

(Ofsted, 2023, pp.4-5)

These 'pillars of progress' can be used to plan the curriculum and to enable physical education teachers to consider carefully, what, why and how they are teaching. Whilst not explicit, links between the 'pillars of progress' and the NCPE (2013) content can be made. For example, across the key stages, pupils are expected to develop increasing levels of competence in a range of movement patterns and activities; develop their knowledge and understanding of strategies and tactics, and their understanding of healthy, active lifestyles.

For the current NCPE in England (DfE, 2013), the Association for Physical Education (AfPE, 2018) has produced a simple guide to progression (see Table 3.1).

These descriptions can help with identifying progression in the curriculum in any one school in relation to the specific content being taught.

One specific aspect for consideration in relation to progression in the content of the curriculum is breadth, depth and balance in the curriculum. This is considered below, starting with descriptions of what is meant by breadth, depth and balance.

Breadth refers to the range of learning. In physical education, this refers to the curriculum, including learning a wide range of movement patterns which can be applied to an appropriate mix of activities in different movement forms.

Depth refers to the extent to which key concepts are explored and revisited. The more time given in the curriculum to progressing an aspect of learning, the greater the depth of learning and hence progress a pupil should be able to make.

Balance refers to the amount of time allocated in the curriculum for different activities in different movement forms to enable pupils to progress to the extent that they are able to identify an (or those) activity(ies) they prefer to participate in outside physical education

Table 3.1 A simple guide to progression in the NCPE in England (adapted from AfPE, 2018)

Early Learning (nursery and reception years; 3-5 years old)

Pupils developing normally will:

- Develop general movement patterns

Be able to

- Negotiate space and obstacles safely, with consideration for themselves and others
- Demonstrate strength, balance and coordination when playing
- Move energetically in general movement patterns, such as climbing, dancing, hopping, jumping, running and skipping

Key Stage 1 (years 1 and 2; 5-7 years old)

Pupils should continue to develop general movement patterns, becoming increasingly competent and confident. They should access a broad range of opportunities to extend their agility, balance and coordination, individually and with others. They should be able to engage in competitive (both against themselves and against others) and co-operative activities in the physical domain, in a range of increasingly challenging situations.

Key Stage 2 (years 3-6; 7-11 years old)

Pupils should continue to develop and apply a broader range of movement patterns, learning how to use them in different ways and how to link them to make movement phrases. They should enjoy communicating, collaborating and competing with each other. They should develop an understanding of how to improve in different activities and learn how to evaluate and recognise their own progress.

Key Stage 3 (years 7-9; 11-14 years old)

Pupils should build on and embed the movement patterns learnt in key stages 1 and 2, becoming more accurate, competent, confident, consistent, efficient and secure in these, and be able to adapt them to apply them across different activities. They should understand what makes learning effective and how to apply these principles to their own and others' work. They should understand the long-term benefits of participating in physical activity and have the confidence, interest and motivation to get involved in physical activity out of school and in later life.

Key Stage 4 (years 10-11; 14-16 years old)

Pupils should tackle complex and demanding activities and should get involved in a range of activities as part of a physically active lifestyle.

---

lessons and after they leave school. For example, pupils should not only be learning a range of different games but also activities in other movement forms (see below).

In some schools, the curriculum covers as many activities as possible (although this may be limited to a range of different games). This decision may be based, at least in part, on an assumption that this enables pupils to select those activities they want to continue outside physical education lessons and after they leave school. In so doing, units of work or blocks of learning are short, such that they could be described as 'taster' courses, which introduce pupils to as many activities as possible but which do not enable them to develop their learning beyond an introductory level (see the multi-activity curriculum above). Unfortunately, if so little time is dedicated to any particular activity – there is unlikely to be enough time for pupils to engage in challenging practices that enable them to establish, revisit, refine and develop their learning so that they make progress and become competent and confident in that activity. As a result of prioritising breadth of learning, there is unlikely to be any real depth of learning, which allows really rewarding and meaningful experiences in the activity. Consequently, it is unlikely that pupils are able to select an (or a number of) activity(ies) they want to continue outside physical education lessons and after they leave school.

For in-depth learning to occur, teachers need to make hard and rational decisions about the content of the curriculum, including how many and what movement patterns and activities should be taught, and how progression is built in to enable pupils to make progress in their learning towards meeting the aims of the curriculum (including adopting a physically active lifestyle).

One way in which this can be achieved is to select a range of activities to focus on and allocate time to so that there is progression in the content, and pupils can progress in these activities. It is stressed that attention needs to be given not only to the number of activities per se but also, in order for there to be breadth and balance in the curriculum, a range of activities should be selected which have different fundamental characteristics, that is, activities should be selected from different movement forms. As a result of each activity being allocated enough time for pupils to have more in-depth learning, pupils are able to transfer their learning to other activities in the same movement form.

Capel, Whitehead and Lawrence (2025) identified five movement forms (these were identified from six movement forms identified by Whitehead, 2010 and Murdoch and Whitehead, 2013). They are: the adventure form, the aesthetic and artistic form, the athletic form, the competitive form and the fitness and health form. These are shown in Table 3.2.

Table 3.2 Movement forms

Movement form	The particular nature of the movement form and examples of activities in the movement form
Adventure	Focus on meeting risk and managing challenge, often in the outdoors within natural and often unpredictable environments. Activities can be carried out alone or as a group co-operative activity. Activity examples include climbing and orienteering.
Aesthetic and artistic	Focus on movement as an expressive medium within a creative, aesthetic or artistic context. Activity examples include artistic gymnastics, dance and synchronised swimming.
Athletic	Focus on physical challenges to reach personal best with regard to speed, distance, power or accuracy, within the context of competition in a controlled environment. Activity examples include athletics (such as long jump and throwing a javelin) and gymnastics.
Competitive	Focus on outwitting opponents both singularly and in teams, managing a variety of implements and objects and coping with changing and challenging conditions and terrain in order to achieve pre-determined goals. Activity examples include basketball, hockey, tennis and volleyball.
Fitness and health	Concerned with the improvement of body functions through regular repetitive participation. Activity examples include aerobics, circuits and Zumba.

Note: The same activity can fit into a number of different movement forms; for example, swimming can be aesthetic and expressive (synchronised swimming), athletic and/or competitive (for speed) or for fitness and health.

How the curriculum content is taught

In order that progression in the curriculum is translated into practice, alongside the specific content to be taught and how it is structured, it is important to consider how the curriculum is taught.

It is well known that any new learning is built upon the foundations of learning already achieved. It is therefore important to understand 'what should come next' in order that new learning builds from where pupils are in respect of current learning and that learning activities and opportunities build on what pupils already know and can do. Where such links are illogical, or jumps in learning are too big, there is more likely to be a breakdown in the learning process.

Further, learning is an ongoing process that occurs over time. To maximise progress, learning must be coherent, with a logical order, going step by step. Thus, not only should prior learning be taken into account when planning new learning, but the learning challenges presented to the pupils must relate to what has come before, showing a gradual increase in complexity towards a more advanced state.

It has been identified that any curriculum must have a clear rationale and be clear in relation to the aims towards which pupils are working. It must be clear what specific concepts are to be learned and show how new learning builds from current learning. However, it must also be flexible, with activities adapted/differentiated to meet the needs of all pupils. For example, many schools now have curriculum statements that clearly outline the aims (the purpose and direction/general intentions, Whitehead, 2021) of the curriculum. These are then supported with learning journeys or planned learning experiences which provide details of how the curriculum builds overtime, including what is to be taught, when and how it will be taught and when learning will be revisited and built upon. Such practices reflect the growing focus within schools on how high-quality teaching and learning can be embedded, influenced by, for example, *the Great Teachers' Toolkit* (Coe et al., 2020) and the Education Endowment Foundation's *Teaching and Learning Toolkit*.

Thus, alongside the content of the curriculum, consideration also needs to be given to the teaching approaches used to support delivery of the content. One frequently used framework of teaching approaches is the Spectrum of Teaching Styles (Mosston and Ashworth, 2002; 2008). Mosston and Ashworth (2008, p.5) argued that the Spectrum is composed of a series of behaviours that teachers can use to support learning, Further, when used effectively, "teachers have the ability to shift among the behaviors, as needed, to accommodate learners' needs, content focus, time constraints, and the myriad goals of education". It focuses on decision-making, particularly on who is making the decisions. Decisions are either made by the teacher or the pupil. The Spectrum moves from a point whereby all decisions are made by the teacher, to one where all decisions are made by the pupil, with styles either reproducing existing learning (reproductive styles) or producing new learning (productive styles).

For example, in reproductive styles, all decisions are made by the teacher, and pupils copy and practice, for example, command and practice styles. Evidence suggests that these are predominant in the teaching of physical education (see, for example, Ofsted, 2022). Such styles make it more likely that pupils copy without thinking, rather than being actively engaged in their learning. In productive styles, pupils make more decisions and hence are more likely to be actively involved in their learning. Thus, if there is to be progression in the curriculum so that pupils can make progress in their learning, productive styles, which enable pupils to gradually move towards taking responsibility for their own learning, need to be adopted. This will take time. The routines/processes applied within each style will need to be learned by the pupils. Pupils will need to become confident and competent in working within the different styles. Consideration will need to be given to the most appropriate style to be adopted based on the concepts and content being taught.

The next sub-section focuses on an aspect of continuity in the curriculum.

Continuity in the curriculum and in pupils' learning

The focus in the chapter so far has been on progression in the curriculum in order to support progress in pupils' learning. However, as stated above, progression is integrally related to continuity in the curriculum. When introducing the National Curriculum in 1989, Her Majesty's Inspectorate (now Ofsted) argued that "The 5-16 curriculum is constructed and delivered as a continuous and coherent whole" (DES, 1989, p.23). However, although guidance on progression (for example, in the current NCPE (DfE, 2013), produced by AfPE (2018; see above)), highlights progression throughout compulsory schooling, this might not occur if continuity is not maintained.

Progression in the curriculum might be disrupted at different times within schooling, for example, as pupils change teachers between units of work or between school years or when they change schools. At such times, teachers might not liaise with colleagues teaching the same class before and after what is being taught either in the same academic year or in the school year above or below the school year. Although continuity may be lost at a number of different times, it is particularly vulnerable when pupils change schools, including when they transfer from primary to secondary school. The challenge is therefore how to get continuity in the curriculum when any change occurs, particularly when the transition between primary and secondary school takes place. It is this transition which is the focus of this brief section.

Particular difficulties in maintaining continuity in learning in the transfer from primary to secondary school arise from, for example,

- pupils joining the same secondary school from a number of different primary schools – each of which has been following a different curriculum
- lack of liaison between a secondary school and its feeder primary schools (that is, the primary schools from which pupils transfer) due to the number of pupils transferring from different schools, or the number of primary schools that feed into one secondary school
- some secondary physical education teachers may assume that there is little or limited teaching of physical education in primary schools. Whilst this was clearly evident in the early twenty-first century (see, for example, Capel, Zwozdiak-Myers and Lawrence, 2003; Capel, Zwozdiak-Myers and Lawrence, 2004), the introduction of the Physical Education and School Sport premium in 2012 has focused attention on the teaching and development of physical education within primary schools. One of the foci of this initiative has been increasing the confidence, knowledge and skills of primary school teachers in teaching physical education (DfE, 2023). Whilst there is a consensus that the impact has not been as strong as potentially first intended (see, for example, Lawrence,

2021; Ofsted, 2023), it is acknowledged that there has been improvement in the teaching and learning taking place in primary physical education in some schools.

There are a range of possible solutions to this. For learning to be continuous, teachers have to know what pupils have learned and consider how to take account of the range of learning which pupils have had in physical education in their primary school. For example, in an ideal situation, the curriculum will be planned as a whole from the start to the end of compulsory schooling – including both content and how it is taught. However, although this may be possible in all-through schools, this may not occur where there are a number of different primary schools feeding into one secondary school and where pupils from one primary school move to a number of different secondary schools. In many contexts, primary and secondary schools plan their curricula independently, and hence pupils have very different experiences and have made different progress in their learning in primary school.

Another is for there to be close liaison between teachers in primary and secondary schools so that each understands what the other is doing and what and how pupils are learning. This includes acknowledging the quality of teaching in primary schools. This will enable physical education teachers in secondary schools to build on what pupils have learned in primary schools and teachers in primary schools to ensure the pupils they teach are prepared for what they will be learning in secondary school.

However, these – and any other solutions – take time and effort. This requires teachers to prioritise continuity in the curriculum. Without this prioritisation, one solution adopted by many secondary schools has been what is frequently called a 'fresh start' approach (generally taken to mean there is little or no consideration or recognition given to what experiences/learning pupils bring with them from primary schools and trying to build on this. Rather, teachers in a secondary school start teaching from a baseline level, irrespective of what pupils have learned in their primary school and irrespective of what information is passed to them about each pupil from their primary school).

In some secondary schools, pupils are initially taught some lessons involving fundamental movement skills, from which teachers try to identify pupils' current level of learning – the learning of pupils as a whole and/or the learning of individual pupils. In other schools, the curriculum identifies activities to be taught, with teachers starting at a basic level. Either way, continuity in the curriculum is lost, as are progression in the curriculum and progress in pupils' learning.

So, how did Lawcap School use this information to improve progression and continuity in their curriculum and hence improve the learning and progress of pupils in physical education? This is identified in the second part of the scenario.

Scenario (part 2) – how the issue identified at Lawcap School was addressed

Having identified an issue around lack of progression and continuity in the curriculum, and then having reviewed and discussed literature related to curriculum design (including content and how it was taught), the physical education department focused on what they needed to do to build progression and continuity into the curriculum to enable pupils to progress in their learning in the subject.

To help them to do this, they used the following seven steps in redesigning a subject curriculum identified by Oak National Academy (2023):

1. Identification of a time frame, outcome and requirements of the curriculum
2. Identification of the core content
3. Organisation of content into big ideas, questions and concepts
4. Sequencing and organisation of content
5. Identify breadth, depth, balance and diversity in the curriculum
6. Design specific content
7. Review and revise.

Curriculum design and content

In undertaking a review of the existing curriculum, the department worked together to identify what they specifically aimed for pupils to achieve and what the curriculum would need to look like to enable them to achieve this. This allowed them to create a curriculum statement that identified the aims of the physical education curriculum at Lawcap and the rationale for this. These aims incorporated the aims of the NCPE in England (DfE, 2013).

This was then shared with the wider school (to ensure that it met the aims of the school curriculum as a whole) as well as with the feeder primary schools to ensure that it reflected and built on what pupils joining Lawcap in year 7 had learned/experienced. Not only did this support better communication between schools, but it also provided an opportunity for the department to showcase what they were doing to support pupils' transitioning to the school. Further, it opened opportunities for both primary and secondary school teachers to work together to gain a better understanding of what they were doing and provide support, where appropriate. As a result, there was clearer progression and continuity in the curriculum from primary to secondary school.

Central to the new curriculum was a focus on what pupils needed to learn rather than focusing on specific activities. Drawing on the 'pillars of progress' (motor competence; rules, strategies and tactics; healthy participation, Ofsted, 2023) and drawing on the principles of progression (Howells et al., 2018), the department created a pupil 'learning journey', which provided an overview of what pupils would learn across the five years that they would be at the school. Each year had a different 'big idea/question', which developed in complexity as they moved through the learning journey.

Underpinning this was a clear curriculum map for each of the five years. Here, the focus moved to ensuring that the pupils were secure in the movement patterns they needed to enable them to learn and engage effectively in a range of activities. To achieve this, activities were taught across a school term (a change to the previous 1/2 term cycle). This meant that pupils had a longer period of time to make progress. Thus, a focus on mastery rather than quantity started to become embedded.

Department considered how the content should build, including the range of content. They also worked on building on what pupils had learned in their primary schools. They identified gaps in progression in the curriculum in relation to some movement forms. As a result, the department at Lawcap adapted their curriculum to help address the gaps – with regard to breadth, depth and balance in the curriculum. In addition, they are continuing to work with the primary schools in relation to what pupils are learning in order that they have effective underpinnings for the curriculum in the secondary school.

Units of work now covered a wider range of activities in different movement forms, building more diversity into the curriculum. For example, boys and girls in key stage 3 (years 7-9) all learned in the aesthetic and artistic (in the form of gymnastics and dance). As they progressed through the school, opportunities for pupils to select the activities they took part in were built into the curriculum. For example, trampolining was introduced in key stage 4 (years 10 and 11) as part of an options programme. Activities that had not previously been on the curriculum were also introduced, for example, handball and pickleball. The purpose of this was to identify activities that developed the movement patterns identified in the curriculum statement but in activities where fewer pupils had previous learning experience, meaning that pupils were being encouraged to apply what they already knew and could do in different contexts.

Central to the revised curriculum was that it was viewed by all teachers as a broad framework. This meant that teachers were able to modify it as appropriate for each class, with a specific focus on ensuring that learning was secure before pupils were moved onto new learning.

Curriculum - how it was taught

Each class was taught by the same teacher throughout the year so that teachers developed a deeper understanding of the classes for which they had responsibility. This enabled them to take account of not only progression and continuity in the curriculum, but also individual pupils' learning needs. To ensure that all teachers could teach all activities in the curriculum, teachers also audited their own subject knowledge around the range of activities in different movement forms that were being taught, and professional development was offered to support those who identified a training need.

Teachers worked together to consider the most appropriate teaching approaches for the activities being taught. Where possible, productive approaches were used (Mosston and Ashworth, 2002; 2008), with pupils provided with more opportunities to use their prior learning to support the creation of new knowledge. As a result, an emphasis on developing independent learning became a central theme within the learning journey.

Over time, spending more time on fewer activities resulted in pupils experiencing more success and becoming more competent and confident and showing a greater willingness to take responsibility for their own learning. They were able to transfer their learning to other activities in the different movement forms. Pupils seemed to be enjoying physical education, were motivated and 'switched on', trying hard to learn and improve in the subject. As a result, pupils were not saying things such as 'not this again' or 'we have already done this'.

Summary and key points

This chapter has focused on progression and continuity in the curriculum-two key components involved in planning and teaching a curriculum, which results in physical education lessons that enable pupils to make progress in their learning.

It has focused on curriculum design, the content and how it is taught, as well as lack of continuity in the curriculum, particularly in the transition from primary to secondary school. A scenario identified the issue at Lawcap School. It described how the department investigated their own practice and used theory, research and evidence to make changes.

It is acknowledged that there are other aspects that could be considered in relation to progression and continuity in the curriculum. However, focus on the four aspects (design of the curriculum, including what and how physical education is being taught, with regard to progression as well as where lack of continuity occurs) was deliberate so that the extent of any changes that need to be made was not overwhelming.

References

AfPE (Association for Physical Education) (2018) 'A simple guide to National Curriculum progression in physical education', *Physical Education Matters*, Summer 8, 49, available at: https://www.afpe.org.uk/page/PublicationsandResources (accessed 10 November 2024).

Benyon, L. (1981) 'Curriculum continuity', *Education 3-13*, 9 (2), 36–41.

Brunsdon, J. (2019) 'Curriculum models and models based practice', *Physical Education Matters*, Summer, 2019, 28-30.

Capel, S., Whitehead, M. and Lawrence, J. (2025) *Progression and Progress in Physical Education*, Abingdon: Routledge.

Capel, S., Zwozdiak-Myers, P. and Lawrence, J. (2003) 'A study of current practice in the liaison between primary and secondary schools in physical education', *European Physical Education Review*, 9 (2), 115-134.

Capel, S., Zwozdiak-Myers, P. and Lawrence, J. (2004) 'Exchange of information about physical education to support the transition from primary to secondary school', *Educational Research*, 46 (3), 283-300.

Coe, R., Rauch, C.J., Kime, S. and Singleton, D. (2020) *Great Teaching Toolkit, Evidence Review*, Evidence Based Education, available at: https://f.hubspotusercontent30.net/hubfs/2366135/Great%20Teaching%20Toolkit%20Evidence%20Review.pdf (accessed 6 August 2024).

DES (Department of Education and Science) (1989) *Physical Education from 5 to 16, Curriculum Matters 16: An HMI Series*, London: HMSO.

DES/WO (Department of Education and Science and the Welsh Office) (1990) *Physical Education National Curriculum Working Group: Interim Report*, London: HMSO.

DfE (Department for Education) (2013) *National Curriculum in England: Physical Education Programmes of Study*, available at: https://www.gov.uk/government/publications/national-curriculum-in-england-physical-education-programmes-of-study/national-curriculum-in-england-physical-education-programmes-of-study (accessed 16 June 2025).

DfE (Department for Education) (2023) *PE and Sport Premium for Primary Schools: Guidance*, available at: https://www.gov.uk/guidance/pe-and-sport-premium-for-primary-schools#about-the-pe-and-sport-premium (accessed 6 August 2024).

Education Endowment Foundation (n.d.) *Teaching and Learning Toolkit*, available at: https://educationendowmentfoundation.org.uk/education-evidence/teaching-learning-toolkit (accessed 12 December 2024).

Education Scotland (2017) *Physical Education, Physical Activity and Sport*, available at: https://education.gov.scot/parentzone/learning-at-home/supporting-health-and-wellbeing/physical-education-physical-activity-and-sport/ (accessed 12 December 2024).

Green, K., Cale, L. and Harris, J. (2018) 'Re-imagination and re-design in physical education: implicit and explicit models in England and Wales', in H.A. Lawson (ed.) *Redesigning Physical Education an Equity Agenda in Which Every Child Matters*, Abingdon and New York: Routledge, pp.156-170.

Howells, K. with Carney. A., Castle, N. and Little, R. (2018) *Mastering Primary Physical Education*, London: Bloomsbury Academic.

Kirk, D. (2010) *Physical Education Futures*, Abingdon: Routledge.

Lawrence, J. (2021) 'Debates in the teaching of primary physical education', in V. Bower (ed.) *Debates in Primary Education*, Abingdon: Routledge, pp.231–242.

Ministry of Education Singapore (2016) *Physical Education Teaching & Learning Syllabus Primary, Secondary & Pre-University*, Singapore: Student Development Curriculum Division available at: https://www.moe.gov.sg/-/media/files/post-secondary/syllabuses/pe/physical_education_syllabus_2014.ashx (accessed 5 January 2025).

Mosston, M. and Ashworth, S. (2002) *Teaching Physical Education* (5th edition), London: Pearson.

Mosston, M. and Ashworth, S. (2008) *Teaching Physical Education* (first online edition), available at: https://spectrumofteachingstyles.org/assets/files/book/Teaching_Physical_Edu_1st_Online.pdf (accessed 20 December 2024).

Murdoch, E. and Whitehead, M. (2013) 'What should pupils learn in physical education?', in S. Capel and M. Whitehead (eds) *Debates in Physical Education*, Abingdon: Routledge, pp. 55–73.

Oak National Academy (2023) *How to Design a Subject Curriculum: A Quick Guide*, available at: https://docs.google.com/document/d/1yfy-OeME9Iv6BVbfna5g9E3vIiEcsMhE5CXhcw0VcE0/edit?tab=t.0#heading=h.80rv7qb93ei (accessed 12 December 2024).

Ofsted (Office for Standards in Education, Children's Services and Skills) (2018) *An Investigation into How to Assess the Quality of Education through Curriculum Intent, Implementation and Impact*, available at: https://assets.publishing.service.gov.uk/media/5fb3e55fe90e07208fd2cb85/Curriculum_research_How_to_assess_intent_and_implementation_of_curriculum_191218.pdf (accessed 20 August 2024).

Ofsted (Office for Standards in Education, Children's Services and Skills) (2022) *Research and Analysis Review Series: PE* published 18 March 2022, available at: https://www.gov.uk/government/publications/research-review-series-pe (accessed 21 December 2024).

Ofsted (Office for Standards in Education, Children's Services and Skills) (2023) *Levelling the Playing Field: The Physical Education Subject Report*, available at: https://www.gov.uk/government/publications/subject-report-series-pe/levelling-the-playing-field-the-physical-education-subject-report (accessed 20 August 2024).

Siedentop, D. (2002) 'Content knowledge for physical education', *Journal of Teaching in Physical Education*, 21, 368–377.

Tyler, R.W. (1949) *Basic Principles of Curriculum and Instruction*, Chicago: University of Chicago Press.

UNESCO (The United Nations Educational, Scientific and Cultural Organization) (2016) *What Makes a Quality Curriculum?*, available at: https://unesdoc.unesco.org/ark:/48223/pf0000243975# (accessed 20 August 2024).

Whitehead, M.E. (2010) *Physical Literacy Throughout the Lifecourse*, Abingdon: Routledge.

Whitehead, M. (2021) 'Learner-centred teaching: A physical literacy perspective' in S. Capel, J. Cliffe and J. Lawrence (eds.) *Learning to Teach Physical education in the Secondary School: A Companion to School Experience* (5th edition), Abingdon: Routledge, pp. 227–240.

Chapter 4 Challenges related to assessment

Developing effective assessment in lessons

Joanne Cliffe and Katie Potter

Introduction

There are multiple ways in which pupils are assessed in physical education, yet they mainly fall into two categories – assessment for learning and assessment of learning. In assessment for learning, the focus is on how pupils make use of information given to them to succeed in their learning; it is a constant learning dialogue between the teacher and pupil as well as between peers (Black and Wiliam, 2010). This ongoing assessment for learning informs assessment of learning, where summative judgements are made on a pupil's attainment at a point in time. Assessment of learning is more likely to take place at the end of a series of lessons; usually a unit of work. Quality assessment is where assessment for learning is an integral part of assessment of learning; where the teacher is fully aware of a pupil's progress against the objectives of a unit of work and intended learning outcomes of a lesson and is confident in articulating a pupil's learning. Whilst it is really assessment for learning that supports pupils' progress (Williams and Cliffe, 2011), this chapter is focused on assessment of learning. The reason for this is that assessment of learning is considered to be one of the weakest aspects of teaching physical education (Office for Standards in Education, Children's Services and Skills (Ofsted), 2023). The chapter will occasionally refer to where assessment for learning contributes to assessment of learning, along with the importance of an assessment policy.

Reporting of inadequate assessment in physical education has been consistent over the last four decades despite changing curricular and a variety of government initiatives over the years (López-Pastor *et al.*, 2013). Assessment per se continues to pose challenges for physical education teachers. Indeed, Ofsted (2023) reported that although some physical education departments operate well-considered assessment policies, where systems have purpose and clarity, for many departments, their assessment procedures are not fit for purpose. The quality of assessment practice remains a concern in terms of the reliability and validity of assessment policies (Hay and Penney, 2009; Thorburn, 2007; Veal, 1988). Further, at the heart of assessment policy is matching pupils' attainment against the unit of work objectives. However, whilst attempts to align assessment with objectives and intended learning outcomes are made, too many variables that have negative impact come into play (Chan, Hay and Tinning, 2011).

This chapter aims to explore reasons for some of the pitfalls of assessment of learning as well as to investigate how effective assessment of learning and/or an effective assessment policy is managed. In doing so, the application of theory, research, evidence and best practice to help address challenges assessment brings to physical education will be considered. In order to illustrate how theory, research, evidence and best practice support teaching and learning in physical education, a case study is provided, which demonstrates areas of weakness in assessment in physical education in a secondary school in the West Midlands (referred to as 'the case study school'). Other difficulties of assessment are also highlighted, and ways to address the challenges posed in part 1 of the case study are considered. The second part of the case study then shows how the weaknesses exposed in the first part of the case study were addressed, utilising a range of theory, research, evidence and best practice. In summary, the chapter presents an opportunity to reflect on what was learnt from this real-life experience in school whilst recapping intervention strategies, which may equip teachers with knowledge and skills to improve assessment and hence pupils' learning.

Case study (part 1)

The following case study is a real-life example of an assessment policy which elucidated a challenge faced by a head of department.

The case study details an ineffective assessment policy designed for pupils in key stage 3. It was intended to provide a structured assessment of pupils' progress in physical education, making use of the 'head, heart and hands' approach (Brühlmeier, 2010; Lynch and Norley, 2024). The head, heart and hands approach has long been considered a holistic approach to education. Johann Heinrich Pestalozzi (1746 to 1827), credited for founding pedagogy (the method and practice of teaching as a discrete subject or theoretical concept), pursued holistic education "to create well-balanced, moral individuals by ensuring that head, heart and hands (the natural powers innate in all humans) are equally and harmoniously developed" (Nair, 2024).

The head, heart and hands approach was adapted for use in the National Curriculum for Physical Education in England by the Association for Physical Education (afPE, 2018) in the form of a 'poster' after the removal of assessment levels (Department for Education (DfE), 2015). Although predominantly aimed at primary physical education, the case study school (a secondary school catering for pupils aged 11-16 years) adopted the approach in devising their assessment policy. This policy aimed to focus on the holistic development of pupils' cognitive understanding, emotional engagement and physical skills. Separate templates were utilised for head, heart and hands (see Figure 4.1 for an example from the department's assessment policy detailing the 'head' template for generic physical education along with the head of department's annotations outlining its faults). Pupils' assessment of learning was against the generic physical education criteria for all taught activities. The assessment 6-point scale ranged from 'emerging' to 'mastery' (see Figure 4.1), as the template aimed to provide a comprehensive measurement of progress. However, its application across the department proved to be ineffective.

In the case study school, a physical education teacher was observed teaching a year 7 gymnastics lesson, the last in the unit of work. This was a 'final assessment' lesson. The pupils were tasked with performing a paired routine based on an 'English Schools Gymnastics' (2019-2020) template (see Figure 4.2), which underpinned the unit of work content for skills such as forward roll, backward roll, headstand, cartwheel, travel and balance. Whilst the criteria for the routine was shared with the pupils during the lesson (and the

Head (Cognitive)

> Three separate assessment grids for head, heart and hands, so difficult to refer to in lesson

> Assessment covers the whole of key stage 3. Unrealistic expectations for year 7 to reach mastery can lead to demotivation

> Criteria trying to fit in with the whole school assessment policy

	0	1	2	3	4	5	6	7	8	9
	EMERGING	DEVELOPING 1		DEVELOPING 2		SECURE 1		SECURE 2		MASTERY
	Can begin to identify why we need to warm up.	Knows the importance of a warmup and can name at least two stages of warming up.		Can explain the importance of warming up and can name the three different stages and begin to identify some of the muscles we use.		Can explain what happens to the body when we warm up and the physical benefits of warming up.		Can explain what happens to the body when we warm up and can explain both the physical and psychological benefits of completing a warmup.		Can explain what happens to the body when we warm up and cool down and can explain both the physical and psychological benefits of completing one.
	Begins to understand why we need to have rules in physical education.	Can describe some skills and rules in some sports. May know simple tactics but needs support to explain them.		Can describe how to use rules and tactics in a game situation.		Can begin to apply knowledge of rules and tactics to attempt to outwit an opponent in a game situation.		Can effectively suggest and apply tactics to outwit an opponent in a game situation.		Can effectively suggest complex tactics to their team, which are applied to enhance team performance.
	Understands the aspects of performance they need to improve on.	Can make suggestions as to how to improve their own and others' performance.		Can identify problems or misconceptions with technique and begins to select the appropriate teaching points to correct mistakes.		Can compare performances. Recognise a good performance and use the information to make suggestions of how to improve their own performance.		Evaluate the strengths and weaknesses of the performance and prioritise the most important mistake to correct.		Critically evaluate and develop targets to have impact on their own and other performances.
	Can point to a location of muscle when provided with the name.	Can identify where some of the major muscles of the body are.		Can identify where some of the major muscles in the body are and can explain the role of a tendon.		Can identify what muscles they are working in an activity and can provide the name of the muscle.		Can explain the differences between agonist and antagonist muscles and can indicate the prime mover in a sporting situation.		Can explain the differences between concentric and eccentric (isotonic) contractions and can explain how muscle groups work isometrically or isotonically.
	Can find their pulse with support and understand what is meant by resting heart rate.	Can explain how to take their resting heart rate and record this data using the correct unit.		Can explain what a normal resting heart rate for an adult should be. Can explain the differences between aerobic and anaerobic exercise.		Can explain the differences between aerobic and anaerobic exercise and can provide sporting examples of each.		Can use the duration and/or intensity of a physical activity in order to identify and justify why it would be aerobic or anaerobic, e.g. marathon (aerobic), sprint (anaerobic).		Can use maximum heart rate to work out whether an athlete is working in their aerobic or anaerobic threshold. Can explain the bi products of aerobic and anaerobic exercise.
	Can identify some ways to be healthy.	Can explain what is meant by health and fitness.		Can explain the relationship between health and fitness.		Can identify some of the different health benefits of physical activity.		Can explain the benefits to the body and mind of regular participation and understand the consequences of a sedentary lifestyle.		Can justify the advantages of following an active and healthy lifestyle on physical, mental, and social wellbeing and the consequences of a sedentary lifestyle. Splitting them into physical, mental and social categories.
								Can explain the short and immediate effects of exercise on the body.		Can explain the immediate, short and long term effects of exercise on the body and can indicate the different timings between each stage.
							Begins to use their knowledge of rules to officiate competitions with support.	Can use their knowledge to rules to officiate competitions on their own but lacks confidence with some decision making.		Can lead and officiate competitions showing a good understanding of the rules.
	Unmanageable to assess for large class	Different criteria relate to different aspects of the physical education curriculum, cannot achieve it all at different assessment points in the year		Difficult for pupils to interpret and understand where they are at and what they need to do to improve			Complex and Overloading			The descriptions rely heavily on subjective interpretations, such as "good level of effort" or "outstanding precision"

Figure 4.1 Case study part 1 – example of a component (the head) in an ineffective assessment policy for key stage 3 physical education with annotations (Figure 4.1 was devised by the case study school and is reproduced here with permission).

Challenges related to assessment 45

Figure 4.2 Lesson criterion shared with the class (based on English Schools Gymnastics, 2019-2020).

(1) Position of Bases arms off the floor. Top shows strong front support position	(2) Base sitting on knees with both ankles together. Top in bent leg headstand in tuck position and toes pointed. Base provides minimal support, arms of base straight.	(3) Top in balanced handstand with the base provides minimal support. A straight handstand is required from the top showing extension & good body tension.
(4) Base legs should be straight. The Top should be in chair position supported by the Base in the lower back.	(5) Feet of B placed above knees of A. Arms of the base bent or straight when top is in balance. Base is kneeling with seat resting on heels.	(6) The top forms an extended flat bodyline, with the hands and shoulders over the knees of the base. Both base and top should have straight arms
(7) The arms of the base should be straight. The support on hands can face either direction but should show an extended bodyline.	(8) Arms of the base and top when in balance straight. Base should be sat in straddle, legs straight toes pointed.	(9) Top shows strong front support position. Base supports below the knee, arms straight.
Gymnasts back to back at the start, each completes a full circle. Finishing where they started	A is in arch; head, arms, shoulders and ankles are clear from the floor. B forward rolls over	A in dish, head, arms, shoulders and ankles are clear from the floor. B: Cartwheels over the waist with one arm either side.
Roll of A should be smooth. Hands of B assist stand. Additional steps not permitted	Cartwheel supported throughout.	The legs of the base must be straight. There must be a flight phase from the top after contact with base.

Figure 4.2 (Continued)

previous lesson), the specific assessment criteria the teacher was expected to use to assess the pupils' performances were not communicated to the class. Therefore, there was a mismatch between the pupils' understanding of what was taught and what aspects of what was taught were being assessed.

Although the pupils had focused on creating their routines in the previous lesson, they were unable to articulate their attainment in relation to the assessment criteria, as noted by the lesson observer. As the pupils could not describe their learning, this lack of clarity left pupils unsure how to refine their routines. Further, as this was the final lesson of the unit

Making up the sequence

(Total value 16.0 marks for each pair of gymnasts)

- **Content:** Include **2 balances, 2 tempo moves,** and **3 individual moves** as shown in the chart above *(Worth 3.5 marks)*

  - **Composition:** Put together sequence with choreography to show:

* Good use of floor with changes in direction and levels (0.5)
* Variety of linking ideas, (leaps, spins, dance)   (0.5)
* Artistry & presentation including use of music   (0.5)
* Synchronisation   (1.0)

(Worth up to 2.5 marks)

- **Execution** faults deducted

  (Worth up to 10.0 marks)

- Can be performed with or without instrumental music. (no words) and to last no longer than **1min 30 secs**.

  - Each pairs balance is held for **3 seconds** and any individual balance for **2 seconds**

Figure 4.2 (Continued)

of work, there was no opportunity for pupils to show progression based on the feedback provided by the teacher.

The teacher struggled to assess every pupil accurately during the lesson due to the demands of simultaneously managing the class and assessing performances. In comments to the lesson observer, the teacher expressed feeling overwhelmed by the complexity of balancing class management with completing the assessments. Consequently, the grades were recorded several days later during the teacher's planning, preparation and assessment time. This therefore relied on the teacher's memory of the lesson. The department's assessment policy outlined six grading categories on a scale from emerging to mastery (see Figure 4.1). When the lesson observer asked about the assessment, the teacher admitted they found it difficult to interpret the difference in the scales between 'emerging' and 'mastery' performance. At the start, 'emerging' refers to taught content, yet pupils are not able to put this into practice. In 'developing', which is split into two developing scales, pupils begin to apply their understanding, first with support, moving to independent learning, where they can express and perform some of the taught content. The 'secure' scale means a pupil is consistent in responding to the taught content. This is again split into two; however, the criteria (as shown in Figure 4.1) show little difference between the two scales and as a result, the teacher found it difficult to distinguish between secure 1 and secure 2. The final scale is 'mastery', where pupils are able to evidence understanding and the application of knowledge and skills without explicit teaching.

Challenges with this assessment policy

This case study provides an example of a weak assessment policy. The policy template (see Figure 4.1) attempts to capture much in relation to a pupil's progress, but in reality, it was difficult for teachers to implement. A concern with the assessment policy template, particularly in its application, was that the content was generic and not directly matched to the objectives of this year 7 gymnastics unit of work. Further, failure by the teacher to share the assessment criteria, which constituted the objectives of the unit of work, left the pupils unaware of what they were being assessed against. During the 'assessment lesson', when asked by the teacher, pupils were unable to identify their strengths or pinpoint areas for improvement. However, this also suggests that assessment for learning in previous lessons was lacking. This resonates with Ofsted's (2023) findings, according to which weak assessment occurred when teachers did not make use of pupil progress from one lesson to inform subsequent teaching in the next. For example, Ofsted (2023) noted that teachers did not always correct pupils' misconceptions or extend pupils' knowledge to enable pupils to progress in their learning.

Assessment was discussed in department meetings, during which teachers shared their concerns regarding the assessment policy generically and specifically in relation to the observed lesson described in the case study. The head of department deemed the assessment template overly complex, as it contained numerous, generic criteria that made it difficult for both the teacher and pupils (when shared) to understand and apply consistently. In addition, vague, subjective language was problematic, leading to inconsistencies in interpretation across the department. As the observed teacher in the case study was unable to provide immediate feedback to pupils, this delay diminished the impact of timely feedback on a pupil's learning and highlighted problems in the assessment process, where assessment for learning should inform assessment of learning. Furthermore, the three separate assessment criteria templates for head, heart and hands (the example of 'head' is shown in Figure 4.1) emphasised the difficulty of applying the template in a practical setting. This was particularly challenging for the observed teacher, who was still developing their subject knowledge and class management. Attempting to assess pupils across these three separate templates reduced the teacher's ability to provide accurate or meaningful assessment, particularly as the selected generic criteria were not embedded in the taught unit of work.

Overall, the reliability of the template was of concern. The difference between the interpretation by the observed teacher and the observer revealed inconsistent practice across the department, which was also raised and discussed in department meetings. In addition, since the assessment policy was designed to cover the entire span of key stage 3, it imposed unrealistic expectations on year 7 pupils, who often struggled to meet criteria that were more appropriate for years 8 and 9. The mismatch between the pupils' learning and the assessment policy led to frustration and demotivation, as year 7 pupils felt overwhelmed and incapable of achieving success within the template (some of which was founded on GCSE criteria). The department collectively surmised that the assessment policy was too generic, attempting to cover the scheme of work, rather than an explicit unit of work which would better inform an overall assessment.

These challenges highlight the need for a more practical, streamlined and transparent assessment policy that can be effectively implemented in physical education lessons.

Reasoning/theory

In addition to the issues explained in the first part of the case study, this section considers relevant theory, research, evidence and best practice that might highlight what makes assessment effective or ineffective. In doing so, ways of addressing the issues that ineffective assessment may pose are considered.

The challenges in assessing physical education

Effective assessment is embedded in good teaching. Some of the issues that lead to ineffective assessment are explored in the following section.

Holistic assessment

From the outset, the department attempted to engage in the holistic nature of learning as mentioned in the first part of the case study. However, the interpretation of these for assessment was overly complicated and did not have a clear focus on how pupils' attainment fit with the head, heart and hands approach. There is a need to consider what constitutes head, heart and hands. In work developed by Islam et al. (2022), the head, heart and hands approach is combined with Bloom's Taxonomy (Bloom et al., 1956) and the three domains of learning. The latter resonates with the holistic teaching of physical education, where pupils learn through the three domains, namely cognitive, affective and psychomotor. The cognitive domain is concerned with thinking and the acquisition of knowledge (head) (Bloom et al., 1956); cognitive elements assist pupils in their thinking and development of knowledge to underpin their learning in the physical. The affective domain is concerned with emotions, feelings and attitudes (heart) (Krathwohl, Bloom and Masia, 1964); affective elements are focused on social and emotional aspects of learning, including leading, teamwork, pupils' thoughts about their work, self-esteem and well-being. The psychomotor domain is concerned with movement and the application of skills (Harrow, 1972); psychomotor elements comprise physical elements, such as acquiring and applying skills (afPE, 2018;

Lynch and Norley, 2024). These domains are useful in physical education, as they combine understanding and practical elements. Further, Gazibara (2013, p.77) highlights "significant connections between movement and learning". Therefore, schools should consider meaningful ways of measuring all aspects of pupils' progress through holistic learning, including communication, social skills, physical development, resilience and independence (DfE, 2015), and these should be captured in an appropriate assessment policy.

School and physical education assessment policies

Schools are encouraged to develop assessment policies that encourage pupils to know more and do more in physical education (Ofsted, 2023). However, the House of Commons Education Committee (2017) suggested there is not enough support in place for schools and departments to implement their own assessment policies effectively and, because of this, many schools have adopted ineffective assessment policies. It is important to note that what happens in one school does not necessarily happen in another, so even when sharing best practice from their physical education networks, another school's policy may not meet the needs of the pupils in their own school context. The variety of different approaches to assessment can be overwhelming for heads of departments when devising their assessment policy. Their first consideration is how the department assessment policy aligns with the school's assessment policy. It is not always straightforward for a physical education assessment policy to fit neatly into a school-wide policy and a school policy may not address the needs of physical education. Therefore, in developing an effective assessment policy, a head of department may face the frustration of their policy being compromised in order to fit with a school-wide assessment policy. For example, in the case study school, the school-wide policy is data-driven. This means that year 9 pupils are awarded an end-of-year (July) grade in October, long before they have been taught the assessed content. This made it difficult for the head of department to ensure that the physical education assessment policy was linked to the school-wide assessment policy.

Some of the challenges of attempting to align a physical education assessment policy with a school's standardised assessment policy are highlighted below. For example, the rigid structure of standardised assessments in schools often lacks the flexibility needed to accommodate the practical nature of physical education. This limitation can result in a physical education department 'shoehorning' their assessment to fit with other subjects. In turn, this restricts the ability of a physical education department to tailor assessments to effectively capture the diverse range of skills, knowledge and understanding developed through physical education. Such a policy results in a negative impact on physical education as a subject (Ofsted, 2023).

Unlike most core subjects that follow standardised assessment points at specific intervals throughout the academic year (such as end of half and full terms), physical education assessments at the case study school may need to be conducted at different points. This is due to pupils' learning being assessed after completing an eight-lesson unit of work which does not coincide with the end of half or full term. This resonates with the argument that physical education is a unique and distinct subject area with its own set of aims, objectives and intended learning outcomes and assessment needs (Walters, MacLaughlin and Deakin, 2023).

Front drop	Emerging:	Developing:	Secure:	Mastery:
	Can demonstrate hand to knee bounces with some mistakes	Can demonstrate hand to knee bounces with the correct timing and can land in front drop position	Can perform hands to knees to a front drop without a throwdown mat	Can perform a front landing without a throwdown mat and can input within a routine

Figure 4.3 Example of assessment for a trampolining front-drop lesson (Figure 4.3 was devised by the case study school and is reproduced here with permission).

Thus, attempting to fit physical education into a standardised assessment framework designed for other subjects may not fully capture the essence and value of physical education, ultimately impacting the quality and authenticity of assessment practices in the subject. An example of this was assessment by 'levels' in England, which have since been removed as a government requirement (DfE, 2015). Removing these was intended to give a head of department freedom in choosing an assessment policy that is fit for purpose and meets the needs of their pupils (Simmons and Maclean, 2018). However, one challenge for a department is where the assessment policy is not robustly embedded in the units of work or overall scheme of work in the physical education curriculum, or left to a sole assessment lesson. A further challenge is to ensure consistency in implementing the policy, as effectiveness in assessment practice remains a significant challenge in physical education (Ofsted, 2023).

The assessment lesson

Physical education departments have a duty to record assessment data, as this informs the writing of school reports, which are sent to parents (DfE and Standards and Testing Agency (STA), 2024). Assessment of learning sometimes leans towards the tendency to treat assessment as a 'bolt-on' at the end of a unit of work in physical education. This can put pupils at a disadvantage if their previous work has not been taken into consideration. For example, teachers often evaluate a pupil's performance in competitive scenarios to gauge the application of skills which were taught throughout the unit. Unfortunately, this approach often isolates assessment as a standalone event, where teachers provide judgements solely based on pupils' performance, knowledge and understanding in that one particular circumstance, rather than an ongoing process throughout the unit. Wiggins and McTighe (2011) suggested teachers should embed assessment in all aspects of their teaching. An effective assessment should not aim to capture everything at once, especially considering the practical constraints of assessing a class of 30-plus pupils within a limited timeframe. An assessment lesson may be useful for pupils to 'showcase' what they have learnt, but if assessment for learning has been implemented throughout a unit of work, a teacher can make a more robust judgement on the pupils' learning.

Indeed, Ofsted (2018) suggested that teachers should check precisely what a pupil knows and can do through carefully designed activities that help to isolate the components of the knowledge required throughout the unit of work.

Assessing content that has not been taught

Too often, teachers focus their assessment on the outcome rather than the process, where the assessment is on what pupils produce rather than consideration of what was taught or not. Further, outcome may not always be learning-related; rather it may be focused on efforts made by pupils and their enjoyment of physical education (Ofsted, 2023). Assessment methods come into question when teachers assess pupils based on criteria outlined in their policy, but these skills or concepts may not have been taught. Expecting pupils to excel in assessments on material they have not been taught is unrealistic. There are various reasons why pupils may not have been taught certain content. For instance, they may have been absent, or the curriculum criteria may lack specificity and may not align with the objectives and/or are too far removed from the taught unit of work. Assessment is known to be weak when it is not aligned with a department's overall scheme of work (Ofsted, 2023). Some assessment designs use generic statements that pupils must meet without providing clear guidance on how to achieve the assessment criteria, as is evidenced in the case study (see Figure 4.1). As a result, pupils may struggle to realise their potential because they have not been adequately prepared or informed about what is expected of them. A teacher can only assess what pupils have been taught. Assessments should reflect the objectives of a unit of work and intended learning outcomes of a lesson and offer a fair opportunity for pupils to demonstrate their understanding and abilities based on what they have learned. This approach promotes transparency and accountability in the assessment process, ultimately benefiting pupil learning and development.

Redesigning the assessment policy

In redesigning their assessment policy, the case study school drew on 'best practice' in order to streamline their assessment criteria. For example, in trampolining, specific criteria may be given for a progressive scale of proficiency in performing a front drop. This kind of detailed assessment criteria helps pupils understand exactly what is expected at each scale (see Figure 4.3). In addition, the case study school recognised issues associated with trying to distinguish between the double scales for developing and secure; hence, they trialled a simplified 4-point scale. At the start, 'emerging' refers to pupils being able to put some of the taught content into practice. In 'developing', pupils begin to apply their understanding and can demonstrate some of the taught content. For the 'secure' scale, pupils understand and can demonstrate the taught content of the lesson. For 'mastery', pupils are able to evidence understanding and the application of knowledge and skills beyond the taught content.

As stated, ongoing effective assessment in physical education is intended to provide feedback so pupils are aware of their attainment at a given time. Feeding forward allows action for correction, or fine-tuning of "learning goals, learning activities and inform[ing] other pedagogical decisions" (Marmeleira et al., 2020, p.120). This feedback is crucial for identifying areas of strength and areas for development in pupils' understanding and performance (see Chapter 5: Feedback). With regard to Figure 4.3, an assessment example to be used as an aide memoire to a lesson shows a 4-point scale related to what pupils can demonstrate from emerging to mastery. However, it is important that teachers do not lose sight of what they want pupils to learn, so they need to plan learning tasks which allow pupils to demonstrate their learning, rather than demonstrate their ability to complete a task (Spackman, 2002). So that assessment for learning can inform assessment of learning, pupils need to be clear about what their learning looks like. In this case (Figure 4.3), the following are learning points to be taught:

- at take-off, bring your arms away from your sides, extend them out in front of you and elevate your arms quickly above your head
- hold this upright position and begin to slightly push your hips backwards as you gain height
- keep your arms up and fingers in a position directly above your toes
- ensure extension of your arms and legs and allow the hip movement to provide the forward rotation
- do not look down and keep your eyes focused towards an end wall
- keep your upper body and head as still as possible
- maintain position (BBC Bitesize, 2024).

When assessment data or information is not utilised to inform subsequent teaching, teachers miss crucial opportunities to address misconceptions or gaps in pupils' knowledge that have been identified through assessment. This failure to respond to identified misconceptions or gaps can lead to a lack of continuity in learning, where pupils are introduced to complex content without the necessary foundation (Leirhaug, MacPhail and Annerstedt, 2016). Building upon secure prior knowledge is crucial for pupils to successfully grasp more complex content and skills (Aarskog, 2020). If assessment data is not used to tailor teaching strategies and adjust learning goals accordingly, pupils may continue to struggle with concepts and thus hinder their ability to progress and engage meaningfully with more advanced material.

Ultimately, the aim of assessment in physical education is not just to assess pupil performance, but also to guide instructional decisions and enhance pupils' achievement of the objectives and learning outcomes. This was an aim of the case study school. It should therefore be embedded in the policy and be used to inform short-, medium- and long-term planning (Arthur and Golder, 2021; Gower, 2021). When assessment data or information is under-utilised or ignored in subsequent teaching practices, it represents a missed opportunity to support pupil development and ensure a more effective and targeted approach to education in physical education settings.

Recording assessment

Immediate feedback is often carried out verbally, but it is important that a teacher plans, monitors and records their feedback either informally or as formal assessment. It has been found that departments that monitor quality in terms of what pupils understand and can do operate effective assessment, where they set out clear expectations and plan regular opportunities to check pupils' understanding (Ofsted, 2023). In contrast, in weak teaching and assessment, teachers' expectations are vague and "focused on broad 'I can' statements, such as 'I can work well in a team' or 'I can link skills to a specific activity'" (Ofsted, 2023,

Table 4.1 Year 7 gymnastics unit of work assessment (based on English Schools Gymnastics, 2019-2020) (Figure 4.4 was devised by the chapter authors and the case study school and is reproduced here with permission).

Year 7 gymnastics unit of work assessment

	Emerging	Developing	Secure	Mastery
Head *Knowledge and understanding*	Will be able to explain the elements that make up a routine	Will be able to explain the elements that make up a routine and will be able to explain fluency	Will be able to explain the elements that make up a routine and be able to understand the difference between execution and difficulty	Will be able to explain the elements that make up a routine and be able to understand the difference between execution and difficulty. Will be able to explain how to extend routine
Heart *Social, feelings, attitude, ability to help others, leadership*	Be able to work together and use communication skills to create a routine	Be able to work together and use communication skills to create a routine, will be able to discuss fluency with a partner	Be able to work together and use communication skills to create a routine and be able to offer advice to others	Be able to work together and use communication skills to create a routine and explain learning points relevant to their routine to others and demonstrate leadership
Hands *Ability to demonstrate the physical skills being learnt*	Will be able to create a routine	Will be able to create a routine with choreography taking into account the difficulty and execution of moves	Will be able to create a routine with choreography taking into account the difficulty and execution of moves and will begin to perform this with correct technique	Will be able to create a routine with choreography taking into account the difficulty and execution of moves and will perform this with correct technique

Challenges related to assessment

	Emerging	Developing	Secure	Mastery
Examples of routines	Present, forward roll, turn, balance1, balance 4, turn, present	Present, forward roll, skip, teddy bear roll, turn, balance1, balance 4, forward roll to stand, backward roll to stand, present	Present, bent-leg headstand, leap, supported cartwheel, cat leap, balance 6, balance7, turn, leapfrog, half turn, backward roll to straight jump, back support, present	Present, back support, cat leap, cartwheel over dish, balance 8, balance 9, forward roll over hallow, full turn, forward roll to straddle sit, turn, headstand, half turn, present
Example learning points to see and hear	Body tension Straight back Counter-tension Walk on tiptoes Rocking, taking weight onto hands then heels	← plus: Forward roll, crouch down, weight on hands, head tucked in, push with legs, tight tuck, reach forward, maintain tuck until on feet, stretch to stand when weight on feet Head stable Eyes focused Weight on balls of feet Backward roll, crouch down, tight tuck, chest on knees, position hands, push hard, keep tuck, keep pushing to land on balls of feet	← plus: Bent-leg headstand, head and hands form triangle pattern on floor, press down hard with hands, keep nose just touching floor Cartwheel, face forward, chest down towards knee, positive push from bent leg, wide straddle of legs, body in same plane, arms straight	← plus: Headstand, back kept firmly straight Forward roll to straddle sit, back straight, legs extended, toes pointed, arms stretched out wide Precision

p.22). Without clear expectations of what the teacher expects pupils to know and do, as well as limited checking of pupil progress, leads to inconsistencies throughout the department. This has a negative impact on pupils' learning.

Teachers who are clear about their intentions also document their scheme of work for each key stage and plan appropriate, progressive units of work. This precision contributes to effective teacher planning, teaching and assessment implementation. All assessment methods rely on good teaching (Ofsted, 2023) and teacher assessment literacy, which is explored next.

Assessment literacy

Assessment literacy is "generally defined as a set of knowledge and skills a teacher needs to effectively enact assessment" (Pastore, 2023, p.1). Assessment dialogue with pupils and teachers alike provides opportunities for critical engagement with assessment (Leirhaug, MacPhail and Annerstedt, 2016). Having established that physical education assessment should be concentrated on what pupils can do and how they can improve, assessment literacy draws attention to the assessment decisions a teacher makes. These decisions include how assessments should be carried out with clarity so that there are no issues with misinterpretation. In the selection of assessment approaches, teachers should aim for the process to provide "information to ensure that pupils know more, do more and remember more" (Ofsted, 2022, p.30). The challenge in selecting meaningful and robust assessment methods is to ensure that pupils are given the opportunity to provide evidence of their attainment. Inappropriate methods may reduce pupils' motivation and bring about feelings of inadequacy, no matter what their attainment. An assessment policy needs to be understood and enacted by all, which requires continuing profession development to be embedded in a department.

Assessment literacy is also demonstrated in recording methods. Clear criteria are used, which are directly related to the objectives of a specific unit of work. This specificity allows a pupil to articulate and demonstrate what they have learned. A teacher will utilise all information available to them, which will include all assessment for learning generated during the process of a pupil's learning. The selected approach will produce meaningful data. As in any good teaching, the assessment should be inclusive, which may require adaptation for any pupil with special educational needs and disability requirements.

The second part of the case study shows how the department took on board some theory, research, evidence and best practice to address some of the issues with assessment highlighted in the first part of the case study.

Case study (part 2)

The first part of the case study revealed an assessment policy which was not fit for purpose. It tried to capture too much, making the policy unmanageable. The head of department recognised that attempting to align the department assessment policy to that of the school-wide policy formed part of the problem, a common issue for physical education (House of Commons Education Committee, 2017). This highlights a misconception that a policy must include 'everything', yet in reality, it captures limited assessment of learning as it is too removed from the taught unit of work. This results in a mismatch of pupils' attainment against the objectives (Chan, Hay and Tinning, 2011). Having separate templates for head, heart and hands was too complex; thus, this assessment 'lost its way' due to a lack of focus. Therefore, the policy was unable to "identify whether pupils' underlying knowledge was secure ... This meant that the information teachers were using to inform subsequent teaching was often not precise [nor] aligned to the curriculum" (Ofsted, 2023, p.37).

Having established that the selected assessment approach to check for understanding was not always appropriate, the department discussed the issues and drew on relevant theory, research, evidence and best practice to devise a streamlined policy to assess pupils' attainment in a year 7 gymnastics unit of work. As was flagged in the first part of the case study, the end of unit assessment of learning lesson did not provide pupils with the opportunity to practice and develop their work. The department therefore ensured there was focus in each lesson on assessment for learning (Williams and Cliffe, 2011; Aarskog, 2020; Ofsted, 2023).

By frequently revisiting their assessment policy and embedding assessment for learning in lessons, the department were able to avoid different interpretations of the assessment criteria by different teachers. In doing so, they identified areas where there was too much focus on doing, with task-driven assessment rather than pinpointing what pupils do well and understand or feel about their work (Spackman, 2002). Ensuring the department shared theory, research, evidence and best practice via critical engagement allowed the teachers to hone their skills and competencies in assessment, thus developing their assessment literacy (Pastore, 2023). The result of this reflection provided opportunities for the department to critically engage with assessment (Leirhaug, MacPhail and Annerstedt, 2016), which led to them exploring the way they conducted assessment for and of learning. The department placed emphasis on clear and precise learning points (see the 'Redesigning the assessment policy' section) and ensuring that assessment for learning informed assessment of learning. To achieve this, the department set about planning for assessment (Arthur and Golder, 2021; Gower, 2021) and engaged in continuing professional development. They streamlined the assessment policy and incorporated an assessment template that captured all learning in the unit of work for gymnastics, as illustrated in Table 4.1.

The department then looked at the assessment for other units of work in other years in order to ensure all assessments were fit for purpose. In addition, the head of department successfully argued the case for keeping their assessment focused on physical education and ensured that precise assessment of learning for each activity and overall best-fit assessment of physical education could be inputted to the school-wide assessment policy. This also meant that the department utilised appropriate age-related assessment for the pupils.

The department addressed the issues raised in the first part of the case study, as illustrated in the second part of the case study informed by theory, research, evidence and best practice. Table 4.1 captures the objectives of the unit of work, through precise examples, and this is embedded in their assessment policy. The department maintained its focus on a head, heart and hands approach (Nair, 2024), as they value holistic physical education and consider this "unity of the cognitive, affective and psychomotor domains of learning" (Gazibara, 2013, p.71) appropriate for assessment of learning. Thus, the streamlined approach adopted (as compared to assessment in the first part of the case study) allowed the teachers to place pupils as a best fit on the 4-point scale of emerging, developing, secure and mastery, which subsequently informed and allowed the teachers to award a best-fit end-of-year assessment of learning comment and grade which, as stated, aligned with the school-wide policy. This resonated with 'the strongest assessment', where "the knowledge to be taught and what pupils need to know and do next has been precisely identified [with a] range of appropriate approaches [to] check what pupils know and can do" (Ofsted, 2023, p.8).

Summary and key points

Faced with the challenge of how to effectively assess in physical education, this chapter identified a real-life, weak assessment policy in the case study school, which was not fit for purpose and unmanageable. In addition, there was inconsistency in the department in how they utilised the policy, with the observed teacher commenting they were overwhelmed in trying to assess pupils at the end of the unit of work through an assessment lesson. Figure 4.1 details a mismatch between the content of the unit of work and the content in the assessment policy. It also provided an example of one of three templates, for the head (with different templates for heart and hands), which highlighted a need to consolidate the templates to make it fit for purpose.

The department therefore decided to look at their assessment by starting with the unit of work highlighted in the first part of the case study. Initially, the department did not find the challenge easy. However, they adopted a collaborative approach, which acknowledged assessment for learning as an integral part of assessment of learning. This was essential in devising a new template for the assessment policy (Table 4.1 details this template for assessment of learning). This came about through the consideration of relevant theory, research, evidence and best practice, which contributed to addressing the challenge of assessment in physical education. One of the key considerations was to ensure that what was to be assessed matched both the objectives and what was taught through the unit of work. By taking an in-depth view of checking for what pupils were learning, lesson-by-lesson and making use of aide memoires (see Figure 4.3), the department found having an assessment lesson at the end of a unit of work was not necessary, unless they utilised it as a method for pupils to showcase their achievement.

With Ofsted (2023) consistently reporting assessment of learning as one of the weakest aspects of physical education, readers may wish to analyse their own assessment policy to ensure that assessment for learning is embedded in lessons and informs assessment of learning. An assessment policy should be fit for purpose and capture pupils' attainment with precise examples of what their learning looks like. This will ensure that the assessment policy is used to support pupils' learning.

References

Aarskog, E. (2020) "'No assessment, no learning': exploring student participation in assessment in Norwegian physical education (PE)', *Sport, Education and Society*, 26 (8), 875–888.

afPE (2018) *Head, Hands and Heart: End of Key Stage One and Two Expectations in Physical Education*, Worcester: afPE.

Arthur, J. and Golder, G. (2021) 'Short-term (lesson) planning in physical education: how planning and evaluation supports effective learning and teaching', in S. Capel, J. Cliffe and J. Lawrence (eds) *Learning to Teach Physical Education in the Secondary School: A Companion to School Experience*, Abingdon: Routledge, pp.87–105.

BBC Bitesize (2024) *Trampolining – Essential Skills and Techniques: Technique for Performing a Front Landing*, available at: https://www.bbc.co.uk/bitesize/guides/zg89dmn/revision/4#:~:text=

Keep%20your%20arms%20up%20and,head%20as%20still%20as%20possible (accessed 9 December 2024).

Black, P. and Wiliam, D. (2010) 'Inside the black box: raising standards through classroom assessment', *Phi Delta Kappan*, 92 (1), 81-90.

Bloom, B.S., Engelhart, M.D., Furst, E.J., Hill, W.H. and Krathwohl, D.R. (1956) *Taxonomy of Educational Objectives: The Classification of Educational Goals. Handbook 1: Cognitive Domain*, New York: David McKay.

Brühlmeier, A. (2010) *Head, Heart and Hand: Education in the Spirit of Pestalozzi* (Translated by M. Mitchel), Cambridge: Sophia Books.

Chan, K., Hay, P. and Tinning, R. (2011) 'Understanding the pedagogic discourse of assessment in physical education', *Asia-Pacific Journal of Health, Sport and Physical Education*, 2 (1), 3-18.

DfE (Department for Education) (2015) *Final Report of the Commission on Assessment without Levels*, available at: https://assets.publishing.service.gov.uk/media/5a808bf9ed915d74e33fb0c7/Commission_on_Assessment_Without_Levels_-_report.pdf (accessed 4 December 2024).

DfE and STA (Department for Education and Standards and Testing Agency) (2024) *Guidance: School Reports on Pupil Performance: Guide for Headteachers*. Last updated 8 May 2024, available at: https://www.gov.uk/guidance/school-reports-on-pupil-performance-guide-for-headteachers (accessed 9 December 2024).

English Schools Gymnastics (2019-2020) *Key Step Forward Competition: For Schools and Active Partnership Entries*, available at: https://www.bsga.org/wp-content/uploads/2019/08/ESGA-Comp-2020.pdf (accessed 30 November 2024).

Gazibara, S. (2013) 'Head, heart and hands learning: a challenge for contemporary education', *Journal of Education Culture and Society*, 4, 71-82.

Gower, C. (2021) 'Long-and medium-term planning in physical education', in S. Capel, J. Cliffe and J. Lawrence (eds) *Learning to Teach Physical Education in the Secondary School: A Companion to School Experience* (5th edition), Abingdon: Routledge, pp.71-86.

Harrow, A.J. (1972) *A Taxonomy of the Psychomotor Domain*, New York: David McKay Co.

Hay, P. and Penney D. (2009) 'Proposing conditions for assessment efficacy in physical education', *European Physical Education Review*, 15 (3), 389-405.

House of Commons Education Committee (2017) *Primary Assessment Contents Conclusions and Recommendations*, available at: https://publications.parliament.uk/pa/cm201617/cmselect/cmeduc/682/68210.htm (accessed 9 November 2024).

Islam, M.A., Haji Mat Said, S.B., Umarlebbe, J.H., Sobhani, F.A. and Afrin, S. (2022) 'Conceptualization of head-heart-hands model for developing an effective 21st century teacher', *Frontiers in Psychology*, 13, p.968723.

Krathwohl, D.R., Bloom, B.S. and Masia, B.B. (1964) *Taxonomy of Educational Objectives: The Classification of Educational Goals. Handbook II: Affective domain*. New York: David McKay Co.

Leirhaug, P.E., MacPhail, A. and Annerstedt, C. (2016) 'The grade alone provides no learning'; investigating assessment literacy among Norwegian physical education teachers', *Asia-Pacific Journal of Health, Sport and Physical Education*, 7 (1), 21-36.

López-Pastor, V.M., Kirk, D., Lorente-Catalán, E., MacPhail, A. and Macdonald, D. (2013) 'Alternative assessment in physical education: a review of international literature', *Sport, Education and Society*, 18 (1), 57-76.

Lynch, S. and Norley, J. (2024) 'Social pedagogy and assessment in physical education: Incorporating students within assessment approaches', in D. Aspasia and C. Farias (eds) *Social Pedagogy in Physical Education*, Abingdon: Routledge, pp.121-133.

Marmeleira, J., Folgado, H., Martinez Guardado, I. and Batalha, N. (2020) 'Grading in Portuguese secondary school physical education: assessment parameters, gender differences and associations with academic achievement', *Physical Education and Sport Pedagogy*, 25 (2), 119-136.

Nair, J. (2024) *Aims of a Pestalozzi Education: The Johann Heinrich Pestalozzi Society*, available at: https://74136823-878f-4b91-94d2dae021f3c2c2.filesusr.com/ugd/c2d99a_e7349214fa364016ac50836f8ea9990e.pdf?index=true (accessed 4 December 2024).

Ofsted (Office for Standards in Education, Children's Services and Skills) (2018) *An Investigation into How to Assess the Quality of Education through Curriculum Intent, Implementation and Impact*, available at: https://assets.publishing.service.gov.uk/media/5fb3e55fe90e07208fd2cb85/Curriculum_research_How_to_assess_intent_and_implementation_of_curriculum_191218.pdf (accessed 20 November 2024).

Ofsted (Office for Standards in Education, Children's Services and Skills) (2022) *Research and Analysis Research Review Series: PE*, available at: https://www.gov.uk/government/publications/research-review-series-pe/research-review-series-pe (accessed 20 November 2024).

Ofsted (Office for Standards in Education, Children's Services and Skills) (2023) *Levelling the Playing Field: The Physical Education Subject Report*, available at: https://www.gov.uk/government/publications/subject-report-series-pe/levelling-the-playing-field-the-physical-education-subject-report (accessed 20 November 2024).

Pastore, S. (2023) 'Teacher assessment literacy: a systematic review', *Frontiers in Education*, 8, 1217167.

Simmons, J. and MacLean, J. (2018) 'Physical education teachers' perceptions of factors that inhibit and facilitate the enactment of curriculum change in a high-stakes exam climate', *Sport, Education and Society*, 23 (2), 186–202.

Spackman, L. (2002) 'Assessment for learning: the lessons for physical education', *The Bulletin of Physical Education*, 38 (3), 179–195.

Thorburn, M. (2007) 'Achieving conceptual and curriculum coherence in high-stakes school examinations in Physical Education', *Physical Education and Sport Pedagogy*, 12 (2), 163–184.

Veal, M.L. (1988) 'Pupil assessment perceptions and practices of secondary teachers', *Journal of Teaching in Physical Education*, 7 (4), 327–342.

Walters, W., MacLaughlin, V. and Deakin, A. (2023) 'Perspectives and reflections on assessment in physical education: a narrative inquiry of a pre-service, in-service and physical education teacher educator', *Curriculum Studies in Health and Physical Education*, 14 (1), 73–91.

Wiggins, G. and McTighe, J. (2011) *Yes, but... misconceptions about standards-based reforms*. Retrieved from Jay McTighe: https://jaymctighe.com/wordpress/wp-content/uploads/2011/04/Yes_but_objections_to_UbDl.pdf (accessed 4 December 2024).

Williams, A. and Cliffe, J. (2011) *Primary PE: Unlocking the Potential*, Maidenhead: Open University Press.

Chapter 5 Challenges related to use of feedback

Using feedback for effective learning in lessons

Joanne Cliffe and Katie Potter

Introduction

Teaching physical education effectively requires teachers to have secure subject knowledge, a deep understanding of the attributes of the pupils being taught and insight into how learning occurs (Shulman, 1986). In essence, teachers simultaneously perform several tasks to support the needs of all pupils whilst checking for their understanding, monitoring their progress and adapting content to allow the pupils to learn. Practical physical education is a 'visual' subject, in that pupils' learning is on show to their teachers and peers alike; thus, "[physical education] in schools is very different to other subjects, as it is one of the few subjects where pupils receive instant feedback on their abilities" (Littlefair, Jopling and Kelly, 2024, p.2). Feedback on pupils' learning is essential as it provides information, judgement and the opportunity for correction. Learning improves faster with feedback than without it (Gibbons, 2004).

However, when feedback is not well matched to pupils' prior learning, their misconceptions, gaps in their knowledge or their specific needs, pupils' progress in their learning is hindered. For example, pupils may be put into situations where they are expected to evidence new knowledge and understanding without receiving meaningful feedback to assist their learning (Office for Standards in Education, Children's Services and Skills (Ofsted, 2023)).

Ofsted (2023) identified a lack of feedback has a negative impact on pupils' learning. This was noted as a weakness in the teaching of physical education. Whilst it is recognised that feedback is a key component of assessment for learning (Black and Wiliam, 2009), the focus of this chapter is to address issues with verbal feedback given or not, in teaching which were identified in a real-life lesson observed in a school in the West Midlands (referred to as the case study school) and in doing so will draw on theory/research/evidence/best practice to explain, understand and ameliorate challenges teachers may face specifically when providing feedback. Such theory/research/evidence/best practice will be addressed under:

- sharing intended learning outcomes
- sharing clear criteria for success
- setting tasks to meet intended learning outcomes
- subject knowledge
- teaching with effective feedback – observation, communication, demonstration, self- and peer feedback.

Part 2 of the case study then details how the teacher addressed the challenges from the first part of the case study by revisiting solutions revealed in theory/research/evidence/best practice. Finally, the chapter offers a summary and key points. First, case study part 1 is presented.

The following case study features an observed lesson, which identifies a teacher's limited use of meaningful verbal feedback.

Case study part 1

Year 7 lesson: badminton backhand serve

The case study features an observed year 7 lesson, where the focus was on the teaching of the badminton backhand serve, with the observer concentrating on a key aspect of teaching, in this case, monitoring how the teacher provided feedback and how the pupils responded.

The class consisted of 30 pupils in a sports hall with three courts and, pupils were split into groups of three.

From the outset, the teacher gave limited information in sharing the intended learning outcomes with the pupils. This consisted of what the pupils were going to 'do' in the lesson, with little dialogue related to what pupils were to learn. The lesson commenced with a warm-up, where the pupils, in groups of three, were instructed to complete 'figure of 8' relays along the lines of the badminton court to help them to learn the service and court lines (see Figure 5.1).

The teacher demonstrated to the class how to complete the relay by running the course and describing it as he went. However, the teacher did not check for the pupils' understanding before they began their relays. This meant that some pupils were not clear about what they had been told to do, so the teacher had to repeat the instructions for the warm-up to help the pupils understand where they needed to go. At the end of the warm-up, when questioned by the teacher about the court markings, most pupils managed to identify where the service line was, but they struggled to identify the lines for the doubles court as the teacher had not shared this information with them. The pupils were motivated to win their relays but did not

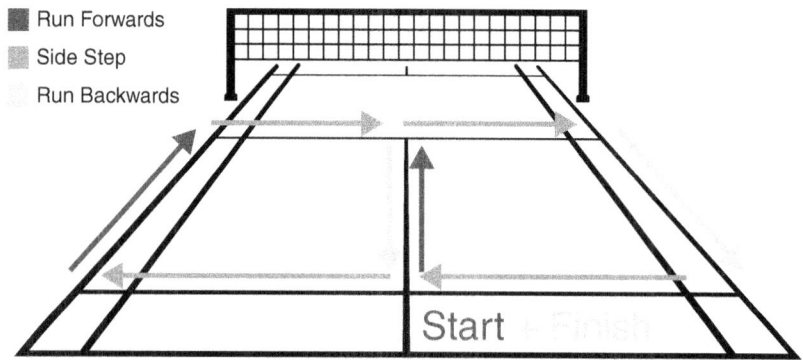

Figure 5.1 Badminton backhand serve 'figure of 8' warm-up relays (reproduced with permission from the case study school).

give attention as to the purpose of the lines on the court. The teacher did not correct any of the pupils' mistakes (for any who did not precisely follow the route) or give any feedback to the class during the warm-up.

The teacher moved on to give the learning points for a backhand serve and then demonstrated the serve correctly, providing the perfect model for pupils to practice. Unfortunately, the teacher did not share with the pupils how to hold the badminton racquet. The teacher provided the pupils with a peer assessment sheet containing the learning points for the backhand serve. However, the teacher had missed teaching the thumb grip, as well as not teaching the pupils how to use the peer assessment sheet to help provide feedback to each other on their learning.

In setting up the playing area to learn the backhand serve, the teacher ensured that the pupils remained in their groups of three, two on one side of the net collecting the shuttles as the third player practised their backhand serve over the net towards them. They all had the chance to perform the backhand serve and, as the pupils practised their backhand serves, the teacher could see that 'something was not quite right' in relation to the pupils' actions, but he did not have the subject knowledge to identify the pupils' misconceptions and how to correct them. Instead, the teacher provided all pupils with feedback on how to improve, but this feedback was generic and did not meet individual pupil learning needs. For example, the teacher said, "Make sure you have the same foot forward", even though the pupils were already achieving this.

Most of the pupils had placed their peer assessment sheet on the floor and disregarded them, although a few pupils were trying to use the sheets to go through the points. There was a lot of information on the sheet, which made it hard for the pupils to identify what they were doing well or pinpoint where their mistakes were being made. Once the teacher had distributed the assessment sheets, he made no reference to them for the rest of the lesson, other than making sure they were collected at the end.

The lesson progressed with pupils attempting backhand serves to start rallies. The pupils remained in their groups of three opposing another group of three. They practised in doubles playing on half a court, taking turns with a timed rotation of the third player waiting for their opportunity to be 'active'. The pupils were motivated in the task and participating well, although the waiting players were not fully engaged until it was their turn 'to play'. At this stage of the lesson, the teacher moved around the class and gave some feedback to each group. This was mainly focused on body stance and positioning. Once the teacher had done this, he moved straight to the next group so he did not wait to see if the pupils understood or took the feedback on board.

The observer noticed that there was little change, if any, in the pupils' standard of performance as they practised after the teacher had spoken to them. The teacher's questions mainly related to the pupils keeping the rallies going, their body stance and positioning rather than checking pupils' understanding and application of the technical skill of a backhand serve.

The teacher had a good relationship with the pupils, who enjoyed 'getting on' with their practice.

The observer in this lesson fed back to the teacher that taking a passing glance of the lesson showed the majority of pupils were active and seemingly enjoying their playing. This could be described as "busy, happy and good" (Placek, 1983, p.46), which, four decades on, is still "alive and well in physical education" (Henninger and Coleman, 2024, p.1). Whilst pupils may be well behaved, active and having fun in their lessons, it becomes problematic if these are the sole elements on which lessons are deemed successful and pupil progress is monitored. Recognising there are a multitude of elements which comprise 'outstanding' lessons (Ofsted, 2012), as previously stated, the observer for the lesson in the first part of the case study focused their observation on one such element, feedback. The observer looked beyond pupils being 'busy, happy and good' and revealed concerns in relation to how the teacher made use, or not, of feedback to promote pupils' learning. A great deal is written about feedback in teaching and in teaching physical education. Not all aspects can be covered in this chapter, but the next section explores theory/research/evidence/best practice in relation to the specific feedback issues which arose from the case study.

Reasoning/theory

The importance of feedback in teaching to promote pupils' learning gained prominence with research into assessment for learning from the 1990s (see the Assessment Reform Group, 2002; Black and Wiliam, 1998a, 1998b; Black et al., 2003), followed by specific research in assessment for learning in physical education (see Casbon and Spackman, 2005; Spackman, 2002). The intention of assessment for learning is to recognise where pupils are in their learning and through planned teaching interventions, progress their learning. As stated in the Introduction, this chapter is considering how feedback per se can be used to promote pupils' learning. It is recognised, however, that there may be some overlap with the principles of assessment for learning (such as setting intended learning outcomes, questioning and peer- and self-assessment) as all feature in good teaching. Indeed, effective feedback is embedded in good teaching (Ofsted, 2023); meaningful feedback promotes learning. In order to move forward in their work, pupils require accurate feedback with strategies to improve. Effective feedback is a pedagogical tool that teachers can utilise and has the potential to motivate pupils (Aarskog, 2021). The challenge as to what makes good feedback in physical education, which can be a tricky process (Shute, 2008), is now explored in relation to the issues raised in the first part of the case study.

Sharing the intended learning outcomes

The information in the first part of the case study resonates with Ofsted's (2023) findings, where poor progression opportunities for pupils were identified, so for pupils to achieve, teachers need to communicate their expectations clearly. They can do this by sharing the intended learning outcome(s) for the lesson and explaining why these learning outcomes have been set. An intended learning outcome is something that the teacher has created to describe what they want the pupils to know, understand and be able to do by the end of the lesson. Explaining why assists the pupils in their understanding (Spackman, 2002). Therefore, sharing intended learning outcomes (and their success criteria, see below) from the outset offers a collaborative feedback approach to pupils as pupils are given the detail needed for learning by their teacher which in turn allows them ownership of their learning (Black and Wiliam, 2009) as they understand what they are aiming to achieve.

Intended learning outcomes for the lesson need to be carefully planned. They are sourced from the objectives of the unit of work. In planning, a teacher needs to take into account what they want the pupils to learn and then frame the intended learning outcomes using vocabulary which is relevant to what is being learned in a way which endorses pupils' learning (Arthur and Golder, 2021). Therefore, intended learning outcomes allow what is being taught to be assessable through expressing expectations for learning, which have a clear focus. Visualising what achievement for pupils looks like at the end of the lesson is key (Cliffe, 2021).

Clear intended learning outcomes assist clear intended feedback. If intended learning outcomes are not shared with pupils, they are left with a vagueness as to what is expected of them, it also runs the risk of learning 'the wrong things' or making too many errors. Therefore, when setting intended learning outcomes, it is helpful for a teacher to consider what they will see and hear from their pupils who will evidence learning, thus sharing clear criteria for success.

Sharing clear criteria for success

For pupils to evaluate their learning and determine how well they meet the intended learning outcomes, teachers must provide them with clear success criteria (Chng and Lund, 2018). Therefore, when sharing the intended learning outcomes, it is crucial that the success criteria for meeting these expectations are shared with the pupils too, so they know what they will learn and why and recognise when they have achieved. As pupils learn better if they have a clear focus, feedback must be carefully aligned to the intended learning outcomes and success criteria.

Ensuring feedback has clear focus, a teacher needs to be both precise and concise in what they articulate to pupils. The teacher can share with pupils 'one thing to see' and 'one thing to hear' in the lesson; this is an approach devised by the authors of this chapter and a network of physical education, teacher education mentors and was utilised in lesson planning by student teachers. This helps break learning into meaningful components with achievable success criteria (Cliffe, 2021). For example, when teaching a seat drop in trampolining, a teacher needs to 'see' a pupil's hands next to their hips with fingers pointing forward. They would want to 'hear' pupils saying "Hips and feet on the cross". In teaching a forward roll, they want to 'see' knees tucked in tightly and want to 'hear' pupils saying "Chin on chest". These can be shared verbally with pupils each lesson but can also be displayed on a whiteboard or success criteria sheet to refer to throughout the lesson (as long as the teacher explains how the pupils should use it). This helps pupils know what they will learn and recognise when they have met the intended learning outcomes. Teachers need to keep revisiting the success criteria throughout the lesson so that the pupils remain focused in their learning.

Setting tasks to meet the intended learning outcomes

Once a teacher has explained the intended learning outcomes for the lesson, along with the success criteria, they should clearly articulate how the pupils can achieve these. Care should be taken to ensure that the intended learning outcomes and tasks are separated. If not, learning may be hindered by a focus on 'doing', whereby the task becomes the focus rather than the intended learning outcomes. For example, in teaching a headstand, the learning points may be 'head and hands form a triangle pattern on floor, press down hard with hands, straight legs and hollow back', yet a pupil may have achieved success performing a headstand on a mat, so the lesson becomes task-driven with the movement being performed on a bench, then on a box top and so forth, rather than developing the learning in the movement. This approach is described as 'teaching to task' (Spackman, 2002, p.185) and it makes it difficult to provide feedback to improve learning. Frequently revisiting the intended learning outcomes throughout the lesson helps to give focused feedback. In the first part of the case study, the teacher appeared to be more centred on what the pupils were doing, rather than giving them precise feedback to improve their learning; this could be due to a lack of subject knowledge.

Subject knowledge

Effective feedback relies on a teacher's secure subject knowledge to set the intended learning outcomes and explain why; the success criteria; and the appropriate tasks in how to bring about pupils' learning. How well a teacher knows their subject reflects in their ability to spot pupils' misconceptions (Smith and Neale, 1989). For example, noticing simple common errors which impact learning, such as a pupil who slaps the basketball with the palm of their hand rather than using their finger pads. It is not unusual for physical education teachers to have more subject expertise in some areas compared to others, but they do have a duty to take ownership of their own subject knowledge development to ensure they can be the best they can. For precise and concise feedback, teachers need to be able to spot errors in isolation. Teachers with a secure understanding of the subject content can easily recognise and resolve pupils' difficulties (Coe et al., 2014). For example, if a teacher has secure subject knowledge in swimming, they will be able to correct a pupil's 'screw kick' in breaststroke. Without secure knowledge, the pupil's 'screw kick' may go uncorrected (Ayvazo and Ward, 2011) and reinforced. It can be challenging for a teacher who may struggle to spot the common mistakes, as it makes it harder for them to plan for suitable strategies to eliminate misconceptions and provide correct feedback. In the first part of the case study, the teacher's subject knowledge was lacking as he could not identify that the pupils were not gripping the badminton racquet correctly.

As teachers gain experience, they learn to spot common misconceptions. As Hendrick and Macpherson (2017, p.30) stated,

> lots of pupils make similar mistakes to other pupils in the class and people who have done the task before, so in many cases [a teacher] can anticipate what is going to be a typical response and how they are going to respond.

Ultimately, a lack of a teacher's subject knowledge can affect a pupil's progress. If teachers are unable to identify the specific skills and concepts that they want pupils to learn, they may not be able to provide appropriate and effective feedback, resulting in a lack of progress and reinforcement of misconceptions.

Teaching with effective feedback

Sharing the intended learning outcomes and explaining why, sharing clear criteria for success, setting tasks to meet intended learning outcomes and having secure subject knowledge are the foundations for effective feedback. As well as these foundations, thinking about what makes effective feedback brings out other aspects, which good teaching entails. These are detailed next.

Effective observation

Feedback involves effective observation and this is a necessary skill for a physical education teacher (and also for pupils). Out of a meeting comprised of a local network of teachers, including the case study school, best practice in observation was shared. Teachers noted that when observing pupils, whilst it was tempting to 'jump in' to provide immediate and instant feedback (Littlefair, Jopling and Kelly, 2024), it was valuable to take a step back and watch. Taking time to observe may not come naturally to all teachers, but it is essential to capture where the pupils are in their learning. This shared best practice resonates with Killingbeck and Whitehead's (2021) stance, where they noted teachers need to see what is occurring in a lesson and that the ability to do this with accuracy and clarity matures with experience. Essentially, teachers should realise that there is more to observation than that which 'meets the eye' and developing a 'with it ness' to see beyond what is immediately in view may bring a sharpness to their teaching.

A useful model for effective observation (see Killingbeck and Whitehead, 2021, p.245) describes the interlinking relationship of a teacher's knowledge and understanding of: activities; techniques; tactics/choreography/environment; and constituents/principles of movement which comprise the components of what is being taught to allow a teacher "to progress from generic observations to apposite, effective and bespoke feedback". Using observation in feedback will show where pupils are in their learning and secure subject knowledge assists in what a teacher may then say to the pupils. This communication via appropriate subject knowledge language should be precise and concise to allow pupils to understand what learning 'looks like'.

Effective communication

Communicating feedback to pupils so that they can improve in their learning requires teachers to know their pupils. Understanding pupils is key when selecting the communication tone, as different pupils may not hear what the teacher may say in the same way. This is less of a problem if the teacher has a firm yet fair approach in their teaching and if effective feedback is embedded in lessons so that pupils understand that the teacher is interested enough in them as individuals to help them to learn. As mentioned above, the subject knowledge language sets out clearly where pupils are in their learning and provides concise information to move them on. The teacher therefore needs to communicate their feedback in a way which is helpful to the pupils.

Communicating feedback may be personalised to one pupil at a time to meet individual needs, to groups or to the whole class rather than repeating the same information or to make the best use of time. It is helpful for teachers to vary how they give feedback and ensure that all pupils receive personal feedback over a series of lessons. No matter how the feedback is communicated, the process of giving effective feedback remains the same in that it is clear for the pupils to understand and it is given in a manageable way so that pupils have the opportunity to address the given learning points. The downside of feedback occurs if it is rushed, if it is not given sincerely, if it does not meet the needs of the pupils or if it is not followed up. The latter happens the most when teachers give feedback to small groups and then move on to the next without checking the pupils' understanding or seeing the results of the given feedback. This is referred to as 'spray and pray', where teachers dash from one group to another. They intend to offer meaningful feedback, but without staying to see if the pupils take advice on board, they move on, which may halt the feedback process. Thus, they spray the pupils with feedback and hope the pupils take it on board (Spackman, 2002, p.189).

Effective demonstrations

'A picture is worth a thousand words'. Demonstrations are very helpful in providing pupils with the perfect model to which they should aim and are equally important in giving feedback, as what is communicated may benefit from a demonstration so that pupils know what their learning looks like. Practical physical education is visual and the power this brings to learning may be underestimated. Where teaching physical education is strong, teachers use demonstrations along with frequent verbal instruction to revisit the intended learning outcomes by re-iterating key points and their criteria for success to their pupils (Ofsted, 2023). This process of feedback thus supports pupils' learning and progression.

Effective self- and peer feedback

As previously mentioned, for pupils to achieve, teachers need to communicate their expectations clearly and plan frequent opportunities to check pupils' understanding. It is also important that pupils have time to respond to feedback to increase their competence before moving on to more complex learning. In addition to making sure feedback is used by pupils, pupils should be taught to give feedback to each other and to themselves. This needs careful planning; a pupil may receive the same feedback from their teachers or their peers in different ways. Pupils should be taught how to assess both their learning and that of their peers.

Self- and peer feedback can be valuable if embedded in the feedback process. However, if a teacher lacks subject knowledge, there is a danger that they can over-rely on pupils teaching themselves and this can have negative consequences for pupils' learning. Learning should be matched to the intended outcomes and, if pupils are not adequately taught, pupils may be prone to subjective evaluations of their own and others' performances, which is more likely to result in negative emotional responses, rather than promoting learning.

When learning how to engage with self- and peer feedback, pupils first draw on feedback provided from the teacher, then with guidance from the teacher, pupils can learn how to provide feedback. Utilising the success criteria, pupils understand the specific aspects or skills they should focus on when providing feedback (Ofsted, 2022).

The theory/research/evidence/best practice presented in this chapter was revisited in relation to the observed lesson in the first part of the case study. They subsequently informed the details illustrated in the second part of the case study, which details what changes were made by the teacher in teaching badminton with a focus on the backhand serve. The observer's focus remained on feedback to support pupils' learning and how these changes impacted the pupils' progress.

Case study part 2

Year 7, lesson 1 – badminton backhand serve

The observer and teacher revisited the observed year 7 lesson detailed in the first part of the case study. Making use of information drawn from the presented theory/research/evidence/best practice, the second part of the case study outlines amended teaching and provision of feedback in the year 7 badminton lesson. The observer's focus remained on how feedback was incorporated in the teaching of the badminton backhand serve and how this impacted pupils' learning.

After recognising that there were poor progression opportunities for pupils in the lesson described in the first part of the case study, as they were unclear with regard to their learning focus but were well behaved, occupied and enjoying the lesson (Placek, 1983), the teacher ensured that for the lesson in the second part of the case study, the intended learning outcomes were identified. These were clearly communicated from the outset of the lesson and described what the teacher wanted the pupils to know, understand and be able to do by the end of the lesson (Spackman, 2002), using appropriate vocabulary (Arthur and Golder, 2021) and explaining why. The teacher wanted the pupils to perform the backhand serve, to know that the serve is used most in doubles and to understand that the backhand serve can have different trajectories, with some pupils being able to perform these. This gave pupils the opportunity to take ownership of their learning (Black and Wiliam, 2009), as having clear intentions and knowing why (having a good backhand serve to start a rally is an advantage) helped pupils invest in their learning.

Along with sharing the intended learning outcomes for the lesson, the teacher gave precise and concise learning points so that the pupils knew what successful learning looked like (Chng and Lund, 2018). The teacher adapted the warm-up from the previous lesson by introducing hoops and shuttlecocks, as well as using the lines from the badminton court. In pairs, the first pupil would be tasked with placing the shuttle in the hoop to the side of the court, with the second pupil removing it back to a hoop on the service line, the pupils then switched roles. The teacher demonstrated with a pupil and explained the purpose of the court lines. For example, the teacher said 'short and fat court' when pointing to the lines for doubles. The teacher checked whether the pupils understood and intervened if the pupils were slightly off-task (for example, throwing the shuttlecock from a distance rather than placing it in the hoop and gripping the shuttle as they would for a backhand serve). With the teacher being more engaged in the pupils' learning since the first lesson, the pupils responded with their work being closely aligned to the teacher's instructions (Arthur and Golder, 2021). For example, the teacher demonstrated the backhand serve and paid attention to the pupils' stance and the way they positioned their racquet and shuttle out in front of their body. The teacher got the pupils to shadow him and first gave some generic feedback, followed by individual feedback to pupils who required it. The teacher recognised that he often 'set pupils off in a warm-up' but rarely intervened. He expressed he had missed learning opportunities for pupils and acknowledged that learning can occur in every aspect of the lesson.

The teacher had engaged with continued professional development, as it was clear he needed to be able to spot pupils' misconceptions (Smith and Neale, 1989) in badminton. The teacher demonstrated the backhand serve and described the key points as well as checking whether all the pupils understood the criteria for success (Ofsted, 2023). As pupils moved to practice the backhand serve, the teacher made sure to check how the pupils were gripping the racquet and then focused his feedback on holding the shuttle 'using your thumb and forefinger, hold the shuttle feather and tilt the shuttle head towards you' and 'hit with a pushing action'. For those pupils who were struggling to do this well, he gave feedback to ensure the 'feathers were facing the net' and said to these pupils that this was one thing he wanted to see the pupils do throughout the lesson (Cliffe, 2021).

Once the pupils were engaged in their practice, the teacher stepped back and, with all in view, he took the time to observe where the pupils were in their learning (Killingbeck and Whitehead, 2021). This allowed the teacher to not only check the pupils' progress but also spot whether pupils were consistent in their practice, whether they were making mistakes or whether they were exceeding the intended learning (Hendrick and Macpherson, 2017).

There was a shift in the teacher's approach to teaching the lesson, from the lesson in the first part of the case study, as the lesson in the second part of the case study was focused on what the pupils were learning, as opposed to what they were doing. The teacher aimed to provide effective feedback, which would close the learning gaps to allow the pupils to progress in their learning (Black and Wiliam, 1998a, 1998b). Being able to spot any difficulties the pupils were experiencing was improved through continuing professional development, as well as the teacher being able to use precise questioning (Coe et al., 2014). Being more focused and sharing precise points to the pupils, such as 'shuttle hit from hand', 'follow through in direction of shuttle', 'shoulders square to the net', 'racquet up ready for next shot', 'ready feet', 'short backswing, slight turn of racquet edge towards stomach' and 'hold shuttle still', provided more opportunities to learn. These points were captured against illustrations and provided on pupil feedback sheets so that any waiting player (waiting for their turn due to limited court space) was engaged in observing and feeding back to their peers. In addition, the information was clear and accessible rather than situated in long sentences.

Instead of rushing from one group to another, the teacher spent longer time with a couple of groups (aiming to address all groups over a series of lessons), to question, feedback and guide the pupils in moving their learning on, thus avoiding the 'spray and pray' technique of teaching (Spackman, 2002). If pupils were feeding back to their peers, the teacher provided feedback to the observing pupils to guide them in moving their peers forward in their learning. One of the most positive aspects as a result of the lesson in the second part of the case study was that the teacher recognised that with any given feedback, pupils required time to practice again and sometimes with new feedback to both consolidate and promote their learning (Ofsted, 2023) to avoid the scenario where pupils receive feedback which is then lost, resulting in a lack of learning. The teacher appreciated the response from the pupils and realised that he impacted their attitude to learning, which also motivated them.

Throughout the lesson, the teacher provided frequent opportunities to check pupils' understanding. This allowed pupils the time to respond to feedback to increase their competence before moving on to more complex learning.

The observer noticed significant change in the pupils' responses to the lesson. The relationship between the pupils and the teacher, whilst good from the start, developed as it was noticeable that the pupils positively engaged and latched onto the learning points provided by the teacher. Pupils were becoming more proficient in their serving, their understanding, and their feedback to one another, ultimately learning was in evidence.

Summary and key points

The first part of the case study detailed a real-life lesson which was found to be limited in the opportunities it provided for pupils' learning through effective feedback. The lesson observation revealed that although pupils were active and enjoying the lesson, the teacher had not engaged with meaningful feedback to allow the pupils to progress in their learning. Over time, this lack of effective feedback in a lesson may mean that pupils do not realise their learning potential (Ofsted, 2023).

The teacher of the lessons described in the first and second parts of the case study embraced the opportunity for continual professional development and made effective use of theory/research/evidence/best practice (particularly from the observer and local network of teachers) and transformed his teaching approach as he understood the power of effective feedback, specifically in the transition from observing pupils 'doing' to observing pupils 'learning'.

There are many elements which constitute good teaching, of which effective feedback is key. To realise effective feedback, there are fundamental aspects to consider. Sharing the intended learning outcomes gives a purpose to the lesson as well as explaining why and sharing the success criteria gives pupils valuable information on what they are trying to achieve. It is essential that the tasks through which learning occurs do not become the main focus of a lesson; the intended learning outcomes should be the catalyst for selecting appropriate learning tasks. Being skilled in observation, communication and demonstration assists pupils in their self- and peer feedback, but to teach with effective feedback, secure subject knowledge is required to ensure that pupils learn.

Although this chapter does not have the scope to cover effective feedback in its entirety, it does aim, through the context of the case studies, to support teachers who may wish to sharpen their feedback skills, in order to allow their pupils to progress in their learning.

References

Aarskog, E. (2021) '"No assessment, no learning": exploring student participation in assessment in Norwegian physical education (PE)', *Sport, Education and Society*, 26 (8), 875-888.

Arthur, J. and Golder, G. (2021) 'Short-term (lesson) planning in physical education: how planning and evaluation supports effective learning and teaching', in S. Capel, J. Cliffe and J. Lawrence (eds)

Learning to Teach Physical Education in the Secondary School: A Companion to School Experience (5th edition), Abingdon: Routledge, pp.87–105.

Assessment Reform Group (2002) 'Assessment for learning: 10 principles – research-based principles to guide classroom practice', available at: https://www.storre.stir.ac.uk/bitstream/1893/32458/1/Assessment%20for%20learning%2010%20principles%202002.pdf (accessed 1st December 2024).

Ayvazo, S. and Ward, P. (2011) 'Pedagogical content knowledge of experienced teachers in physical education: functional analysis of adaptations', *Research Quarterly for Exercise and Sport*, 82 (4), 675–684.

Black, P., Harrison, C., Lee, C., Marshall, B. and Wiliam, D. (2003) *Assessment for Learning: Putting it into Practice*, Maidenhead: Oxford University Press.

Black, P. and Wiliam, D. (1998a) *Assessment and Classroom Learning: Assessment in Education*, Abingdon: Routledge.

Black, P. and Wiliam, D. (1998b) *Inside the Black Box: Raising Standards through Classroom Assessment*, London: School of Education, King's College.

Black, P. and Wiliam, D. (2009) 'Developing the theory of formative assessment', *Educational Assessment, Evaluation and Accountability (Formerly: Journal of Personnel Evaluation in Education)*, 21, 5–31.

Casbon, C. and Spackman, L. (eds) (2005) *Assessment for Learning in Physical Education*, Leeds: Coachwise.

Chng, L. and Lund, J. (2018) 'Assessment for learning in physical education: the what, why and how', *Journal of Physical Education, Recreation and Dance*, 89, 29–34.

Cliffe, J. (2021) 'Medium- and short-term planning: units of work and lesson plans', in S. Capel, J. Cliffe and J. Lawrence (eds) *A Practical Guide to Teaching Physical Education in the Secondary School: A Companion to School Experience* (5th edition), Abingdon: Routledge, pp.51–69.

Coe, R., Aloisi, C., Higgins, S. and Major, L.E. (2014) *What Makes Great Teaching? Review of the Underpinning Research*, available at: https://www.suttontrust.com/wp-content/uploads/2014/10/What-Makes-Great-Teaching-REPORT.pdf (accessed 11 June 2025).

Gibbons, E. (2004) 'Feedback in the dance studio', *Journal of Physical Education, Recreation and Dance*, 75 (7), 38–43.

Hendrick, C. and Macpherson, R. (2017) *What Does This Look Like in the Classroom? Bridging the Gap Between Research and Practice*, Woodbridge: John Catt Educational.

Henninger, M.L. and Coleman, M. (2024) 'Don't look now - "Busy, Happy, and Good" is still very much alive', *PE Links 4U*, available at: https://www.pelinks4u.org/articles/henninger1008.htm (accessed 16 December 2024).

Killingbeck, M. and Whitehead, M. (2021) 'Observation in physical education', in S. Capel, J. Cliffe and J. Lawrence (eds) *Learning to Teach Physical Education in the Secondary School: A Companion to School Experience* (5th edition), Abingdon: Routledge, pp.241–261.

Littlefair, D., Jopling, M. and Kelly, N. (2024) 'Pupil voice in physical education and the desire for (in)visibility', *Sport, Education and Society*, 1–14.

Ofsted (Office for Standards in Education, Children's Services and Skills) (2012) *Beyond 2012 – Outstanding Physical Education for all Physical Education in Schools 2008-12*, available at: https://www.gov.uk/government/publications/beyond-2012-outstanding-physical-education-for-all (accessed 13 November 2024).

Ofsted (Office for Standards in Education, Children's Services and Skills) (2023) *Levelling the Playing Field: The Physical Education Subject Report*, available at: https://www.gov.uk/government/publications/subject-report-series-pe/levelling-the-playing-field-the-physical-education-subject-report (accessed 20 November 2024).

Placek, J. (1983) 'Conceptions of success in teaching: busy, happy and good?' in T. Templin and J. Olson (eds) *Teaching in Physical Education*, Champaign, IL: Human Kinetics, pp.46–56.

Shulman, L. (1986) 'Paradigms and research programs in the study of teaching: a contemporary perspective', in M. C. Witrock (ed.) *Handbook of Research in Teaching* (3rd edition), New York: Macmillan, pp.3–36.

Shute, V.J. (2008) 'Focus on formative feedback', *Review of Educational Research*, 78 (1), 153–189.

Smith, D.C. and Neale, D.C. (1989) 'The construction of subject matter knowledge in primary science teaching' *Teaching and Teacher Education*, 5 (1), 1–20.

Spackman, L. (2002) 'Assessment for learning: the lessons for physical education', *The Bulletin of Physical Education*, 38 (3), 179–195.

Chapter 6 Challenges related to motivation

Enhancing the motivational climate for year 10 girls

Victoria Clements and Kevin Morgan

Introduction

The World Health Organisation (WHO, 2017, p. 5) advocates high-quality physical education that provides opportunities for all pupils to "establish and reinforce lifelong health and physical literacy, and promote the enjoyment of, and participation in, physical activity". Physical literacy (PL) is defined as "the motivation, confidence, physical competence, knowledge and understanding to maintain physical activity throughout the lifecourse" (Whitehead, 2010, p.5). Whilst acknowledging that all the elements of PL are inter-related (Whitehead, 2010), the specific focus of this chapter is on the first of these crucial components, the motivation to participate and learn in secondary physical education lessons. Motivation is an internal process that activates, guides, and maintains behaviours over time (Morgan and Sproule, 2023). Given that motivation is an internal process, physical education teachers cannot motivate pupils to participate, as the motives must come from the pupils themselves. However, what physical education teachers can do, is to promote a motivational climate that inspires and enables pupils to discover their own motives for participation (Morgan and Sproule, 2023).

The participation and dropout rates of teenage girls in physical education is a particular issue in secondary schools in the UK and internationally (Mitchell, Gray and Inchley, 2015). This is even more of a challenge for girls from lower socio-economic groups (Charlton et al., 2014). Therefore, the aim of this chapter was for a university professor to work with a physical education teacher to facilitate the application of motivational climate theory within her school practice, to improve the motivation and participation of a purposively selected group of year 10 (aged 14-15 years) female pupils. Whilst the overall responses from the group were observed and reflected upon, the responses of two pupils, both from a lower socio-economic background, were of particular interest within this case study.

The specific objectives were to: (1) identify a group of year 10 girls who were low in motivation to participate in physical education, with a particular focus on two girls from a low socio-economic group (that is, eligible for free school meals (eFSM)); (2) consider and select the most appropriate motivational theory to apply to improve the pupils' motivation to participate; (3) collaborate (physical education teacher and university professor) to apply the most appropriate theory in practice to address the problem; (4) observe the impact of the applied theory on the pupils' motivation and participation; and (5) reflect on the application of the theory and the collaborative process.

Case study part 1 – setting the scene and identifying the girls (Vicky the physical education teacher)

Within our physical education department, girls' attitudes towards physical education and their declining participation levels had been a growing concern at the time of this case study. Whilst we had always prided ourselves on high participation levels amongst both boys and girls, evidence suggested a trend of dwindling participation in girls (see Table 6.1), particularly following the COVID-2019 pandemic. Consistent with the concerns about girls' participation in physical education nationally (Mitchell, Gray and Inchley, 2015), this was a significant worry and challenge for our department.

The school is located within an area of deprivation in Wales with an increasing number of eFSM pupils. At the time, there was a whole school drive to raise educational aspirations of eFSM learners, so it seemed an ideal opportunity to attempt to improve the participation and engagement levels of all girls in physical education, with a specific focus on two of them, for several reasons. First, we were curious as to whether there was a link between eFSM girls and non-participation in physical education; and if so, what were the reasons for that connection? We were also interested to discover if this had been a growing trend as the girls progressed from years 7 (aged 11-12 years) to 11 (aged 15-16 years). Further, it had previously been identified within our physical education department that a low number of eFSM pupils (girls in particular) opted for GCSE Physical Education, and we wanted to increase that number for subsequent years.

The challenge identified led to the gathering and examination of our own data regarding participation to establish any significant trends (see Table 6.1). On analysis of the data, it was apparent that there was an increasing trend of non-participation through years 7-11, with a higher percentage of non-participation of eFSM girls as the school year progressed. Worryingly, in year 11, of the 39% of eFSM pupils that we identified as frequent non-participants in physical education, 32% were girls. In contrast, the level of non-participation amongst the boys was much lower and had remained more consistent throughout years 7-11, suggesting that this was significantly more of a problem for girls than boys.

Table 6.1 School eFSM data for 2022-2023

eFSM data for the 2022-2023 Academic Year				
Year group	Pupils eligible for free school meals	% of high-frequency non-participation	% of high-frequency non-participants – girls	% of high-frequency non-participants – boys
7	52 out of 169 (31%)	11	6	5
8	29 out of 125 (23%)	13	10	3
9	45 out of 160 (28%)	22	14	8
10	63 out of 231 (27%)	22	19	3
11	46 out of 197 (23%)	39	32	7

Following informal conversations between myself and the two identified eFSM girls at the initial stage of the case study, contrary to my assumptions, access to out-of-school sporting opportunities at a younger age had not been an issue for them. Indeed, both girls had been physically active whilst growing up and had fully participated within school physical education lessons and in a variety of local community club sports. When further discussing the potential reasons for their non-participation as they got older, both girls alluded to social comparison as a key factor. They revealed that they felt inadequate and threatened when they compared their physical skills and techniques to those of others within the class. This was heightened by the fact that they participated in physical education with other girls who were in extracurricular school sports teams and perceived them to be quite cliquey. Interestingly, when I posed the scenario of introducing a new activity to them, that all the girls within the class would have little to no experience of, they both said that they would feel more comfortable and be more likely to participate.

As an experienced physical education teacher, I was fully aware of the changing attitudes of girls towards physical activity as they became older, and I had always aimed to employ an inclusive approach to teaching and learning in my physical education lessons. However, the pupils' voice (identified above) led me to question my own pedagogical approach. Had I inadvertently created an environment that focused on social comparison, resulting in girls' negative attitudes towards physical education? Could I use a different approach to promote an environment that focused on personal development and self-reflection, rather than social comparison? Would this, in turn, have a positive impact on non-participation levels, particularly amongst eFSM girls? These were the key questions I asked myself and shared with Kevin, the university professor, as the starting point of this case study.

Case study part 2 - selecting the most appropriate motivational theory (Kevin the university professor)

Whilst there were alternative motivational theories that could have been applied to this scenario, such as self-determination theory (Deci and Ryan, 1985), the girls' overt concerns about social comparison pointed more towards motivational climate theory (Ames, 1992; Morgan, 2017). Indeed, the chosen pupils' negative perceptions of their own competence and ability in comparison to others in class is a classic reaction from individuals who are strongly ego-involved (that is, they compare themselves with others), particularly those who have a relatively low perception of their own ability (Ames, 1992; Morgan, 2017). I therefore felt that if Vicky could change their perceptions of the motivational climate from ego to mastery (where ability is perceived as self-referenced), then the girls would be increasingly likely to focus more on themselves and their own individual progress, according to motivational climate theory (Ames, 1992).

The reflective and critical questions that Vicky asked herself, as identified in the previous section, were crucial to addressing the issue. Despite her best efforts to avoid overt social comparison in her lessons, Vicky was battling against the comparative culture of physical education, sport and, indeed, society in general, particularly in the age of social media. This meant that Vicky needed to be clear and explicit about the mastery motivational climate she wanted to create in her lessons, to counter the existing culture. It was not enough for Vicky to simply avoid emphasising public comparison and competition with others. She had to be more explicit in stating that success in her physical education lessons was to be 'the best that you can be', and that the pupils should be self-referenced and not compare themselves with others. Indeed, even though the public nature of physical education means that some social comparison is inevitable, it became apparent during our discussions that Vicky needed to redefine success for the non-participating girls, to try to focus them on developing their own individual PL journey (Whitehead, 2010). Ames (1992) proposed that a mastery climate can be created in sporting contexts by manipulating the task, authority, recognition, grouping, evaluation and time (TARGET) structures. Morgan (2017) re-conceptualised these TARGET structures for a physical education setting (see Table 6.2) and further argued that they can be applied to enhance PL (Morgan, 2019). Using some or all structures of the TARGET theoretical framework was, therefore, the focus of the case study intervention by Vicky.

Case study part 3 – collaborating to apply the theory in practice and observing the impact of the applied theory on the pupils' motivation and participation

Vicky's actions and the observed impact

Following some initial meetings with Kevin, where we discussed different motivational theories and pedagogical models, I was excited to explore the impact of TARGET as a pedagogical approach to enhance the girls' motivation within their physical education lessons. With the aim of achieving this, I manipulated four of the TARGET structures in particular, as follows. I also met with Kevin every few weeks to discuss the impact of the intervention and the next steps in the process.

Table 6.2 TARGET structures (Ames, 1993; Morgan, 2017)

TARGET structure	TARGET description
Task	Encourage pupils to set their own self-referenced learning goals.
	Differentiate/individualise the activities.
	Design tasks for variety and novelty.
Authority	Provide pupils with decision-making and leadership opportunities.
Recognition and relationships	Recognise individual effort and improvement.
	Develop caring and nurturing relationships with pupils.
Grouping	Encourage pupils to work together and support each other.
	Organise mixed-ability, cooperative groups.
	Re-group the pupils regularly for greater social interaction.
Evaluation	Base assessments (both formative and summative) on pupils' individual self-referenced progress and effort.
	Encourage assessment for learning strategies, including self- and peer evaluation.
Time	Allow flexible time for different rates of learning.
	Optimise the time to learn in lessons.

Task

As an experienced physical education teacher, I was eager to spend time considering the *task* design, as my previous experience had identified this as a key area for pupils' motivation. Providing variety within tasks was something that I was already familiar with in my practice, and I was aware that differentiation within mixed-ability group lessons was vital for pupil engagement. Therefore, when considering the theory of motivational climate that I had been introduced to by Kevin, my focus within the *task* structure was to design lessons that included a variety of different tasks, at various levels of difficulty, rather than simply allowing the pupils to participate on a rotational basis around pre-determined undifferentiated tasks. This allowed them to opt for an activity that both suited and challenged their ability level and increased their autonomy within the activities.

Practically, pupils had the opportunity to explore each game variation and choose the activity they wished to do from several variations of games and practices that I had designed. For example, each game had slightly different rules and choices within it, including the team numbers, the level of complexity, different equipment, and ways of scoring. This variety provided the pupils with a freedom of choice that resulted in enhanced motivation due to them feeling a sense of autonomy and comfort with the activities they chose to participate in. Consequently, ability comparisons were promptly decreased amongst the pupils, as they focused on organising themselves and participating in an activity that they were both comfortable and interested in.

Consistent with another aspect of the *task* structure, as the pupils became more competent at the activity, I encouraged them to set personal learning goals. Here, they worked individually, as part of their group, to identify strengths and areas for development during subsequent lessons. This increased level of pupil ownership resulted in an observable improvement in focus, determination, independence and skill level. Therefore, whilst my primary focus was to maintain the fun and enjoyment level of the pupils, their level of competence in the physical skills, and overall engagement and learning in the lessons, also noticeably improved.

Authority

As already identified in the previous section on *task*, my first consideration in relation to the *authority* structure was to actively involve the pupils with regards to the choice of activity they wished to pursue. Historically, as the teacher, I would have sole control of the lesson plan. However, with the specific aim of increasing the level of pupil *authority*, I was eager to engage their voices as soon as possible, at the beginning of a new block of teaching. Therefore, lesson 1 of the new teaching block included the pupils and I discussing a possible range of new activities they could pursue for the next half-term of lessons. To provide new opportunities, I presented a range of different activities, such as handball, pickle ball and basketball, all chosen due to their novelty and relative ease of organisation. During the lesson, I collaborated with the pupils by investigating how each game was played and what equipment was needed, and then we identified the skills required to play each game. Interestingly, this discussion led to the pupils voicing concerns that some of the activities were too similar to the traditional invasion games curriculum of hockey and netball, in terms of skills and tactics. In my opinion, these activities were less appealing to the girls because overt social comparison would have continued to exist, particularly amongst the less physically able pupils. After further discussion with the pupils, it was clear to me that there was an appetite amongst them for some kind of new invasion game that required teamwork, movement and novelty. Following some more careful questioning from me, the pupils decided to pursue a variation of ultimate frisbee, a totally new activity to all pupils (and the school).

To further promote pupils' *authority* throughout the teaching block, they were able to choose from three variations of the games selected for each lesson, focusing on core elements such as passing, receiving, scoring and tactics. It is important to note that the pupils also had the option of continuing with the same game variation from the previous lesson if they so wished. The structure of the lessons was consistent each week and started with a discussion on which game variation the group wanted to pursue. Then, in their groups, they would share and rotate the leadership responsibilities, such as captain, umpire and equipment organiser. In my discussions with Kevin, we had identified that this was consistent with a Sport Education approach, which has been linked to a mastery motivational climate (Hastie *et al.*, 2014). Pupils were excited to participate in this way, trying new game variations each week, which added variety and responsibility, and noticeably enhanced their motivation and engagement as a class. As you might expect with a new and technically challenging game, initially, skill levels across the whole class were quite low. This level did improve, but most importantly, it was clear that fun and enjoyment levels were high.

During the initial planning and preparation phase of the teaching block, the two girls in focus within this case study were fully engaged and expressed that they were happy to participate. When I questioned them further on this change of engagement, they both agreed that the activity was more fun and less boring than the activities that they had been pursuing in the past. Both also mentioned that they had become bored of participating in the same traditional invasion games activities within the physical education curriculum throughout years 7-10, and that the opportunity to participate in a new and novel activity was exciting. During subsequent weeks, pupil 1 maintained her initial higher levels of participation and enjoyment. This was clear to see, as she did not miss a week of physical education (compared to previous blocks, where participation had peaked at a maximum of 25%). Interestingly, her whole outlook on physical education seemed to have shifted, with a genuine and stated anticipation towards the next lesson, alongside a marked shift in her ability to seek and receive feedback. Disappointingly, however, pupil 2 reverted to her previous levels of non-participation in the actual physical activities. When questioned on this, her apathy for physical education in general remained and when presented with the opportunity to help uncover potential solutions to how she might engage more, she still seemed entirely disinterested. However, on a more positive note, she did actively participate in the lesson as an official and organiser within one sub-group. Here, she adopted the roles of referee, record keeper and team captain, thereby developing her learning about the game, and her personal and social skills, which demonstrated some improvement in her motivation, and showed potential signs of a move towards full physical participation in the future.

Recognition and relationships

When reflecting on the recognition structure in my previous practice, it became clear to me that I may have inadvertently been promoting an ego-motivational climate. Role modelling through demonstration had always been a mainstay of my physical education practice, and I had utilised this within my lessons for many years. Prior to engaging with the literature on motivational climate, I was unaware that this could, unintentionally, lead to pupils' perception of an ego-oriented motivational climate. My prior physical education experience had led me to ask high-achieving pupils to model good practice within my lessons, whilst I supplemented this with positive public feedback. From a skill acquisition perspective, this made complete sense, but, following further reflection and discussion with Kevin, I realised that I had quite possibly been creating pupils' perceptions of an ego climate, resulting in increased social comparison amongst them. This led me to reflect upon and question whether this common physical education practice had contributed to the levels of non-participation that I had witnessed within that class, as well as other classes. Therefore, to apply the theory and foster a mastery motivational climate, consistent with the theory, I felt that I had to create a shift from public recognition to more private, individual feedback. To achieve this, I increased my level and focus on individual observations, and ensured that the feedback I was providing was on a more personal and private 'one-to-one' basis (although this is difficult to achieve in physical education lessons). I attempted to achieve this by moving around more during the lessons and being more purposeful with my individual interactions with the pupils. Little gestures, such as using their names more frequently when providing feedback, helped with this personal connection and ensured the pupils knew I was talking to them individually, leading to a visible appreciation on their part. Added to this, I had to ensure that my feedback shifted from simply recognising performance, to also praising effort more frequently. As a teacher who had always aimed to praise effort in my practice, being more purposeful about this throughout my lessons increased pupils' motivation levels across the class, and this was clear to see. Being more aligned to a mastery *task* design also allowed me to provide additional 'stretch goals' privately for certain pupils.

The change in my approach had an immediate positive impact on pupil 1 and her levels of self-confidence, and motivation to participate and improve markedly increased. On reflection, our relationship had shifted dramatically from regular negative conversations regarding a lack of participation to frequently praising her practical efforts in lessons. Consequently, she began to feel more valued and appreciative of the fact that her hard work and progress were being recognised in the same manner as those of the more able pupils in the class.

Grouping

Mixed-ability grouping was a common strategy that I had frequently used within my lessons, and I was already aware that the grouping strategy could potentially have a major consequence on the pupils' motivation and participation. Having tried various strategies (for example, identifying the teams pre-lesson, or grouping specific pupils for various tasks), it was evident that social comparison still existed between the pupils prior to this intervention. Fortunately, working with a group of relatively mature year 10 pupils allowed me to offer them more freedom within group selection. So, in a shift from the grouping being solely organised by me, I leant further on the idea of *authority* (demonstrating the inter-relatedness of the TARGET structures) and encouraged the pupils to take ownership of their own groupings, prompting them to group themselves based on the practices that motivated and excited them the most and the people they wanted to work with.

Initially, to make this work, the pupils were provided with information about three different game variations (as previously mentioned in the *Task* section) and could choose the game variation that interested them the most. This strategy helped me integrate the more reluctant pupils by providing them with autonomy over their own participation. The idea behind this decision was that new groups would potentially be formed each week, based on a common task interest. I didn't want to force reluctant participants into participating in an activity or a group that didn't appeal to them. Rather, I wanted to give them freedom of choice, allowing them to feel in control of their own participation. However, in practice, the pupils naturally formed friendship groups and subsequently agreed on a task they would all enjoy. While this was not the intended outcome of my grouping strategy, and perhaps does not speak directly to the idea of mixed-ability groupings, pupils worked well together, physical activity levels increased and they were highly motivated within their chosen groups. This prompted me to consider whether social comparison is less of a concern when working within friendship groups? And whether girls are more confident and less critical of each other when working within such groupings, where they feel more comfortable? Within the friendship groups, the range of abilities remained mixed, and pupils naturally supported and encouraged their friends, which is consistent with the cooperative grouping emphasis within a mastery motivational climate. However, on a cautionary note, I am aware that this class was composed of mostly quite mature and confident girls and had strong friendship groups within it, so that no pupils were excluded in this process. In some classes, where different relationship dynamics exist and where some pupils are not naturally part of a friendship group, this strategy would have to be changed, emphasising the variety of grouping strategies the theory alludes to.

In relation to the two girls specifically observed within the case study, working within their friendship groups allowed for different levels of transition from non-participation. Pupil 2 was still a reluctant physical participant, and unfortunately her reluctance continued throughout this unit of work. I was unable to engage her practically within her group; therefore, (as identified above) to actively involve her within the lesson, with the longer-term goal of eventually increasing her level of physical participation, I encouraged her to take on additional roles, such as umpire, record keeper and team captain, where she was happy to participate. I was pleased for the small gains with pupil 2 and aware that this was the first steps towards what I hoped would be a move back towards full participation in the future. Pupil 1 was more fully integrated into the group and the physical activities, as described above.

Case study part 4 – reflecting on the application of the theory and the collaborative process

The key take-home messages from Vicky

Reflecting on the case study, I have found the TARGET framework and the theory of motivational climate very applicable and beneficial in relation to planning and delivering my lessons. Indeed, there are several aspects of the TARGET structures that have had a profound impact on the way I now teach. The most notable and impactful for me were *task, authority* and *recognition and relationships,* which I will discuss further here. As already identified, it is also important to note that, as I went through the process, it became clear to me that all elements of the TARGET structures were inter-related and could not be easily separated. Indeed, although *evaluation* (assessment) and *time* were not specifically focused upon, they both exist in every other aspect of TARGET, which is consistent with Ames' (1992) original theory.

Task

Task design was an area that I really enjoyed developing throughout the case study and one that I feel I improved upon significantly. The importance of designing tasks that promote self-referenced improvement and limit social comparison was one of the main take-home messages for me, and one that will impact on the type of tasks that I will embed in my lessons moving forward. Linked to this, whilst recognising the need to challenge different ability levels, I will continue to work hard to ensure that the different levels of tasks are not overtly evident to the other pupils, thus protecting pupils' levels of self-esteem and confidence. Both case study pupils identified that comparison with others was a reason why they were reluctant to participate prior to the case study.

Having had the opportunity to have professional development dialogue with Kevin and to access academic journal articles, I have learned the importance of supporting pupils to set personal targets and will definitely embed this strategy into my lessons moving forward. Supporting pupils to focus on personal development and progress, rather than comparison with others, is essential. While I believe the environment I had created prior to the case study was both caring and nurturing, the importance of overtly emphasising a self-referenced pedagogical climate became clearer to me as a result of this case study.

Engaging with the TARGET framework also encouraged me to be more creative when considering the *task* element of the framework. As highlighted throughout this case study, the novel activities that I introduced for pupils to learn in the ultimate frisbee lessons were clearly a positive element that the pupils enjoyed, resulting in higher levels of engagement.

Authority

The structure of *authority* within the TARGET framework resonated with me a great deal. As we move towards a new curriculum within Wales, a pupil-centred curriculum, where pupils are encouraged to take ownership over their learning, is key. When constructing curriculum programmes in the past, pupils through years 7-11 had limited ownership over the activities that they participated in. However, it is now clear to me that the more we engage with pupil voice, and provide them with choices, the more self-motivated they are likely to become.

Interestingly, the way I provided *authority* within the *task* design clearly increased autonomy across the group. Allowing the pupils to select tasks gave them the opportunity to choose the level of challenge that suited them best and allowed them to move between activities at their own pace. This again highlighted the close and inter-related links between the different elements of TARGET. Moving forwards, the Sport Education model is a pedagogical approach I will trial further to enhance autonomy, personal goal setting and leadership opportunities (see Hastie *et al.,* 2014).

Recognition and relationships

On reflection, one of the most impactful outcomes of the case study came as a consequence of reflecting and improving the way I provided *recognition* to the pupils. As mentioned within the case study, technique or skill modelling through pupil demonstrations had been a key element of my prior physical education practice. Before engaging with TARGET, I was unaware that this practice could potentially enhance social comparison within my lessons (particularly amongst pupils with a high ego orientation and low perceived ability) and could result in a decrease in their motivation. Engaging with the theory resulted in a change of how I delivered praise and feedback during the case study. For example, when I recognised effort, I made a conscious decision to ensure that this was done as close to a 'one-to-one' basis as possible. This led me to share public *recognition* a lot less, unless I felt it was really necessary for the motivational benefits of certain pupils in the class. For example, if I saw a pupil who didn't usually get much recognition, successfully engage in an activity, and I knew that they would 'feed' positively off the *recognition* of their peers, I would still purposefully provide that public recognition on occasions, in an attempt to boost their confidence.

Finally, having had an opportunity to reflect deeply on my teaching approach, it has made me re-evaluate the importance of using a more pupil-centred approach and re-examine guided discovery and reciprocal teaching styles (Mosston and Ashworth, 2002). It has also encouraged me to do additional reading into the similarities between TARGET and the principles behind the Sports Education model, as identified by Hastie *et al*. (2014). Finally, this case study has resulted in some excellent professional dialogue with colleagues in my school, and this book chapter will hopefully be an excellent resource for me to disseminate what I have learnt to my physical education colleagues and, more broadly, to other subject teachers in my school and beyond.

Kevin's final reflections

It was an absolute pleasure to work on this project with Vicky and to learn from her application of motivational theory in practice. The key ingredient for me in this case study was Vicky's open-mindedness to question her assumptions and existing practice. Vicky's desire to learn was admirable and essential for this type of theory to practice relationship to work. It was also deeply rewarding to see the TARGET theory, which I have researched and espoused for over 20 years, having such a profound impact on Vicky's practice and on her pupils' learning experiences. The fact that one of the case study pupils fully bought into the application of the theory, whilst the other did to a much lesser extent, is also very interesting and realistic, demonstrating that TARGET theory doesn't have all the answers, but can still make significant inroads into the engagement of pupils in physical education, and indeed all school subjects. The other key take-home message for me from a research/theory perspective was that although the mastery TARGET guidelines are well established and evidenced in school physical education research, Vicky was still able to use them whilst also adopting what Van Manen (2015) refers to as pedagogical tact, that is, in a way that is best for the individual pupil in a particular context and situation.

It is hoped that this chapter will enable readers to reflect and be as open minded as possible to, for example, question their assumptions and beliefs about their teaching practice and the fact that they may inadvertently be creating an ego-involving motivational climate through some of their teaching practices; apply TARGET structures in their own teaching; aim to change their teaching behaviours to foster pupils' perceptions of a mastery motivational climate; and observe the impact on the pupils' behaviour and learning.

References

Ames, C. (1992) 'Achievement goals, motivational climate and motivational processes', in G. C. Roberts (ed.) *Motivation in Sport and Exercise*, Champaign, IL: Human Kinetics, pp.161-176.

Charlton, R., Gravenor, M.B., Rees, A., Knox, G., Hill, R., Rahman, M., Jones, K., Christian, D., Baker, J., Stratton, G. and Brophy, S. (2014) 'Factors associated with low fitness in adolescents – a mixed methods study', *BMC Public Health*, 14, 764-774.

Deci, E.L. and Ryan, R.M. (1985) *Intrinsic Motivation and Self-determination in Human Behaviour*, New York: Plenum Press.

Hastie, P., Sinelnikov, O., Wallhead, T. and Layne, T. (2014) 'Perceived and actual motivational climate of a mastery-involving sport education season', *European Physical Education Review*, 20 (2), 215-228.

Mitchell, F., Gray, S. and Inchley, J. (2015) '"This choice thing really works..." changes in experiences and engagement of adolescent girls in physical education classes, during a school-based physical activity programme', *Physical Education and Sport Pedagogy*, 20, 593-611, https://doi.org/10.1080/17408989.2013.837433.

Morgan, K. (2017) 'Reconceptualising motivational climate in physical education and sport coaching: An interdisciplinary perspective', *QUEST*, 69 (1), 95-112.

Morgan, K. (2019) 'Applying the TARGET pedagogical principles in physical education to enhance students' physical literacy', *Journal of Physical Education, Recreation and Dance*, 90 (1), 9-14.

Morgan, K. and Sproule. J. (2023) 'Motivation in sport and exercise', in J. Sproule (ed.) *Course Companion for Sport, Exercise and Health Science, International Baccalaureate* (2nd edition), Oxford: Oxford University Press, pp. 231-241.

Mosston, M. and Ashworth, S. (2002) *Teaching Physical Education* (5th edition), San Francisco: Benjamin Cummins.

Van Manen, M. (2015) *Pedagogical Tact*, Abingdon: Routledge.

Whitehead, M. (2010) *Physical Literacy: Throughout the Lifecourse*, Abingdon: Routledge.

WHO (World Health Organization) (2017) *Physical Activity for Health: More active people for a healthier world: draft global action plan on physical activity 2018-2030*, EB 142/18, Geneval: World Health Organization.

Chapter 7   Challenges related to managing behaviour

Using behaviour for learning in lessons

Joanne Cliffe and Chris Ewing

Introduction

Effective teaching is complex and multi-faceted. It involves, among other things, an understanding of what is being taught and how it is being taught, positive interactions with pupils, an effective learning environment and effective behaviour management. The latter is the focus of this chapter.

Behaviour management is important in all teaching. However, in physical education, it is an essential component of all lessons. If there is poor class management, little or no order and control in practical lessons and/or if pupils are misbehaving, pupils are more at risk of getting seriously hurt than in a 'classroom' environment. Misbehaviour covers a multitude of actions, which include disobedience, flouting rules, insolence and stubbornness. All of these aspects hinder learning in lessons.

There is a lot written about behaviour management, both in education in general and in physical education in particular. In this chapter, the focus is on some general considerations for teachers in managing behaviour in physical education lessons, not on detailed ways of doing this. Such detail can be found elsewhere.

The chapter starts with the first part of a case study, in which behaviour management was an issue for teachers. Although we recognise there are other potential foci in relation to behaviour management, in this chapter, four different aspects of behaviour management are considered. They are:

- misbehaviour and good behaviour
- school behaviour policy
- learning environment
- positive approach to behaviour management/behaviour for learning.

These four are then considered in the second part of the case study in relation to the teachers' responses to the issues raised in the first part of the case study.

Case study part 1

The majority of misbehaviour issues are those that may occur on a regular basis and, if they are not addressed, may escalate to the point where the teacher has limited control over a class. Such low-level behavioural issues in lessons include pupils who, for example,

- deliberately arrive late to lessons
- consistently forget their kit
- always have their phone out in the changing room
- do not engage in the lesson
- talk while the teacher is talking
- blatantly ignore a teacher's request
- frequently pester other pupils who are trying to work in the lesson
- are prone to swear at the teacher
- are likely to forge excuse notes.

When misbehaviour manifests from poor class management, this negatively impacts the learning of all pupils and takes its toll on the teacher. This case study describes several scenarios which demonstrate the low-level disruptive incidents that have been witnessed in a school in the West Midlands.

Example 1

In a lesson focused on the activity of football, the teacher sent 26 pupils to get a football each from the bag of balls. The bag was tied up at the side of the pitch. The first pupil struggled to open the bag quickly enough, so another pupil grabbed the bag and tried to open it whilst the pupils behind began to push and shove. This resulted in pupils falling over the bag. At this point, no pupil had a ball. The teacher then spent at least 20 minutes of the lesson managing the behaviour of the pupils, which resulted in significant lost learning time.

Example 2

Following a teacher's instruction to a year 10 class to 'go and warm up' for a lesson focused on the activity of basketball - pupils stood in groups chatting, with some doing token static stretching. The teacher did not address this lack of engagement and, when he called them in, the pupils wandered over at a slow pace. When the teacher started explaining the learning outcomes for the lesson and the practice the pupils were to do, at least half of the class were talking, as well as fidgeting by occasionally tapping or kicking other pupils. The teacher had his back to some of the pupils. Therefore, because they had not listened, not only were the learning outcomes for the lesson 'lost', but as the pupils were sent to get on with their practice, many were confused as to what they were supposed to do.

Example 3

Gymnastics lessons occurred in a shared space, which also doubled as a dining hall. The pupils were told to get 15 mats out of the gymnastic cupboard, but all the pupils just gathered around the door so much that they struggled to get the door open. Once the door was eventually open, the mats were pulled out and dragged to areas of the hall, with groups too close to each other or to the walls. Some pupils also jumped against the mats as they were being dragged. As a result of the pupils' actions, the proximity of the mats did not lead to a purposeful learning environment and there were also issues regarding safety.

Example 4

As the pupils were changing for a netball lesson, they were shouting across to each other. The teacher was late; thus, the changing rooms were unsupervised. When the teacher entered the changing rooms, the pupils did not notice her and continued to behave in a boisterous manner until the teacher starting shouting 'shush'. A chorus of 'shush' then rang back at her from the pupils. The lesson got off to a distracted start and it took a while for the teacher to bring control to the class.

Example 5

An engaged class were warming up for their GCSE dance lesson, except for one pupil. This pupil isolated herself from the rest of the class and when she was given instructions she 'tutted, huffed and puffed' and, answered back. The pupil complained the lesson was boring and that she was not going to work with anyone. The teacher separated the pupil and left her sitting on a bench all lesson.

As a result of the time spent dealing with behavioural issues such as these in lessons, pupils' learning in many physical education lessons was impacted. In order to address behavioural issues such as these so that pupils are able to learn in lessons, it is important to understand the reasons for the inappropriate behaviour. The examples in the first part of the case study are revisited in the second part of the case study, which details teachers' reflections, analysis and actions taken to address the issues, drawn from the theory, research and evidence that follow. First, we look at misbehaviour and good behaviour.

Misbehaviour and good behaviour

The focus on behaviour in schools is commonly on misbehaviour, rather than good behaviour. It is important to note that a variety of different terms are used in relation to misbehaviour. For example, antisocial, challenging, disruptive, inappropriate, off-task, unacceptable (Department for Education (DfE), 1994). The specific term used may be due a number of reasons, including the personal preference of the teacher concerned, the type of behaviour being described or the terminology used in a particular school. In this chapter, the term misbehaviour is generally used.

In the Elton Report (Department of Education and Science (DES), 1989, p.102), misbehaviour was described as "behaviour which causes concern to teachers". Misbehaviour ranges from low-level unacceptable conduct, for example, distracting other pupils, occasionally arriving late in class or talking out of turn, to more serious misbehaviour, such as 'acting out', including bullying, cyberbullying, non-attendance, verbal or physical aggression, or wilful disobedience.

In order to manage behaviour, it is important to try to understand why a pupil is misbehaving. Debate as to why pupils misbehave in school is constant. For example, from questioning whether is it an unmet need or whether it is down to the lack of relationship with the class teacher. For example, it may be because the teacher does not know the pupils, does not match the learning in the lesson to the learning needs of the pupils and/or with the intended learning outcomes of the lesson or because pupils are bored, tired, annoyed or lacking in motivation. Garner (2019) provided a list of causes of misbehaviour (what he called unacceptable behaviour), including individual factors, cultural factors, curriculum relevance factors (linked to both individual and cultural), school ethos and relationship factors and external barriers to participation and learning factors. Bennett (2020, pp.66-72) cited ten reasons why pupils do not enjoy behaving in school - each of which can be specifically applied to a physical education setting.

1. We ask pupils to do what they might not be inclined to do.
2. We ask pupils to think.
3. We judge pupils.
4. We ask pupils to focus.
5. Distractions are abundant.
6. Schools exist to teach ... secondary skills (things which evolution has not fitted [pupils] to find easy to learn or to feel motivated to learn).
7. Pupils are not successful.
8. Pupils think they are not supposed to like school, and nobody counteracts this.
9. Pupils are happier misbehaving than behaving.
10. Pupils have bigger problems.

For example, in a physical education setting, the average pupil, if they had the choice, may not want to go barefoot in the dance studio or gymnasium. Pupils may not wish to embrace being judged publicly by the rest of the class as they run up the home straight of the running track. Pupils may be distracted in their lessons as physical education teaching often happens in 'public' spaces.

While there may be misbehaviour across the school in all subjects, the physical education setting can exacerbate many of the issues, partly at least due to added concerns about safety. For example, pupil behaviour is important from the time they arrive at the changing rooms at the start of a lesson. If pupils take a long time to change because they are misbehaving, the learning time in the lesson is shortened. When they leave the changing area, pupils may be asked to help collect and carry resources (including equipment) to the teaching area, sometimes in difficult weather conditions. During the lesson, pupils need to follow instructions. For example, stopping when the whistle blows, when to fetch javelins from the throwing area, how to sensibly and safely support their peers who are about to attempt a handstand, or not being rough or fouling in a game. If they do not, their behaviour may have a direct result on both their own and other pupils' quality of work and safety.

Rather than just reacting to misbehaviour when it occurs, Bennett (2017) emphasised the importance of planning for each individual pupil, especially when setting behaviour goals. McGill (2012) developed a series of 5-minute plans, which included an example behaviour proforma. The vast majority of behaviours, both negative and positive, can be planned for and, this proforma can be used to plan for teaching generically, for particular classes and particular lessons and/or particular pupils. This allows the teacher to plan ahead in order to prevent potential issues occurring as well as enabling the teacher to consider what they may do at different stages of an intervention. This planning may include, for example,

- the class rules, expectations, assertiveness, cooperation, support needed
- class arrangements, grouping plans (or seating plans if in a classroom)
- start- and end-of-lesson routines
- transitions between activities
- proportionate and escalating responses to any issues through stages initial, secondary and final
- consideration of what rewards and sanctions are available.

Evidence Based Education (2022) defined 'good behaviour' within a framework of negative good behaviour and positive good behaviour. Negative good behaviour is the absence of misbehaviour, while positive good behaviour is the good habits and individual characteristics which allow pupils to flourish.

Negative good behaviour may include, for example, pupils all arriving on time, not calling each other names and not talking when the teacher does (Bennett, 2017). However, this is not as powerful as positive good behaviour. Positive good behaviour refers to pupils exhibiting the types of behaviours that will make the most of the opportunity to learn and make progress. This includes, for example, pupils: proactively planning to get to physical education lessons on time with their full kit in their bag; actively forming good relationships and mutual respect for peers; being fully focused on what the teacher is saying, so when the teacher is demonstrating, for example, a badminton serve, pupils are picking up key pointers, such as the grip on the racquet and the positioning of feet. Indeed, as stated by Whitehouse (2013, p.166).

> pupils who demonstrate positive behaviour in a physical education lesson not only learn more effectively, develop positive relationships with others and grow in confidence, they also promote teacher well-being, raise teacher confidence and revitalise even the most experienced of practitioners.

Good behaviour in lessons enables learning to flow. To achieve this, expected behaviours from the pupils should be clear. However, teachers are at the whim of the behaviour culture, ethos and systems in the school. In addition to the culture, ethos and systems in which teachers and pupils operate, teachers themselves are also important in encouraging good behaviour. Rogers (2015) highlighted the importance of 'teacher agency' and the fact that teachers have more of this than perhaps they realise. Teachers need to be empowered by the capacity they have. They need to be on the front foot, adapting and shaping the behaviour in their teaching space. Further, teaching pupils about 'behaviour' should be embedded in the curriculum and, as Bennett (2020, p.26) stated "being well behaved is a combination of skills, aptitudes, habits, inclinations, values, and knowledge. These can be taught".

One of the difficulties in defining what constitutes misbehaviour or good behaviour is that different teachers view it differently according to, for example, their perceptions, experience, management approach and tolerance level. What one teacher may regard as misbehaviour or good behaviour may differ to what another teacher may regard as misbehaviour or good behaviour. This is true in relation to different physical education teachers, but may be more diverse between a physical education teacher (or a teacher of another practical subject) and a 'classroom' teacher. It can also vary from one school to another. As a result, what one teacher in one context may regard as normal in relation to misbehaviour or good behaviour may be regarded differently by another teacher or in another context. In light of this, it is important to take full account of a school's policy concerning behaviour and apply it with consistency. This is considered next.

School behaviour policy

Government guidelines detail headteachers' duties as to the expected behaviour of pupils in their schools. Whilst these guidelines are non-statutory, advice is given in relation to supporting pupils to behave well. In addition, the guidance covers misbehaviour by pupils and the powers with which teachers have to respond. It does not offer a uniform approach to be taken by all headteachers; rather, it is provided to encourage schools to devise their own policies for behaviour management. In essence, the focus centres on the creation of a school culture which sets high expectations for the benefit of all (DfE, 2024).

Schools operate as hierarchies and, such policies are initiated from the school leadership team, through middle leaders to each and every teacher and into every learning space. It is important that pupils are not left to try and work out what good behaviour and conduct looks like. The more consistency there is across all classrooms and teaching spaces (see the 'Learning environment' section), the easier it is for pupils to understand what is expected and so conform. Consistency gives rise to predictability and this makes it feel safer for pupils and easier for them to follow what the majority are doing. Although most schools have guiding principles on behaviour, teachers may also be left alone to implement them and to look after behaviour in their teaching space. If a whole-school approach is lacking, a head of physical education could identify guiding principles for teachers in the department.

Therefore, all schools adopt a behaviour policy, which is adhered to across the school. Behaviour policies are expected to be embedded in school life with training for teachers to ensure the policy is consistently applied. Whilst headteachers are free to design their policies, they must ensure that the national minimum expectation of behaviour is in line with the then Office for Standards in Education, Children's Services and Skills (Ofsted) grade for 'good' (DfE, 2024). The minimum requirements are:

- "the school has high expectations of pupils' conduct and behaviour, which is commonly understood by staff and pupils and applied consistently and fairly to help create a calm and safe environment
- school leaders visibly and consistently support all staff in managing pupil behaviour through following the behaviour policy

- measures are in place and both general and targeted interventions are used to improve pupil behaviour and support is provided to all pupils to help them meet behaviour standards, making reasonable adjustments for pupils with a disability as required
- pupil behaviour does not normally disrupt teaching, learning or school routines. Disruption is not tolerated and proportionate action is taken to restore acceptable standards of behaviour
- all members of the school community create a positive, safe environment in which bullying, physical threats or abuse and intimidation are not tolerated, in which pupils are safe and feel safe and everyone is treated respectfully and
- any incidents of bullying, discrimination, aggression, and derogatory language (including name calling) are dealt with quickly and effectively" (DfE, 2024, pp.6-7).

The policy and any resulting department behaviour policies should identify systems to discourage misbehaviour and to encourage appropriate behaviours, as well as applying appropriate rewards and sanctions. When a teacher's attempts at managing behaviour are not successful and they have followed the steps as outlined in a policy, they can apply the sanctions as decided by the school. Likewise, when pupils' behaviour is regarded as good, teachers can apply the rewards in the policy.

It is important that all teachers are familiar with the school behaviour policy, take full account of it and apply it consistently. To stress, it is important that a teacher is consistent with rewards and sanctions. Inconsistency builds resentment, undermines not only the teacher but also their colleagues. Consistency here refers not only to an individual teacher applying the policy consistently with different pupils and classes, but also to the policy being applied consistently by all teachers in a department and across a school. Without this consistency of use, there can be tension between teachers in a department and/or school. Further, pupils may be confused about how they should be behaving.

A school behaviour policy adapted for physical education will encompass the rules of the department. For example, it will include what kit should be worn, treating equipment with respect, no-go areas without supervision, no chewing and so forth. Pupils are expected to follow the rules as well as being full participants in their lessons and interacting with others with respect. The policy sets the tone and contributes to establishing a positive learning environment, as experienced by all those who come in contact with it, including teachers, pupils and any class visitors. Learning environment is considered next.

Learning environment

A learning environment often refers to the 'space' in which learning takes place. The majority of taught lessons in schools occur in classrooms, whereas practical physical education lessons take place in a number of spaces. These include a gymnasium, sports hall, swimming pool, courts, track and pitches outside or in offsite environments. Whilst consideration of space is important in planning and teaching, the 'culture' and 'expectations' set in this space contribute to the learning environment. There may be different terms for this, for example, a learning environment is sometimes referred to as a 'learning climate'. In essence, it is where the teacher sets out a purposeful and positive learning environment.

This may incorporate the character or 'feel' of the space in which pupils learn. Therefore, it is the 'mood' developed in a lesson that places the pupils and their learning at the heart of lesson planning and implementation. A lesson with an effective learning environment has a caring and positive climate whereby pupils feel respected and accepted by their teacher and peers (Whitehouse, Barber and Pepperell, 2021). Interactions and relationships between the teacher and pupils and between pupils are positive and effective. In turn, this leads to positive pupil behaviour.

Lessons that have clear expectations for positive pupil behaviour, which are embedded into class routines, are characterised as follows: pupils are expected to learn, to be on task and be supported by a committed and enthusiastic teacher who is confident, authoritative and clearly in control of the lesson, yet one who is also caring, understanding and sensitive to the needs of individuals, perhaps with a firm yet fair approach. This resonates with the '3 Rs of the behaviour curriculum' framework, as outlined by Bennett (2016). Teachers who are able to use a range of appropriate strategies around the three Rs are better prepared to deal with a variety of class circumstances they may encounter. The 3 Rs are as follows:

1 *Routines*: these are understood and well-practised by pupils in the learning environment. They include, for example, handling equipment, moving to and from working areas.
2 *Responses*: these are strategies and interventions used to de-escalate unproductive and confrontational behaviours, resolve conflict and promote positive and effective learning environments. These may include, for example, positive body language, verbal and non-verbal cues and rewards and consequences from school behaviour policies.
3 *Relationships*: this means understanding the variety of pupil needs, including special education needs and disability. For example, understanding what causes pupils' personal triggers and how pupils regulate their own emotional state, which will enable positive and effective relationships to be developed.

Clear routines for pupils to follow promote positive behaviour in the learning space. They are particularly important in physical education, where the movement of pupils and equipment should be carefully thought through to prevent pupils going off-task. Movement to the learning space from the changing rooms may have the same routines; however, routines in lessons will vary depending upon a number of factors. For example, in the activity taught, pupils should take on the character required for the activity. In gymnastics, this means wearing the appropriate kit and working barefoot, as opposed to a lesson in rugby, which will require different kit and equipment. The health and safety considerations for each activity should be communicated and adhered to, such as how to carry specialised equipment in athletics. Overall, a well-organised learning environment and class ethos allows pupils to demonstrate positive behaviour and optimum attainment.

Creating a learning environment which promotes positive behaviour and in which pupils spend more time on-task learning effectively should therefore be a priority for all physical education teachers. However, it is important to stress that although positive behaviour is promoted, poor behaviour is not necessarily prevented from occurring. Although these need to be managed, these can be minimised by teaching strategies that can promote positive behaviour in a lesson.

In order to achieve a well-organised learning environment, there will be some basic guiding principles in place for the class. For example, Marzano and Pickering (2010) outlined four key rules for successful lessons:

1. Pupils are quiet when the teacher is talking.
2. Pupils follow directions right away.
3. Pupils let others get on with their work.
4. Pupils respect each other.

These rules resonate with three key rules identified by Strickland (2023), which underpinned his behavioural approach. Pupils should:

1. Respect the teacher and their peers, following all instructions without question.
2. Complete all of the work set to the best of their ability, giving 100% effort and without distracting others.
3. Arrive at lessons ready to learn (on time, fully equipped and appropriately dressed).

Such principles provide a sound basis for a teacher to successfully manage the space and provide a positive learning environment. However, the teacher's teaching style and teaching approaches are also very important as they play a part in forging positive relationships and contributing to an effective learning environment. To develop a positive learning environment, Lemov (2015, p.344) advocated what he called a 'warm strict' approach. In this approach, the teacher is strict and is consistent and firm with the pupils whilst being positive, enthusiastic and caring in equal measure. It is important to help the pupils understand that the teacher's actions are designed to help them learn and make progress.

A positive learning environment is likely to be associated with a positive approach to behaviour management or what might be termed behaviour for learning (Ellis and Tod, 2018). Thus, it is important that teachers know how to establish and maintain a learning environment which promotes positive behaviour. This requires understanding the importance of school and department policies and practices for promoting positive behaviour and appreciating the need for rules, rewards and consequences. A positive approach to behaviour management/behaviour for learning is considered next.

A positive approach to behaviour management/behaviour for learning

Good teachers put time into planning their lessons in order that pupils can work towards achieving the learning outcomes. They evaluate the success of their teaching by the quality of the pupils' learning, the mistakes they have made, misconceptions that have been picked up and whether or not they have achieved the learning outcomes. The same approach must be used with behaviour management in lessons.

A positive approach to behaviour management or 'behaviour for learning' refers to the development of appropriate, positive behaviour that brings significant benefits for all pupils (Garner, 2011) and enables them to focus on learning. However, taking such an approach to pupil behaviour does not reduce the importance of clear and explicit class rules to govern pupil behaviour and their consistent application, nor does it prevent misbehaviour from occurring in lessons. A positive approach to behaviour management emphasises the teacher's role in creating an appropriate learning environment, in which all pupils can learn effectively (see the 'Learning environment' section).

There are a number of ways in which positive behaviour can be promoted by the strategies teachers use and relationships they build and maintain with pupils to enable pupils to feel safe and happy and hence promote positive behaviour and learning. Relationships between teachers and pupils play a key role in teaching to promote positive behaviour. What a teacher says and does in a lesson, their body language, verbal communication and expectations all impact the way pupils respond to the teacher.

It is important for teachers to focus on developing positive relationships with pupils in their lessons and apply principles which support them in demonstrating positive behaviour. These include: making expectations explicit by giving both verbal and visual clues; giving a rationale for expectations that show these are for the pupils' benefit and not for the benefit of the teacher; expecting pupils to comply and being surprised rather than angry if they do not comply; modelling required behaviour; keeping things simple and sentences succinct (Roffey, 2011). According to Burnett (2002), the promotion of positive relationships is one of the most successful strategies for developing a positive learning environment.

Bronfenbrenner (1979) identified three interlinked relationships:

- pupils' relationship with themselves (how pupils feel about themselves, their self-confidence as learners and their self-esteem)
- pupils' relationship with the learning they are undertaking (the curriculum) (how accessible they feel a lesson is and how best they think they learn)
- pupils' relationship with others (how they interact socially and academically with all others in their class and school (both teachers and other pupils)).

The interrelationship between these is shown in Figure 7.1.

In the relationships in the behaviour for learning model, each of the three relationships is important in developing a positive learning environment in the lesson, something the teacher is at the very heart of managing in order to promote good behaviour. Such relationships take time and effort to develop in order to establish a learning environment in which pupils' learning can flourish.

Further, according to Garner (2019), all three 'relationships' need to be taken into account when planning a strategy to tackle unacceptable behaviour. In the case of a pupil who is consistently misbehaving, it is suggested that there has been a breakdown in one (or more) of these three relationships. Morgan and Ellis (2011) highlighted the interaction between these three relationships as the basis of a positive approach to behaviour. They also emphasised the role of the pupils themselves in learning to manage their own behaviour. This requires pupils taking responsibility for their own behaviour and enabling them to make their own positive choices about behaviour. In order to achieve this, teachers can, for example, enable pupils to make decisions about the structure and content of the lesson, assign jobs to pupils and encourage pupils to volunteer or collaborate with pupils.

In following this approach, pupils develop skills that enable them to learn within a variety of learning contexts. Taking behaviour for learning as a positive description, it informs pupils what the teacher wants them to do and why this helps them to learn, rather than focusing on behaviours that the teacher does not want in the lesson. A teacher who places value on pupil

94 *Maximising Learning in Physical Education*

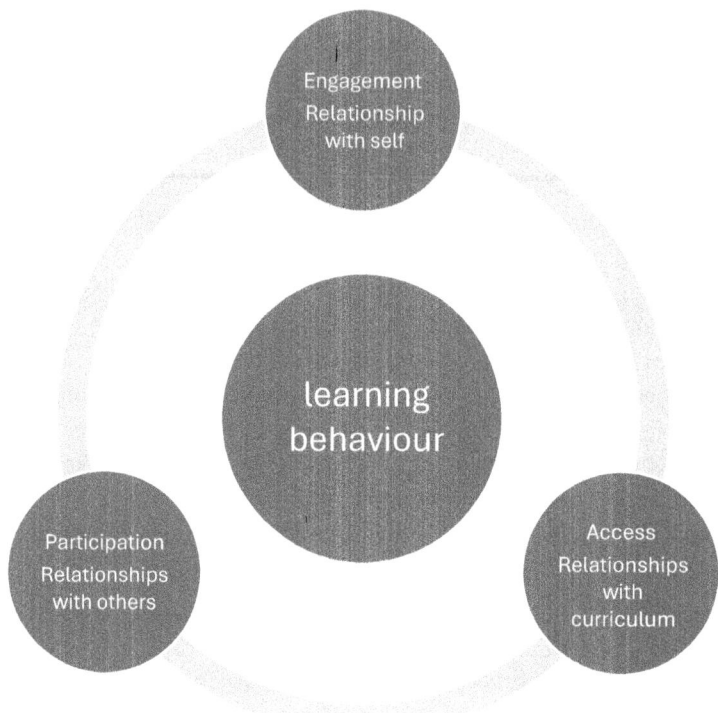

Figure 7.1 Relationships in the behaviour for learning model (taken from Garner, 2019).

Source: After Tod and Powell (2004)

behaviour (and praises appropriately) facilitates and enhances learning. Effective behaviour for learning strategies emphasises setting targets that are reachable by pupils.

Garner (2019) also recognised that this approach incorporates aspects of 'emotional intelligence' (Goleman, 1995). This awareness can assist teachers in helping to create a positive learning environment and culture for learning in which good relationships between a teacher and pupils are paramount. It is based, in part, on the premise that "generally a punitive approach tends to worsen or sometimes even create the very problems it is intended to eradicate … punishment alienates children from their teachers and does nothing to build up trust that is the bedrock of relationships" (Weare, 2004, p.63).

Building meaningful, positive and personalised relationships with pupils' parents is also a valuable strategy for promoting effective pupil behaviour. Positive two-way communication with parents to gain their support will lead to significant benefits when communicating expectations with pupils. Physical education teachers tend to have more access to parents than teachers of other subjects if parents support their children in after-school extra-curricular activities or in school-club links.

There are other approaches which are both well-established, which seek to address the challenges of managing behaviour in lessons. For example, Dix (2017) focused on preparing interesting and exciting activities that actively engage pupils, modelling social and emotional literacy and encouraging pupil self-reflection. Garner (2019) highlighted the crucial link between the way in which pupils learn and their social knowledge and behaviour. These approaches recognise that behaviour in lessons and social settings does not occur in isolation, but is the product of a variety of influences and relationships (Roffey, 2011).

We now return to the case study. Teachers face different behaviours every day, so it is important they are aware of the theory, research and evidence and how they can use it to develop solutions to the problem. All examples in the first part of the case study led teachers to reflect on their practice. The second part of the case study revisits the examples from the first part of the case study to illustrate the teachers' reasoning and solutions to address the issues and hence improve their teaching and pupils' learning.

Case study part 2

Example 1

Lesson focused on the activity of football and the misbehaviour of pupils as a result of the teacher mismanaging the handling of equipment.

Whilst it may have seemed a simple error to have the bag in which footballs were kept tied up, it resulted in mayhem. The teacher realised that preparation of the learning environment was key to ensuring a smooth start and effective transitions in a lesson. For a purposeful practical positive learning environment, the teacher understood that management of the equipment is essential. The teacher took a 'warm strict' approach (Lemov, 2015) and set clear expectations of pupils (DfE, 2024; Roffey, 2011), for example, in moving to the learning area and being clear about the routine for the collection of equipment. The teacher in this instance then gave a named pupil the responsibility for distributing the footballs. Therefore, clear routines assisted the teacher in their firm but fair approach. The teacher ensured the pupils practised handling equipment in an organised manner moving to and from the working areas (Bennett, 2016).

Example 2

During the year 10 lesson focusing on basketball, the teacher asked pupils to "go and warm up", which led to pupils' lack of engagement and misbehaviour.

The teacher reflected on his relationship with the class and also his assertiveness as a teacher. This made him more aware of his 'teacher presence', his way of being with the class, using his 'agency' (Rogers, 2015) by encouraging pupils to show more enthusiasm, work harder and perform better. There are times when some pupils are happier misbehaving than behaving (Bennett, 2020), so it is essential that the teacher adopts a firm but fair approach (Lemov, 2015). The teacher built on his presence (way of being) and adapted his positioning (physical presence) when teaching so that he could see all pupils and they could see him. He made sure he was thorough in his planning, which included teacher positioning (McGill, 2012). With this approach, the pupils could not hide, as the teacher maintained eye contact to aid the promotion of good behaviour and curtail misbehaviour (DfE, 2024).

Example 3

Gymnastics lesson where the teacher did not give clear instruction when pupils mishandled the mats.

The teacher reflected on the lesson and realised he should have stepped in rather than let the poor handling of equipment proceed. The lesson was disjointed and lacking in quality; the teacher recognised that he had poor expectations and organisation from the outset. He acknowledged that he struggled to get the pupils on task and to stay on task. For example, in giving instructions, pupils chatted or 'rolled around'. The teacher sought advice and, with the benefit of receiving guidance from a very experienced and knowledgeable teacher, he made adjustments to his lesson. He gave clear instruction to the pupils and laid out that he had high expectations of them as well as reminding the pupils they should be adhering to the school behaviour policy (DfE, 2024; Roffey, 2011). Pupils were led to the working space, where they were tasked with taking on the character required for the activity by walking as a gymnast should, encouraging head high and holding firm body tension. This approach resonates with teachers setting out pupils' routines (Bennett, 2016). Pupils were taught from the outset how to handle the equipment. Pupils were instructed when to collect and where to place their mats, a task they did in pairs, carrying a mat between two. Whilst giving instructions, pupils were expected to sit up and pay attention. Such were the changes in this lesson that pupils met the intended learning outcomes with some excelling. The teacher made use of the rewards as outlined in the school behaviour policy.

Example 4

Netball lesson where pupils were unsupervised in the changing rooms and did not notice their teacher arrive due to making too much noise.

The teacher described her class as 'lively', yet up to the point of trying to shout over them in the changing rooms, the teacher had not considered that she inadvertently contributed to the loudness of the class. The teacher knew she needed to make changes in how the class were taught, as they were not fully engaged in their learning. The teacher realised that although she felt she 'got on' with the class, she had never set out clear rules to allow lessons to be successful (Bennett, 2016). This was particularly the case in establishing that pupils should be quiet when the teacher is talking (Marzano and Pickering, 2010). Two key small yet significant changes allowed the teacher to set a purposeful learning environment. First, the teacher had got into a habit of being late after break and she understood that for pupils to have high expectations, then she should lead by example and be waiting for the class before the start of the lesson. Being present in the changing rooms gave an authoritative vibe and less opportunity for pupils to misbehave (Rogers, 2015). Second, the teacher took more notice of the tone and volume of her voice, realising that if you start a lesson with your loudest voice, there is nowhere left to go. The teacher took a more proactive role in her planning to establish a positive approach to behaviour management (Garner, 2011).

Example 5

One pupil not engaged in her learning in a GCSE dance lesson.

The teacher analysed her handling of the situation of the pupil not engaged in her learning. The pupil's lack of engagement demonstrated she had a poor relationship with herself (Garner, 2019). The teacher realised that she aided the pupil's negative behaviour by allowing her to 'sit out' of the lesson. The teacher knew that she had to get the pupil engaged as she was concerned her behaviour would impact on her GCSE grade and perhaps influence others to misbehave. The pupil displayed the same behaviour in the following lesson. Once all other pupils commenced their work, the teacher addressed the pupil's behaviour with her. This did not have the desired effect, so the teacher initiated the school behaviour policy, to the point where the head of year was involved to make contact with the pupil's parents. The outcome of this action enabled the teacher to build a meaningful, positive and personalised relationship with this pupil's parents. Thus, the interaction between relationships as the basis of a positive approach to behaviour (see Figure 7.1) emphasises the importance of others as well as the pupil themselves in learning to manage their own behaviour (Morgan and Ellis, 2011). Unbeknown to the teacher, the pupil was a high-attaining dancer out of school and her reasons for withdrawing were because she did not want to display her talent in front of her peers. This situation resonates with Bronfenbrenner's (1979) interlinked relationships and, having knowledge of this theory allowed the teacher to adapt her teaching. The teacher was able to meet the needs of this pupil by utilising her prior experience and talent to her advantage. Thus, she was able to build relationships with her peers and build her confidence and self-esteem by contributing to peer learning.

Summary and key points

This chapter has focused on the challenges related to effective management of pupils' behaviour and focusing on behaviour for learning. Drawing on relevant theory, research and evidence, particular attention is given to what constitutes misbehaviour and good behaviour, the school behaviour policy developing a positive learning environment and promoting positive behaviour or behaviour for learning – where positive behaviour evidences pupil engagement, their conduct and their attitude to learning.

Part 1 of the case study detailed real examples of pupil misbehaviour from a secondary school in the West Midlands. This was followed by relevant theory, research and evidence, which can inform practice and address the issues in the first part of the case study. The outcomes of teacher reflection and intervention to create a positive learning environment and promote good pupil behaviour were addressed in the second part of the case study. Key points to emerge from these examples include the communication of expectations; the importance of teacher presence; the importance of rules, routines and responses; the necessity for planning; careful management and handling of equipment; consideration of adopting the character of the activity being taught; meaningful interaction of relationships; and the need for consistency in adhering to school behaviour policies. All these points promote behaviour for learning.

There are, of course many features relating to behaviour, which have not been covered in this chapter. The aim here was to investigate theory, research and evidence, which may provide solutions and make a difference. Central to this information is the school behaviour policy, which sets the scene for schools and their departments. However, consistency is key in promoting good behaviour and sanctioning misbehaviour.

The focus of this chapter has been behaviour management. Teaching to promote positive behaviour does not happen by chance, it needs to be planned, consistent, well organised and supportive of a learning environment where pupils feel safe, where positive relationships are developed and where pupils take responsibility for their behaviour and learning. Further, reflection by teachers is essential. This allows a teacher to recognise when the behaviour in lessons falls short of expectations and by engaging with relevant theory, research and evidence, teachers are equipped with knowledge and skills to enhance pupils' learning to enable them to address particular challenges by sourcing intervention strategies. Therefore, teachers should reflect and apply solutions to their own practice.

References

Bennett, T. (2016) *Developing Behaviour Management Content for Initial Teacher Training (ITT)*, available at: https://assets.publishing.service.gov.uk/government/uploads/system/uploads/attachment_data/file/536889/Behaviour_Management_report_final__11_July_2016.pdf (accessed 23 November 2024).

Bennett, T. (2017) *Creating a Culture: How School Leaders Can Optimise Behaviour*, London: Department for Education.

Bennett, T. (2020) *Running the Room: The Teacher's Guide to Behaviour*, Woodbridge: John Catt Educational.

Bronfenbrenner, U. (1979) *The Ecology of Human Development*, Cambridge, MA: Harvard University Press.

Burnett, P. (2002) 'Teacher praise and feedback and students' perception of the classroom environment', *Educational Psychology*, 22 (1), 5-16.

DES (Department of Education and Science) (1989) *Discipline in Schools (The Elton Report)*, London: DES, available at: www.educationengland.org.uk/documents/elton/elton1989.html (accessed 23 November 2024).

DfE (Department for Education) (1994) *The Education of Children with Emotional and Behavioural Difficulties* (Circular 9/94), London: DfE.

DfE (Department for Education) (2024) *Behaviour in Schools: Advice for Headteachers and School Staff,* **February 2024**, available at: https://assets.publishing.service.gov.uk/media/65ce3721e1bdec001a3221fe/Behaviour_in_schools_-_advice_for_headteachers_and_school_staff_Feb_2024.pdf (accessed 12 November 2024).

Dix, P. (2017) *When the Adults Change, Everything Changes: Seismic Shifts in School Behaviour*, Bancyfelin, Carmarthen: Independent Thinking Press.

Ellis, S. and Tod, J. (2018) *Behaviour for Learning: Promoting Positive Relationships in the Classroom* (2nd edition), Abingdon: Routledge.

Evidence Based Education (2022) *Student Behaviour: What Is 'Good' Behaviour and How Can Teachers Encourage It? Reflecting on Great Teaching*, available at: https://f.hubspotusercontent30.net/hubfs/2366135/What%20is%20good%20behaviour%20and%20how%20can%20teachers%20encourage%20it%3F.pdf (accessed 23 November 2024).

Garner, P. (2011) *Promoting the Conditions for Positive Behaviour to Help Every Child Succeed, Review of the Landscape: Professor Philip Garner*, Nottingham: NCSL, available at: https://dera.ioe.ac.uk/id/eprint/12538/1/download%3Fid%3D158591%26filename%3Dpromoting-the-conditions-for-positive-behaviour-to-help-every-child-succeed.pdf (accessed 23 November 2024).

Garner, P. (2019) 'Managing Classroom Behaviour: Adopting a Positive Approach', in S. Capel, M. Leask, S. Younie, E. Hidson and J. Lawrence (eds) *Learning to Teach in the Secondary School: A Companion to School Experience* (9th edition), Abingdon: Routledge, pp.171-189.

Goleman, D. (1995) *Emotional Intelligence: Why It Can Matter More Than IQ*, London: Bloomsbury Publishing.

Lemov, D. (2015) *Teach Like a Champion 2.0: 62 Techniques that Put Students on the Path to College* (2nd edition), Totnes: John Wiley and Sons.

Marzano, R.J. and Pickering, D.J. (2010) *The Highly Engaged Classroom*, Bloomington, IN: Marzano Research Laboratory.

McGill, M.R. (2012) *TeacherToolkit: The 5 Minute Lesson Plan*, available at: https://www.teachertoolkit.co.uk/5minplan/inset-for-5minplan/ (accessed 28 November 2024).

Morgan, N. and Ellis, G. (2011) *A Kit Bag for Promoting Positive Behaviour in the Classroom*, London: Jessica Kingsley Publishers.

Roffey, S. (2011) *The New Teacher's Survival Guide to Behaviour* (2nd edition), London: SAGE Publications Ltd.

Rogers, B. (2015) *Classroom Behaviour: A Practical Guide to Effective Teaching, Behaviour Management and Colleague Support* (4th edition), London: SAGE Publications.

Strickland, S. (2023) *They Don't Behave for Me: 50 Classroom Behaviour Scenarios to Support Teachers*, Woodbridge: John Catt Educational.

Tod, J. and Powell, S. (2004) *A Systematic Review of How Theories Explain Learning Behaviour in School Contexts*, London: EPPI.

Weare, K. (2004) *Developing the Emotionally Literate School*, London: Paul Chapman Publishing.

Whitehouse, K. (2013) 'Teaching to promote positive behaviour', in S. Capel, P. Breckon and J. O'Neill (eds) *A Practical Guide to Teaching Physical Education in the Secondary School* (2nd edition), Abingdon: Routledge, pp.166-179.

Whitehouse, K., Barber, L. and Pepperell, R. (2021) 'Developing and maintaining an effective learning environment', in S. Capel, J. Cliffe and J. Lawrence (eds) *Learning to Teach Physical Education in the Secondary School: A Companion to School Experience* (5th edition), Abingdon: Routledge, pp.161-182.

Chapter 8 Challenges related to promoting learning in the physical domain

Developing physical competence – curriculum, pedagogy and assessment

Richard Blair and Neve Blair

Introduction

Blair and Capel (2020, p.137) wrote "in both work and leisure time and across all aspects of modern life, there is now greater *choice* and potential for physical activity, but also more options for physical inactivity". For children and young people to be in a position to make choices about engaging in different forms of physical activity, it is important that they develop their physical competence (Whitehead, 2010). In this context, the chapter aims to discuss how physical competence is developed through school-based physical education. Connections between practice and theory are highlighted, in order that a reflective position can be considered. As the chapter develops to consider the details of its overall aim, *developing pupils' physical competence through school-based physical education*, there is an awareness that the development of competence is considered a motivator for human behaviour (Mascret, Elliot and Cury, 2015) and (Deci and Ryan, 2000). This connects to what Blair and Capel (2020) discussed regarding physical activity and choice and reinforces the point that learning in the physical domain and the development of physical competence supports children and young people to consider and make a wide range of positive choices to be physically active throughout the different stages of their life course (Whitehead, 2010).

Learning in the physical domain and the development of physical competence is discussed critically against the real-world experience of secondary school physical education. An introductory case study is used to present a real-world example of a current challenge in relation to the physical education curriculum, learning in the physical domain and the development of physical competence; there is a focus on pre- and early teenage pupils. The case study has been developed from the real-world experiences of the authors and is presented from the perspective of the younger author. The authors of the chapter differ from other chapters in that they are a father and daughter team, a combination that allows for a perspective on physical education and specifically learning in the physical domain and the development of physical competence from the experiences of a young person.

To help readers navigate the chapter, a short bit about us. At the time of writing Neve was in year 11; she was taking GCSE Physical Education; with her three non-examined assessments sports being rowing, swimming and climbing. Neve is a rower and spends much of her spare time on the river, rowing either a Gig (a fixed seat, 6-person boat, usually made of wood) or a skiff (a single, double, four or a coxed quad). As part of a coxed quad, she took part in the 2023 U15 regional championships at Holme Pierrepont; in a Gig, she has represented her county, at U15, U16 and U18 and is a member of the Girls National and International Championship winning crews. Richard is an academic, a qualified physical education teacher and sports coach with an interest in understanding aspects of education and physical education, considering the relationship between curriculum, pedagogy and assessment. He spends some of his spare time helping to launch and retrieve wooden boats. He also coaches his son's U14 football team.

A note from Neve: I feel very lucky to have found a physical activity, a sport, that I love. As I develop my knowledge, passion, and competence as a rower, and as a physically active young person, I can appreciate how being physically competent adds value to my life. Physical competence impacts not only my physical health and well-being but helps with my self-confidence and identity; in every sense, it supports my agency as a young person. Dad tells me that Professor Henry Giroux states, "education in its final analysis is really about the production of agency", and therefore how we experience education questions the kind of agents we are going to become. Dad asks what kind of agents does physical education produce? I am not sure about a fuller answer to his question, but for me, being physically competent has helped me navigate the bumps, twists, and turns of my early teenage years. It has supported me in understanding who I am and how I connect and engage with different people, communities and broader society. I know a lot of people through being a rower and more generally taking part in physical activity and sport. These experiences have given me a lot of opportunities to develop physically, socially and psychologically.

I cox a women's four, a veteran's crew, a boat made up of four older ladies (they won't mind me saying that …). We row at 8.00 AM on a Sunday morning. Rowing is a very technical sport; there is a need to concentrate and commit yourself. The vet ladies are a perfect example for any young person of how fulfilling, and how important, it is to be physical competent as you move through the different stages of the life course. For me, they demonstrate how being physically competent can add significant value to your life, not only physically but also socially and emotionally. As a four, the ladies are physically and technically competent, we work hard on the water, and then we enjoy breakfast, a chat and a laugh in the boat house. It is often during breakfast and the lively, humorous chatter that I can appreciate and understand how important physical activity and being physically competent is for our sense of self and our broader health and well-being. This is not elite-level rowing, far from it (they won't mind me saying that …), but it is inspiring. The opportunity to cox the four ladies has given me an insight and a broader perspective and understanding; it provides a context that has shown me the relevance and importance of developing physical competence that, if looked after, will last you a lifetime.

A note from Richard: we feel very lucky that both Neve and her younger brother have found physical activities, sports that they love and that are developing their physical competence. I can see as they develop their competence, how it is adding to their motivation to be healthy and active, and if I'm honest, to be competitive. However, beyond competition, their developing physical competence is supporting and shaping their identities, their confidence and their agency, allowing them to develop their understanding of how they contribute to our family, our local communities, in which they access so much support and encouragement, and the wider society.

Case study part 1 – year 7 swimming

Curriculum – swimming was the next activity on the curriculum map for my year 7 all-girls group. The week before the swimming block started, our teacher, who we all really liked, sat us down in the changing room and informed us that we would be doing swimming for the next 5 weeks. This would require a short walk to the local swimming pool. As we live near the sea, she placed an emphasis on swimming being a very important physical activity, as it could save your life. As a strong swimmer, I was looking forward to the lessons, but I was very aware there were others who were not. A combination of not being competent swimmers, some of the girls were also starting their first experience of menstruation, and having to wear a swimming costume was an uncomfortable idea in such a public setting; the changing room chatter was clear. Interestingly, this is still the case with my year 10 and 11 GCSE classes, which may explain why we haven't done whole-class swimming as part of our GCSE course. Despite these concerns, Miss did a really good job of explaining the importance of swimming and reassuring the whole class.

Pedagogy – the following week, on the day of our first swimming lesson, we headed down to the pool. To our surprise, our class teacher wasn't waiting for us; instead, we were met by a cover supervisor and part-time swimming coach. He informed us that Miss was away at a sports fixture and that he would be taking this week's lesson. To be honest, it didn't bother me, the cover supervisor had taught me when I was younger and, because I am a competent swimmer, I was confident and not fazed by this change. However, as most of the girls were not as competent and therefore not as confident or motivated to take part in the lesson, their feelings were heightened by the change of teacher; the changing room chatter was clear. The context of a male teacher further compounded the challenges for some of the girls, the less competent swimmers, those who had started their periods and those developing their awareness of body image and our changing body shapes.

The first swimming lesson focussed on finding out the different levels of swimming abilities; effectively, it was an assessment of physical competence through swimming. For the next 5 weeks, we had a different teacher each week, a combination of male and female teachers. Each lesson looked and felt much like the first, until the final lesson, which was 'ok girls, get in and swim'. The final lesson had more girls sitting out than taking part.

Assessment – since we had a different teacher each week, I can only reason that there was very little assessment of our swimming abilities. I reach this view by the fact that the lessons were the same; we started again each week. Perhaps it is more accurate to say that none of the assessments undertaken by any of the teachers were used to inform the following lesson or to provide feedback on how we might improve of swimming competence.

Discussion

This case study highlights a range of issues, including a lack of communication to the pupils, lessons not being planned and therefore principles of learning not being applied. To solve any given issue or challenge, it is important to identify where the problem begins. In the case study, the development of the girl's physical competence through swimming is significantly challenged due to a department-level curriculum issue, potentially connected to whole-school challenges of timetabling and staffing, that is, the activity of swimming was chosen and the lesson was timetabled during a period that, due to how the school prioritised the teachers' time, did not allow the swimming lessons to be taught by the same teacher each week. The curriculum and organisational challenges of timetabling and staffing had significant implications for teacher pedagogy and assessment, and therefore pupil learning in the physical domain and the development of the physical and swimming competence. Swimming as an activity for developing physical competence had been timetabled through the year 7 curriculum; this is a department-level decision. However, in this case, the department did not align their curriculum planning with the staffing structure, that is, as highlighted above, there was not a class teacher who could teach a 5-week block of swimming, a teacher who could teach the curriculum subject, through an appropriate range of pedagogies supported and developed using ongoing assessment opportunities. In relation to developing physical competence, the case study highlights the importance of curriculum planning (Bowler et al., 2020, Cliffe, 2021) and introduces the importance of a learning theory that supports the acquisition and consolidation of knowledge, understanding and competence, while connecting to pedagogy and assessment (Blair and Capel 2020, Hattie and Donghue, 2016, 2018).

The issue starts with curriculum planning, a department issue. The physical education department made a choice to timetable swimming during a specific time of the year and during a certain period of the day. In the case of the first lesson, the department prioritised the class teacher missing the lesson to attend an extra-curricular sporting event. This is an interesting decision given the context, that is, it was the first swimming lesson for a year 7 class who had shown signs of concern the week before. It is an issue that connects to planning and staffing, and the values of what is prioritised by the department, the physical education curriculum or, in the case of the first week, extra-curricular school sport? The staffing issue is potentially a joint issue shared between the department and the whole school. In addition, clearly, an issue of this nature is not simple, and there will be levels of complexity and detail unbeknown to pupils and parents. However, the implications of this decision-making on pupils developing their physical competence through swimming are significant. Having a different teacher for all five lessons acted as a significant blocking mechanism to how the relationship between a curriculum plan, teacher pedagogy and how assessment could be developed and used. For the relationship between curriculum, pedagogy and assessment to work, there needs to be a consistency in how the teacher and the pupils communicate; in the case of the example provided through the case study, this was not possible due to the class having a different teacher each week. As such, the curriculum, pedagogy and assessment relationship was, in effect, broken at a meso- and micro- or class level. It is also reasonable to conclude that because of the department-level planning and the prioritisation of staffing, questions can be raised regarding pupils missing an opportunity to develop their physical competence through swimming.

Physical competence: a connected perspective

The position taken in this chapter is developed from what Bernstein (1977), and subsequently Penney *et al.* (2009), considered the three message systems of education: the relationship between curriculum, pedagogy and assessment. The alignment of the three systems provides the overarching structure through which the challenges and opportunities of intentionally facilitating pupils' learning and the specific focus of this chapter, learning in the physical domain and the development of physical competence in school-based physical education. Within the broader structure of curriculum, pedagogy and assessment, this section presents a social, cultural view and a narrower psychological perspective that together consider how pupils experience the development of their physical competence through curriculum-based physical education. It discusses why in a society with more opportunities to be active or inactive, there is a greater need for individuals to make informed educated choices (Blair and Capel, 2020). It is suggested that it has never been more important for schools and physical education departments to plan for the intentional development of physical competence, through a taught programme of study; a point supported by Stidder and Blair (2020). This broad view is presented with an awareness that children and young people are faced with an increased number of opportunities and choices (Ziehe, 2018), which require a broader and transferable range of competence to make the best decisions for any individual.

The importance of a school-based physical education programmes that support pupils to develop their physical competence is referenced by Bowler *et al.* (2020), Jess and Carse (2020) and Ní Chróinín, Fletcher and O'Sullivan (2018), who discussed issues around the values, aims, meaning and content of physical education. Bowler *et al.* (2020) discussed different approaches to curriculum design and to teaching physical education and highlighted the perspective of physical literacy. Whitehead (2010), in her definition of physical literacy, made the explicit connection between an individual's physical competence, their confidence and motivation and how they connect to support the physically literate person. An individual who possesses the knowledge and understanding to engage with physical activity, albeit in potentially different forms, is more likely to participate across and through the different stages of their life course (Whitehead, 2010). The discussions around the importance of a structured programme of study are developed in relation to the points made by Whitehead and connected to the position of Penney *et al.* (2009), Kirk (2013) and Stidder and Blair (2020), who all suggested that, to fully develop pupils' physical competence, there is a need for structured support at a meso- (school or college) level; through a well-organised physical education curriculum. If such a curriculum is in place and it is suitably resourced, learning in the physical domain and the development of physical competence can be achieved across a medium-term block of lessons, connected to units of work and across year groups, although this is further dependent on teachers adopting appropriate pedagogical approaches and assessment opportunities. If there is a clear structured programme of physical education, intentional learning will take place over extended periods of time; both in the medium and longer terms (Cliffe, 2021). If appropriate pedagogy and assessment are not in place, learning in the physical domain and the development of physical competence are less likely to occur, as seen through the real-world example used in the case study.

In relation to learning in the physical domain and the development of physical competence, there is further connection back to Whitehead (2010), who discussed physical competence as a central attribute to the physically literate individual and suggested that "individuals who are physically literate will move with poise, economy, and confidence in a wide variety of physically challenging situations" (Whitehead, 2010, p.44). For all pupils to develop physical competence, they need to rehearse, repeat and refine patterns of movement, using different environments, contexts, activities and through engaging in different ways of practicing (Farrow, Baker and MacMahon, 2013; Patterson and Lee, 2013). The intentional rehearsal and repetition of movement patterns were not possible in the case study. This was fundamentally because the systems of curriculum, pedagogy and assessment were not connected, due to the class having a different teacher during each of the 5 weeks. It is at this micro-level of classroom, or in this case a swimming pool, where the importance of curriculum, pedagogy and assessment is brought to life. The importance and relevance of this structure in relation to intentional teaching, learning in the physical domain and the development of physical competence can be further reinforced through making the connection to psychological literature and theory.

To apply psychological theory to aid the development of pupils' physical competence, it is important that a well-organised curriculum is in place that allows for progression in learning and development. At its most fundamental point, this would mean that lessons and activities are scheduled with class teachers, who, barring any unforeseen circumstances, can teach the class over a medium-term unit of work. It is within this overall curriculum structure that the relationship between physical competence and motivation connects with both achievement goal theory (Elliot, Murayama and Pekrun, 2011; Mascret, Elliot and Cury, 2015) and self-determination theory (Deci and Ryan, 2001). Achievement goal theory and self-determination theory are described in greater detail in the next paragraph. Psychological theory supports the development of competence – specifically, in this case, physical competence – through nurturing the relationship between motivation and how competence is achieved and developed. In the specific case of physical competence through different practice organisation including blocked, variable and random (Lawrence, Kingston and Gottward, 2013). These are explained further in the section on pedagogy below. Therefore, with specific reference to the development of all pupils' physical competence, it is suggested that the stronger the meso-level structure, the relationship between curriculum, pedagogy and assessment, the better the connections of competence, confidence and motivation can be achieved. This allows for psychological theory to be applied to practice at a higher, stronger and more transferable level. This increased level of application is achieved because a clearer curriculum, pedagogy and assessment structure allows for the development of strong, positive teacher-pupil relationships (Jowett et al., 2023) – relationships that are supportive of the application of psychological theory in practice. A moment's reflection on the swimming case study makes it clear that the application of psychological theory, with the specific intent of developing physical competence, was not possible due to the breakdown of the systems, curriculum, pedagogy and assessment.

Achievement goal theory considers a person's constructions of the meaning of competence and thus of the goals they strive to achieve. Initial work in this area by Nicholls (1984) and Dweck and Leggett (1988) considered two broad categories of goals, mastery and performance. Mastery goals orient pupils to try and improve and to attribute personal outcomes to the amount of effort they apply (Elliot, Murayama and Pekrun, 2011; Mascret, Elliot and Cury, 2015). Mastery goals require the definition and evaluation of competence to be developed relative to the demands of the activity or previous outcomes of an activity. Thus, it requires an understanding of difficulty or challenge in relation to the need for further learning. This requires a response that either increases effort or uses different strategies, including asking for additional help or feedback (Elliot, Murayama and Pekrun, 2011; Mascret, Elliot and Cury, 2015). Based on the experience presented in the swimming case study, it is argued that, for both pupils and teachers to access this level of goal-orientated development, there needs to be a structured programme of physical education, and crucially this needs a high level of consistency in relation to how the programme is taught and assessed. On the other hand, a performance goal-orientated individual demonstrates their ability to define and evaluate competence relative to others. A performance orientation attributes outcomes to ability. It understands setbacks as signs of lower ability and avoids exposing inadequate ability by asking for help (Elliot, Murayama and Pekrun, 2011; Mascret, Elliot and Cury, 2015). Furthermore, achievement goal theory concludes the most desirable and productive form of motivation is based on a mastery position. This connects to the work of Deci and Ryan (2002) on motivation and self-determination.

Self-determination theory (Deci and Ryan, 2002) makes connections between three psychological needs, namely, competence, autonomy and relatedness, that support self-determined motivation (Haerens et al., 2013, Aelterman et al., 2012). The need for competence aligns with the human need to feel capable and confident when undertaking behaviour. The psychological literature supports the view that there is a relationship between learning in the physical domain and the development of physical competence and an individual's motivation (Aelterman et al., 2012; Elliot, Murayama and Pekrun, 2011; Haerens et al., 2013; Mascret, Elliot and Cury, 2015). As with achievement goal theory, reflection on the swimming case study highlights the fact that the application of the theory is not possible in a formal educational context if the three systems of curriculum, pedagogy and assessment are not aligned and working together.

This section makes the point that to develop pupils' physical competence, physical education teachers, individually and as a department, need to understand the connected perspective of curriculum planning and pedagogy, including the importance of positive teacher–pupil relationships (Jowett et al., 2023) that allow for connection between pedagogy and assessment and continuous feedback to the participant, as noted by Black and Wiliam (2018). If this environment is achieved, the self-determined pupil is supported. Therefore, it is important that at a meso-level of organisation, there is a clearly structured and resourced curriculum that allows teachers to engage with relevant pedagogies and assessment opportunities. If the meso-level structure is in place, it allows for the micro-psychological, the face-to-face interactions between teachers and pupils to develop. The next three sections consider, respectively, the three educational systems of curriculum, pedagogy and assessment.

The importance of curriculum planning

As Bernstein (1977) and Penney et al. (2009) stated, the issue of curriculum planning has a direct relationship to pedagogy and assessment. The three systems are interconnected and, in every sense, cannot be separated in relation to a pupil's experience of education or physical education (Penney et al., 2009). These points are extended by Marsh (2009), who stated that pupils should learn through a framework of aims, purposes, content, pedagogy and assessment. Therefore, if the aims of the National Curriculum for Physical Education are to be achieved, and pupils are to develop their physical competence, it is important that the curriculum is seen as a framework for intentional learning (Blair and Capel, 2020). This point reinforces what the educationalist Lawrence Stenhouse (1975, p.53) said when he defined curriculum as "an attempt to communicate the essential principles and features of an educational proposal in such a form that it is open to critical scrutiny and capable of effective translation into practice".

In the swimming case study above, it is argued that the breakdown in learning in the physical domain and the development of physical competence can be traced back to curriculum planning and the management of staffing; the implications of this will be discussed in relation to teacher pedagogy and assessment in the following sections. The importance of a high-quality curriculum that is broad and balanced has been documented and supported by a significant number of academics, including (Bowler et al., 2020). However, it should be noted that Kirk (2010) and others have questioned just how broad a curriculum should be. They argued that too much breadth - or a curriculum that is "a mile wide, but an inch deep" (Guy, cited in Kirk, 2010, p.7), can make any depth of content and knowledge impossible to achieve. This is a point that could be made against the swimming case study; the activity was beyond the resources and capacity of the department. Swimming took up curriculum space, but due to not being resourced or staffed effectively, it did not enable pupils to achieve the required learning or development. To move forward and make suggestions regarding how the scenario in the swimming case study could have been avoided or indeed changed for the future, reference back to Stenhouse (1975) is made. The school, physical education department and the teachers should be encouraged to think carefully about the educational purpose of units of work and how they are translated into practice, in order that the curriculum aims - macro, meso and micro - are achieved. In the specific case of this chapter, clarity regarding the curriculum aims are encouraged to ensure that pupils develop their physical competence, to make informed decisions about how they engage in being physically active throughout the life course.

The curriculum and staff planning led to an interpretation of content that was disconnected and fragmented. It did not allow any of the teachers to engage and develop supportive relationships with the pupils (Jowett et al., 2023). Furthermore, it did not support the development of an effective learning environment (Lawrence, 2021; Rosenshine, 2012; Whitehouse, Barber and Pepperell, 2021). It was noted that while there were girls who were competent swimmers, some, indeed most, were not, and therefore lacked confidence and, in some cases, the motivation to take part in lessons, as evidenced through the dropout rate throughout the 5 weeks. The curriculum planning prevented teachers and pupils from developing positive relationships. Without appropriate, positive teacher-pupil relationships, it is harder to communicate and motivate pupils. It is very difficult to engage pupils in formative assessment opportunities that will lead to them developing their awareness and skill to self-assess.

As noted above, clearly, an issue of this nature is not simple, and there will be levels of complexity and detail unbeknown to pupils, parents and perhaps even beyond the direct control of the physical education department, that is, whole-school decisions made by senior managers. Therefore, how do physical education departments negotiate curriculum issues? It is suggested that this may be achieved through clearly communicating the importance and value of the subject aims and how they will be met through the management of curriculum time, resources and ultimately pedagogy and assessment. Clearly, this is not a straightforward matter and will require a localised response relevant to the specific context in which a teacher works. However, some general points for consideration:

- at a meso-school level, the curriculum offered should be planned with care, detail and an awareness of the local social, cultural, political, economic and geographical context. Clear learning aims should be included, with unit of work objectives that can be developed into lesson learning outcomes by individual teachers. A range of activities and assessment opportunities should be planned that align learning with the aims of the macro-curriculum
- documentation, policy and curriculum should communicate the organisational expectations for school, teachers, pupils and all stakeholders
- at a department level, a clear understanding of the aims and purpose of physical education and a shared view on how learning in physical education should take place should be developed so that it is clear what physical education looks like in this specific context
- a departmental approach should be developed that supports an agreed accountability for pupils' learning and development. An emphasis should be placed on formative assessment and the development of strong, healthy relationships between pupils and teachers. In these healthy relationships, teachers and pupils know each other and feel comfortable engaging in dialogue, sharing understanding and gathering evidence that learning is taking place.

The importance of pedagogy

Blair and Capel (2020) discussed pedagogy as an intentional act of communication that supports learning, a communication that is socially, culturally and politically aware, and formed through the relationship between pupils, teachers and significant others. It demonstrates an understanding of the environment, context and circumstances in which it is undertaken. Pedagogy is complex; it connects the physical act of teaching or communication with a broader awareness of who, why, where and how a communication should take place. The act of pedagogical communication differs from teaching communication because it is rooted in policy, theory, values and beliefs (Alexander, 2008). Pedagogical communications are formed from an epistemological (the view of knowledge) and ontological (the meaning of, in this case, teaching) position, and cannot be separated from the social, cultural, political and economic context or circumstance in which it is undertaken.

In relation to learning in the physical domain and the development of physical competence in physical education lessons, and the importance of teachers, schools and other organisations who work with children and young people, for example, youth sport settings, understanding and valuing pedagogy has, perhaps, never been more important than it is today. Potentially, there has never been a more critical period in history for teachers to have a clear understanding of pedagogy and their own pedagogical identity. It is accepted that this is a bold statement; therefore, a short rationale is provided below.

There are now more opportunities for children, young people and adults to make a *choice* to be active or inactive (Blair and Capel, 2020). Increased choice is generated, in part, because children and young people are experiencing a more individualised society (Ziehe, 2018). A society with far less reliance on broad social norms and values, with an increased need for everyone, particularly younger people, to make decisions, without the support of a broader structural, social, cultural reference (Ziehe, 2018). Therefore, in order to make good decisions, decisions that are supportive of enhancing lives, their own and those of others around them, it is important that children and young people are informed regarding the consequences and potential outcomes. To achieve this in an educational setting, there is a need for teachers to be skilled pedagogues to communicate ideas, activities, knowledge and understanding from a position of theory, belief and value in order that their communication supports the development of meaning and understanding for all pupils. An understanding of intentional communication aligns with the views of Marsh (2009) regarding learning being connected to aims and values but, and this is the critical point, the aims and values connect with the lives and experiences of younger people. Therefore, at a curriculum level, a physical education department should aim to deliver an interpretation of curricular that has belonging in the lives of children. The department should therefore carefully consider how they communicate, using pedagogies that are relatable for pupils. This position of awareness and understanding allows for the development of positive teacher-pupil relationships (Jowett et al., 2023), which in turn leads to higher-quality assessment and feedback.

To extend this discussion, consideration should also be given to what could be viewed as a broader position through which physical competence can be developed using an ecological dynamics approach. This is an approach that aims to understand how participants relate to environmental factors and how the environment supports the development of competence and behaviours (Vaughan et al., 2021). Ecological dynamics considers how the learner and the environment become interconnected, making it challenging to practice the development of skilled competent performance without the support of a clear, well-structured and supported environment, a notion that was challenged in the swimming case study. This connects to points made by Jones et al. (2010) which, although writing in a sports coaching context, relate to the swimming case study. Jones et al. (2010) made a plea for the need to re-conceptualise and re-humanise sports coaching. Considering the year 7 girls' swimming experience, the same plea is made in this chapter for the teaching of physical education and specifically learning in the physical domain and the development of physical competence. It is accepted that in many schools and colleges, there are clear and visible connections to an ecological approach to teaching physical education and school sport. In every sense, the essence of an ecological viewpoint is the strong, tightly connected relationship between curriculum, pedagogy and assessment, with teachers understanding how to connect the three systems. However, the work of Kirk (2010, 2013, 2019) should be acknowledged regarding the de-contextualised, sport-technique approach to teaching physical education, specifically through a games-based curriculum. While accepting that swimming differs significantly from games in relation to movement requirements, the de-contextualised and de-humanised experience presented through the swimming case study presents, albeit different challenges but with a familiar feel, to the points made by Kirk (2010, 2013, 2019).

An ecological approach emphasises learning and development being continuously regulated and adapted through engagement and interaction with information from the environment. As far back as 1966, James Gibson discussed how performers or athletes enhanced physical competence or functional interactions by becoming more attuned to the environmental factors. This is further supported by Araújo et al. (2017), who reported that participant behaviour, physical skill and competence can only be fully understood through the connected lens of the performer and the environmental characteristics. The ecological dynamics model supports the need for children, participants or performers to fully connect with the environment. In relation to teaching physical education, the approach would allow teachers, pupils and the learning environment to be viewed as interconnected in the development of the physically literate agent; of which physical competence is a central component (Whitehead, 2010). In the case study of the year 7 swimming, the weakened relationship between curriculum, pedagogy and assessment acts as a block to an ecological understanding, due to the constantly changing teacher and the start-again approach of each lesson. This inconsistency affects the stability and understanding of the social, emotional environment in which the pupils were attempting to develop their physical competence through the aquatic activity of swimming.

While the focus remains on pedagogy, the aim is to narrow the lens and discuss the specifics of pedagogies for learning in the physical domain and the development of physical competence. The spectrum of teaching methods (see styles), Mosston and Ashworth (2002), discusses the reproduction cluster of teaching styles (A–E) including approaches to communication such as 'command', where the teacher makes all the decisions, and 'practice', where pupils practice teacher-prescribed tasks. Both these teaching methods align with the development of motor or physical competence (Morgan and Sproule, 2013; Mosston and Ashworth, 2002). In basic terms, this is achieved through the repetition of patterns and movement. This has relevance to the swimming case study. Metzler (2011) suggested that when safety is a key consideration, as in situations such as swimming, the direct or command method of teaching maybe the best approach. Therefore, it could be argued that having a different teacher every week makes less difference in swimming, as a recommended approach to teaching is more direct, or teacher-focussed, and thus requires less reflection and consideration when using approaches to teaching underpinned by constructivist theories of learning (Jones and Kingston, 2013). This notion can be questioned, based on the points made by Jowett et al. (2023) around the importance of positive teacher-pupil relationship in physical education, and as a connected point, there is still a need for ongoing assessment and feedback to support learning in the physical domain and the development of physical competence, regardless of the chosen method communication.

If it is accepted that a direct, command or practice method of teaching is appropriate for the swimming case study, there is still the issue presented by Rosenshine (2012) regarding principles of instruction. For Rosenshine (2012), a principle of instruction is that all lessons should start with a review of prior learning. In the context of the swimming case study, this principle is challenging, but not impossible. Here the connection between curriculum, pedagogy and assessment is seen. Due to curriculum planning, teacher pedagogy is limited and therefore assessment and feedback opportunities are narrowed, which, in theory, results in a lower quality of intentional learning. This is especially the case if it is acknowledged that learning takes places, that is, knowledge is acquired and consolidated, over the medium term. Research by Hattie and Donoghue (2016, 2018) concluded that the acquisition and consolidation phases of learning are achieved through using different pedagogical approaches.

In considering the acquisition phase of learning, Hattie and Donoghue (2016, 2018) suggested that for successful learning, it is important that pupils 'know the success criteria'. This is a point that is addressed in the next section on assessment. They suggested that during the acquisition phase of learning, which a significant number of pupils in the swimming class were in, it is important to teach pupils how to connect, summarise and organise (Hattie and Donoghue, 2018). What does this look like in relation to learning in the physical domain and the development of physical competence? For many people, learning in the physical domain and the development of physical competence is achieved through continuous practice or repetitions, the replication of an ideal movement pattern being confirmed into the central nervous system, a memory of the correct executed action (Patterson and Lee, 2013).

Therefore, in the specific context of a learning outcome that is connected to learning in the physical domain and the development of physical competence, an appropriate learning activity would include a repetition of a specific movement pattern. For example, when practicing swimming, the front crawl, a one-armed pull, using a float to stabilise (Patterson and Lee, 2013). This is a popular notion and understanding but a point that was developed further by Scott (2004), who suggested that learning in the physical domain and the development of physical competence and movement skill consist of three fundamental components, which he called the 3 Bs, the connection between the brain, biomechanics and behaviour. Scott (2004) described the process of developing motor or physical competence as the brain engaging and understanding the goal of the motor task, followed by the brain organising a plan for successful movement and then communicating with the musculoskeletal system to achieve the desired movement task (Patterson and Lee, 2013). Therefore, what is an appropriate learning activity for the development of motor or physical competence? A classic study by Shea and Morgan (1979) found that practicing using an unpredictable repetition schedule, for example, a random practice, produced superior learning than a more stable or blocked practice condition, where the learner repeated what was done in the previous attempt. In a blocked practice, movement patterns can be planned and then used for all repetitions. In contrast, in a random practice, where repetitions are changed during the practice, the learner is required to actively think about and continuously construct a new plan, connecting brain, biomechanics and behaviour (Scott, 2004). The findings from the Shea and Morgan (1979) study were surprising in that a blocked practice design produced superior results to a random practice during the practice stage. However, when learners returned to be tested for retention and transfer, the findings were reversed. The broader point to make is that learning and developing physical competence are complex and detailed and are not possible if the learning conditions, environment or pedagogy is not supportive. Careful planning, evaluation and pedagogy are required. It is not something that can be achieved through ad-hoc lessons taught by different teachers, who may, but equally may not, have found time to engage in joint planning and sharing of assessment feedback and detail. It is acknowledged that in the case study of swimming, a blocked practice would be supportive, as the movement outcomes are repetitive, with fewer environmental variables. The development of physical competence through swimming, requires the constant refinement of what are complex biomechanical movements to achieve maximum efficiency or, and maximum speed or endurance that require support, through ongoing assessment and feedback.

The importance of assessment

Ongoing formative assessment plays an important role in connecting lesson-to-lesson pedagogy (Blair and Capel, 2020) and the development of positive, professional and constructive teacher–pupil relationships (Jowett et al., 2023). It allows the teacher to know and understand how and what pupils are learning and at what rate. Assessment supports an understanding of what pedagogical approaches and learning activities are working, and what are not working, for individual pupils and for the class. It supports a position that considers how learning activities might be changed or adapted to best support the learning and development of all pupils. Opportunities for assessment form the glue that makes the pedagogy and practice organisation connect and operate together to support the goal of intentional learning. In the real-world example presented through the swimming case study, the constructive use of assessment was largely prevented due to the change in teacher each week. To use assessment constructively, a teacher needs to observe, record and monitor changes in pupil behaviours, knowledge and understanding. In the swimming case study, this would have been achieved if a single teacher had been able to observe, ask questions and provide feedback to the pupils. This issue would have been resolved through the school and the department prioritising their approach to staffing the lessons.

Hay and Penney (2013, p.3) considered assessment from a social-cultural perspective and suggested that "assessments are required by people, developed by people, implemented by people, are performed by people, and have implications for people, across the education system". This point connects critically to the swimming case study; assessment, like pedagogy, is centrally about the connection of people, in this case, teachers and pupils. The teachers are in a position where they are required to make ongoing judgements against the agreed or presented criteria, communicating information to pupils in the form of feedback to support learning in the physical domain and the development of physical competence. As noted above, through the work of Hattie and Donghue (2016, 2018), learning is supported by assessment, which is best supported through the use of 'success criteria', enabling judgements and feedback to be made against a set of desired qualities. As an example from swimming, 'arm action in front crawl, keep your elbow slightly bent as you reach your hand in front of your body to enter the water. Your hand should enter the water between the centre line of the head and the shoulder line. Your hand should be directed with the palm facing down and out, so the thumb first enters the water first, etc.'

In addition, teachers are tasked with using ongoing assessments to develop and adapt learning activities. In the specific context of learning in the physical domain and the development of physical competence, assessment is increasingly fluid and complex, depending on the learning activities being blocked, variable or random (Lawrence, Kingston and Gottward, 2013). As noted above, an increase in competence is linked to an increase in motivation (Deci and Ryan, 2002). Motivated pupils can access a higher level of autonomy and independence (Deci and Ryan, 2002). This position supports the development of self-assessment, a reflective state that supports the possibility that children and young people will continue to be physically active beyond school, in family, community, performance and representative settings. Swimming is a good activity through which pupils can be taught to engage with the success criteria and develop their knowledge, skill and understanding of self- and peer assessment. In part, this is due to the relatively stable nature of the repetitive movement patterns. There are multiple opportunities to observe the repetition of the movement. If this takes place against clearly communicated success criteria or assessment guidance, pupils will be empowered to contribute to the feedback process of assessment and learning.

Case study part 2 - my brother's experience

Three years later and my brother was in year 7, and it was his turn for swimming in the curriculum. This was at the time when this chapter was being written; therefore, I asked him about his experience.

Curriculum - it was an all-boys group, they had 'the talk', the next 5 weeks will be swimming and like my group, some of the boys appeared nervous and apprehensive. My brother was fine, he's a very good swimmer. Like our talk, there was an emphasis on the importance of swimming as a life-saving activity. There was a difference, though. Ellis's talk presented some additional details about what content would be covered in the block and why it was important. The teacher also explained to the boys how they would be assessed and showed them examples of resources for peer and self-assessment, which Ellis thought were 'cool'.

Pedagogy - the same teacher taught the group for all 5 weeks. Learning activities were differentiated for the more and less able or confident pupils. Although only two swimming strokes were covered in the 5 weeks, these were done with a good level of detail, with most of the time spent learning the front and back crawls and, for some pupils, water confidence. The teacher used a range of different practices and activities to support water confidence and the development of both the front and back crawl strokes. Ellis was very clear in stating that the swimming pool white boards were used extensively, with learning outcomes, assessment guidance, activities and key words presented, referred to and actively used throughout the lessons. The visual resources for peer and self-assessment were designed in such a way that it promoted the boys to develop their self-regulation and awareness. Ellis said this didn't work for all the boys, but for his group of more able swimmers, the resources were helpful and engaging as they had enough prior knowledge to use the resources independently; thus, presenting a pedagogy for swimming that supported independence and confidence. Ellis said it allowed the teacher to focus on the less able swimmers, who, in some cases, were still developing their general water confidence.

Assessment - as the same teacher taught the lesson each week, this allowed for assessment to take place and be critically used in every lesson. There was evidence of teacher, peer and ongoing self-assessment across all five lessons.

Summary and key points

To successfully develop physical competence through school-based physical education, there are several important factors that need to be considered and understood. At the broadest point, an understanding of the relationship between curriculum, pedagogy and assessment is needed at both department and school levels; there also needs to be appropriate resourcing and staffing. It is accepted that the introductory case study of swimming presents what some might consider an extreme example of the realities of school-based physical education programmes. However, please note this is a real-world example. Even a watered-down version presents challenges in relation to understanding the curriculum, pedagogy and assessment relationship.

This broader structural response to the learning and development of physical competence forms the framework for a more detailed consideration of the micro-interactions between teachers and pupils. For example, given an understanding of the relationship between, curriculum, pedagogy and assessment, teachers are placed in a position to further consider a range of different pedagogical approaches and practice organisation needed to develop physical competence. The swimming case study makes several points that highlight the importance of teacher continuity in relation to both pedagogy and assessment. For example, what the pupils experienced was effectively a repeat of the same lesson five times, as each teacher was, somewhat understandably, making sure everyone was safe; this was achieved through the repetition of the introductory lesson. In every sense, this is a version of the criticism presented by Kirk (2013) regarding a sports technique-based approach to teaching physical education, an approach that sees the teacher take a surface-based approach to 'covering' the curriculum content (Blair and Capel, 2020; Bowler et al., 2020), with little reflection or use of assessment to support their planning, pupil learning in the physical domain and the development of physical competence.

It is not until this level of structure is understood that focus can be given to teacher–pupil relationships and developing an understanding of appropriate pedagogies that connect to the experiences of pupils, and how they are currently experiencing their childhoods. An understanding of pedagogy leads to the focussed use of assessment. Combining pedagogy and assessment supports the development of practice organisation that connects and develops across several lessons and weeks, acknowledging the progress that the pupils are making. This point supports the research of Hattie and Donoghue (2016, 2018) regarding the acquisition and consolidation of learning over medium-term cycles. The specific focus on learning in the physical domain and the development of physical competence is developed through the work of Scott (2004) regarding the 3 B's – brain, biomechanics and behaviour. While it is beyond the scope of this chapter to present a more detailed explanation, readers are encouraged to give further consideration to the pedagogy of blocked, variable and random practice design (Lawrence, Kingston and Gottward, 2013) and how the different designs connect to pedagogy and assessment, allowing the repetition, rehearse and isolation of specific and connected movement patterns.

There has, perhaps, never been a more important time in history for pupils to develop their physical competence through an intentional, planned and well-resourced physical education curriculum. The broader value of being physically competent connects to the sense of developing confidence that, in turn, supports the development of sense of self, identity and agency. Finally, as noted by Neve earlier in the chapter, in relation to her experiences with the ladies four, it ... has shown me the relevance and importance of developing physical competence, *that if looked after, will last you a lifetime.*

References

Aelterman, N., Vansteenkiste, M., Van Keer, H., Van den Berghe, L., De Meyer, J. and Haerens, L. (2012) 'Students objectively measured physical activity levels and engagement as a function of between-class and between-student differences in motivation towards physical education', *Journal of Sport and Exercise Psychology*, 34, 457–480.

Alexander, R. (2008) 'Pedagogy, curriculum and culture'. In K. Hall, P. Murphy, and J. Soler. (Eds) *Pedagogy and Practice Culture and Identities*. London, Sage, pp.3–27.

Araújo, D., Hristovski, R., Seifert, L., Carvalho, J. and Davids, K. (2017) 'Ecological cognition: expert decision-making behaviour in sport', *International Review of Sport and Exercise Psychology*, 12 (1), 9858, 1–25, https://doi.org/10.1080/1750984X.2017.1349826

Bernstein, B. (1977) *Class Codes and Control, Towards a Theory of Educational Transmissions* (Volume 3), London: Routledge, and Keegan Paul.

Bernstein, B. (2000) *Pedagogy, Symbolic Control, and Identity. Theory Research, Critique*, London: Roman and Littlefield.

Bowler, M., Newton, A., Keyworth, S. and Mckeown, J. (2020) 'Secondary school physical education', in S. Capel and R. Blair (eds) *Debates in Physical Education* (2nd edition), Abingdon: Routledge, pp.170–189.

Black, P.J. and Wiliam, D. (2018) 'Classroom assessment and pedagogy', *Assessment in Education*, 25 (6), 551–575, https://doi.org/10.1080/0969594X.2018.1441807

Blair, R. and Capel, S. (2020) 'Physical education knowledge and learning', in S. Capel and R. Blair (eds) *Debates in Physical Education* (2nd edition), Abingdon: Routledge, pp.132–148.

Cliffe, J. (2021) 'Long-term planning: schemes of work', in S. Capel, J. Cliffe and J. Lawrence (eds) *A Practical Guide to Teaching Physical Education in the Secondary School*, Abingdon: Routledge, pp.39–50.

Deci, E.L. and Ryan, R.M. (2002) *Handbook of Self-determination Research*, Rochester, NY: University of Rochester.

Dweck, C.S. and Leggett, E. (1988) 'A social-cognitive approach to motivation and personality', *Psychological Review*, 95, 256e273.

Elliot, A.J., Murayama, K. and Pekrun, R. (2011) 'A 3 ✕ 2 achievement goal model', *Journal of Educational Psychology*, 103 (3), 632–648, https://doi.org/10.1037/a0023952

Farrow, D., Baker, J. and MacMahon, C. (2013) *Developing Sport Expertise Researchers and Coaches put Theory into Practice*, Abingdon: Routledge.

Gibson, J.J. (1966) *The Senses Considered as Perceptual Systems*, Boston, MA: Houghton Mifflin.

Haerens, L., Aelterman, N., Van den Berghe, L., De Meyer, J., Soenens, B. and Vansteen-kiste, M. (2013) 'Observing physical education teachers' need-supportive interactions in classroom settings', *Journal of Sport and Exercise Psychology*, 35 (1), 3–17.

Hattie, J.A.C. and Donoghue, G.M. (2016) 'Learning strategies: a synthesis and conceptual model', *NPJ: Science of Learning*, 1, 16013, https://doi.org/10.1038/npjscilearn.2016.13

Hattie, J.A.C. and Donghue, G.M. (2018) 'A model of learning, optimising the effectiveness of learning strategies', in K. Illeris (ed.) *Contemporary Theories of Learning, Learning theorists… in Their Own Words*, Abingdon: Routledge, pp.97–113.

Hay, P. and Penney, D. (2013) *Assessment in Physical Education*, Abingdon: Routledge.

Jess, M. and Carse, N. (2020) 'Primary physical education', in S. Capel and R. Blair (eds) *Debates in Physical Education* (2nd edition), Abingdon: Routledge, pp.151–169.

Jones R.L. and Kingston, K. (eds) *An Introduction to Sports Coaching: Connecting Theory to Practice* (2nd edition), Abingdon: Routledge.

Jones, R.L., Potrac, P., Cushion, C. and Ronglan, L.T. (2010) *The Sociology of Sports Coaching*, Abingdon: Routledge, https://doi.org/10.4324/9780203865545

Jowett, S., Warburton, V., Beaumont, L.C. and Felton, L. (2023) 'Teacher-student relationship quality as a barometer of teaching and learning effectiveness: conceptualization and measurement', *British Journal of Educational Psychology*, 93 (3), 842–861, https://doi.org/10.1111/bjep.12600

Kirk, D. (2010) *Physical Education Futures*, Abingdon: Routledge.

Kirk, D. (2013) 'Educational value and models-based practice in physical education', *Educational Philosophy and Theory*, 45 (9), 973–986.

Lawrence, J. (2021) 'Lesson organisation and management', in S. Capel, J, Cliffe and J. Lawerence (eds) *Learning to Teach Physical Education in the Secondary School: A Companion to School Experience*. London, Routledge, pp.106-127.

Lawrence, G., Kingston, K. and Gottward, V. (2013) 'Skill acquisition for coaches', in R. Jones and K. Kingston (eds) *An Introduction to Sports Coaching: Connecting Theory to Practice* (2nd edition), Abingdon: Routledge, pp.31-46.

Marsh, C.J. (2009) *Key Concepts for Understanding Curriculum* (4th edition), Abingdon: Routledge.

Mascret, N., Elliot, A.J. and Cury, F. (2015) 'Extending the 3x2 achievement goal model to the sport domain: The 3x2 Achievement Goal Questionnaire for sport', *Psychology of Sport and Exercise*, 17, 7-14.

Metzler, M.W. (2011) *Instructional Models for Physical Education* (3rd edition), Scottsdale, AZ: Holcomb Hathaway.

Morgan, K. and Sproule, J. (2013) 'Pedagogy for coaches', in R. Jones and K. Kingston (eds) *An Introduction to Sports Coaching Connecting Theory to Practice*, Abingdon: Routledge, pp.15-28.

Mosston, M. and Ashworth, S. (2002) *Teaching Physical Education* (5th edition), San Francisco, CA: Benjamin Cummings.

Nicholls, J.G. (1984) 'Achievement motivation: conceptions of ability, subjective experience, task choice, and performance', *Psychological Review*, 91, 328e346.

Ní Chróinín, D., Fletcher, T. and O'Sullivan, M. (2018) 'Pedagogical principles of learning to teach meaningful physical education', *Physical Education and Sport Pedagogy*, 23 (2), 117-133, https://doi.org/10.1080/17408989.2017.1342789

Patterson, J.T. and Lee, T.D. (2013) 'Organising practice', in D. Farrow, J. Baker and C. MacMahon (eds) *Developing Sport Expertise Researchers and Coaches Put Theory into Practice*, Abingdon: Routledge, pp.132-150.

Penney, D., Brooker, R., Hay, P. and Gillespie, L. (2009) 'Curriculum, pedagogy, and assessment: three message systems of schooling and dimensions of quality physical education', *Sport, Education and Society*, 14 (4), 421-442, https://doi.org/10.1080/13573320903217125

Rosenshine, B. (2012) 'Principles of instruction: research based strategies that all teachers should know', *American Educator*, 36 (1, Spring) 12-19, 39.

Scott, S.H. (2004) 'Optimal feedback control and the neural basis of volitional motor control', *Nature Reviews: Neuroscience*, 5, 534-546.

Shea, J.B. and Morgan, R.L. (1979) 'Contextual interference effects on the acquisition, retention, and transfer of a motor skill', *Journal of Experimental Psychology: Human Learning and Memory*, 5 (2), 179-187, https://doi.org/10.1037/0278-7393.5.2.179

Stenhouse, L. (1975) *An introduction to Curriculum Research and Development*, Oxford: Heinemann Educational.

Stidder, G. and Blair, R. (2020) 'Inclusion and curriculum in physical education', in S. Capel and R. Blair (eds) *Debates in Physical Education* (2nd edition), Abingdon: Routledge, pp.223-238.

Vaughan, J., Mallett, C.J., Potrac, P., López-Felip, M.A. and Davids, K. (2021) 'Football, culture, skill development and sport coaching: extending ecological approaches in athlete development using the skilled Intentionality framework', *Frontiers in Psychology*, 12, 635420, https://doi.org/10.3389/fpsyg.2021.635420

Whitehead, M. (2010) *Physical Literacy Throughout the Life-course*, Abingdon: Routledge.

Whitehouse, K. Barber, L, and Pepperell, R. (2021) 'Developing and maintaining an effective learning environment', in S. Capel, J, Cliffe and J. Lawerence (eds) *Learning to Teach Physical Education in the Secondary School: A Companion to School Experience*. London, Routledge, pp.161-182.

Ziehe, T. (2018) 'Normal learning problems' in youth', in K. Illeris (ed.) *Contemporary Theories of Learning, Learning Theorists... in Their Own Words*, Abingdon: Routledge, pp.204-2018.

Chapter 9   Challenges related to promoting learning in the cognitive domain

Developing pupils' declarative knowledge and thinking

Julia Lawrence

Introduction

In teaching physical education, the focus should be on much more than developing pupils' physical competence. Acknowledging pupils as holistic (see, for example, Capel, Whitehead and Lawrence, 2025), pupils' learning across different domains of learning needs to be supported. In this book, these have been identified as the physical (see Chapter 8), the affective (see Chapter 10) and the cognitive domains (the focus of this chapter).

Learning in the cognitive domain focuses on building knowledge and the ability to think. It is seen as "the development of thinking, knowledge and understanding" (Tan, 2022, p.33). With regard to knowledge, Anderson and Krathwohl (2001) referred to factual, conceptual, procedural and metacognitive knowledge. Within the context of physical education, the Office for Standards in Education, Children's Services and Skills (Ofsted, 2022; 2023) argued that the knowledge expected to be learned in physical education focuses on declarative knowledge (facts and information about a topic or knowing what) alongside procedural knowledge (knowledge about how to do something or knowing how). Table 9.1 provides a summary of types of knowledge by both Anderson and Krathwohl (2001) and Ofsted (2002; 2003) and the relationship between them.

Thus, when planning and teaching lessons, it is important to be clear what knowledge (declarative, procedural or both) pupils are expected to learn, as well as identifying and providing opportunities for this knowledge to be learned and demonstrated, for example, verbally (through for example questioning), in writing and through practical demonstration. In this chapter, the focus is on learning declarative knowledge and how this can be assessed in its own right, not as applied to the practical, as procedural knowledge.

Using a focused case study, this chapter looks to identify how teachers can support pupils to develop cognitively, focusing specifically on strategies that support pupils to develop their declarative knowledge and their ability to think.

Case study (part 1)

Sam is an early career teacher (ECT). During her teacher training, Sam developed knowledge about how pupils learn and the cognitive processes involved with this. However, she is finding

Table 9.1 Types of knowledge

Anderson and Krathwohl (2001)	Ofsted (2022; 2023)
Factual – knowledge of specific facts	Declarative – facts and information about a topic or knowing what, for example, knowing how to: move efficiently and effectively; rules, tactics and strategies; about how to participate effectively
Conceptual – knowledge of concepts and principles	
Procedural – knowledge of how to apply factual and conceptual knowledge	Procedural – knowing how to do something, knowing how to apply declarative knowledge or knowing how
Metacognitive – knowledge of the learning process – for example, learning to learn	

it increasingly challenging to draw out pupils' understanding in relation to the key declarative knowledge and concepts they are expected to learn.

Sam is therefore concerned that the declarative knowledge pupils are learning is not sufficiently embedded within their long-term memory. Whilst the pupils can demonstrate their knowledge through their performances in the physical domain, when responding to questions, their ability to recall key facts and information and explain and talk about what they are doing (declarative knowledge) is less developed.

Following observations as part of her ECT programme, feedback demonstrated that how Sam is using questions is potentially impacting the pupil's ability and willingness to respond. Some pupils are reluctant to answer questions, and when they do, the responses lack depth. Too frequently, Sam seeks out the same pupils to respond to the questions, and this results in other pupils becoming disengaged. Sam's challenge is therefore to seek ways of developing her ability to use questions and ensure that all pupils feel able to respond to questions during the lesson in order that they can demonstrate the knowledge they are acquiring.

This case study identifies a number of key issues that need to be considered when thinking about learning in the cognitive domain. Namely:

1. what declarative knowledge should pupils be learning?
2. how can questioning be more effective and support pupils to develop their declarative knowledge and their ability to think more deeply?

These are now considered in turn.

What knowledge should pupils be learning?

Although a number of types of knowledge that pupils can learn were identified in the introduction to this chapter (see Table 9.1), the focus here is on declarative knowledge, that is, knowledge about facts and concepts. Therefore, as well as considering learning in the physical domain in planning and teaching lessons, it is important to plan and teach for what declarative knowledge pupils should learn. Further, if pupils are to develop their declarative knowledge, opportunities need to be provided for them to learn key facts and concepts and for this to be embedded, recalled and utilised. It is then important to check that this information has been retained through an appropriate assessment process, for example, through effective questioning.

As regards the declarative knowledge that pupils should learn in physical education, Ofsted (2023) identified three 'pillars of progress', that is:

- "motor competence - knowledge of the range of movements that become increasingly specific to sport and physical activity
- rules, strategies and tactics - knowledge of the conventions of participation in different sports and physical activities
- healthy participation - knowledge of safe and effective participation" (Ofsted, 2023, pp.4-5).

More recently, Capel, Whitehead and Lawrence (2025) identified declarative knowledge that pupils should learn as the constituents and principles of movement, which includes knowing how to move efficiently and effectively and recognising the effects of physical activity; as well as knowledge about adopting a physically active lifestyle, which includes knowing the nature and purpose of movement activities, knowing the importance and benefits of participating in physical activity, and planning for participation in physical activity.

How can pupils be supported to develop this knowledge?

Bloom *et al.* (1956) argued that learning in the cognitive domain takes place as a result of engagement with a number of cognitive processes. These being:

- remembering or recalling existing knowledge - being able to retrieve or activate prior learning
- understanding - being able to use existing knowledge to interpret new material
- application - being able to apply existing knowledge to a new context
- analysis - being able to break down existing knowledge, problem solve and make connections
- evaluation - being able to use existing knowledge to appraise and re-design new learning
- creation/synthesis - being able to bring existing knowledge together to create new knowledge.

These cognitive processes are hierarchical; therefore, pupils must first learn basic, foundational knowledge about any given topic before they can progress to more complex processes in relation to that knowledge, such as analysing and evaluating it. Pupils must therefore work through these levels of cognitive process in order and master one level before they can progress to the next. Thus, for example, pupils need a basic understanding of the rules of a game in order to apply them in practice, and as they learn the rules in more detail, they are able to respond creatively within the rules.

Central to pupils' cognitive development, and the development of knowledge, is the process of thinking. Thinking enables the information being learned to be processed so that what is already known might be used to learn new knowledge. Thus, thinking links to the cognitive processes identified by Bloom *et al.* (1956) (above) and Piaget (1962) with regard to how pupils process, retrieve, attend to, remember, use and apply knowledge. More recently, Ritchhart, Church and Morrison (2011, p.5) argued that "If we want to support students in learning, and we believe that learning is a product of thinking, then we need to be clear about what it is we are trying to support".

Whilst acknowledging the value of Bloom *et al.* (1956) in relation to learning objectives, Ritchhart, Church and Morrison (2011, p.8) argued that

> Thinking doesn't happen in a lockstep, sequential manner, systematically progressing from one level to the next. It is much messier, complex, dynamic, and interconnected than that. Thinking is intricately connected to content; and for every type or act of thinking, we can discern levels or performance.

Learning new knowledge requires drawing on, recalling, retrieving and thinking about existing knowledge and understanding already stored in a learner's memory.

Thus, a challenge for teachers is to develop pupils' knowledge, and their ability to think in order that they can apply their knowledge in different contexts. For example, within the national curriculum in England, explicit reference is made to the knowledge, skills and understanding required to be effective (Department for Education (DfE), 2013).

Ritchhart, Church and Morrison (2011, p.10) argued that if thinking is valued, teachers need to ensure they engage pupils in activities that support them to learn about and apply knowledge within the context of the subject being studied. As a result, they identified eight thinking moves – "kinds of thinking that are essential in aiding our understanding" (p.11), including describing, explaining, reasoning, connecting, considering different perspectives, forming conclusions, asking questioning and seeking depth of understanding.

To support these thinking moves, Ritchhart and Church (2020, p. xvii) argued for the establishment of thinking routines, that is, "structures ... to carefully prompt, scaffold and support students' thinking", allowing for thinking to become visible. They also highlighted that making thinking visible can support:

> Deep learning–"the significant understanding of core academic content, coupled with the ability to think critically and solve problems with that content" (Hewlett Foundation, 2013, cited in Ritchhart and Church, 2020, p.6).
>
> Pupil engagement – pupils interact and engage with others and ideas resulting in them challenging their thinking.
>
> A move away from a transmission model of learning to one where the teacher is a facilitator, guiding pupils to take increasing levels of responsibility for their own learning.
>
> The adoption of ongoing formative assessment strategies that engage pupils in thinking about and applying the knowledge that they have acquired, to new contexts.
>
> Improved learning through increased engagement by pupils in the active process of learning.
>
> The development of a thinking disposition – that is the inclination, awareness, motivation and ability to use a skill
>
> (Ritchhart and Church, 2020)

Thus, making thinking visible seeks to build pupils' capacity to respond to and apply existing knowledge and understanding in more complex and challenging situations.

In support of this, Coe et al. (2020, p.5), in their *Great Teaching Toolkit*, identified that to support pupils to learn, teachers should "present content, activities and interactions that activate their students' thinking". This they refer to as "activating hard thinking" (Coe et al., 2020, p.6). To support this, they identified six key strategies: structuring, explaining, questioning, interacting, embedding and activating. A summary of these and how they are reflected in a physical education context is provided in Table 9.2.

Whilst all six strategies identified above support the activation of pupils' thinking, the next section looks to expand upon the first three as these reflect the focus of the chapter.

Structuring

How activities are structured and sequenced can either support or detract from the learning process. One way in which this can be done is through the use of effective scaffolding (see Bruner, 1966).

Wood, Bruner and Ross (1976, p.90) defined scaffolding as a process that enables a learner "to solve a task or achieve a goal that would be beyond his unassisted efforts". Rosenshine (2012, p.18) suggested that "teachers provide students with temporary supports and scaffolds to assist them when they learn difficult tasks". Further, Bates (2019) argued "that scaffolding could be used by a practitioner to help people safely take risks and reach higher levels of understanding than would be possible by the individual's efforts alone" (p.49). More recently, the Education Endowment Foundation (2021, p.26) described scaffolding as "a metaphor for temporary support that is removed when no longer required… It may be visual, verbal or written".

The premise of scaffolding aligns with Vygotsky's (1978) concept of the social construction of learning, whereby pupils develop their knowledge through the support of others. In particular, in relation to Vygotsky's (1978) concept of the zone of proximal development – proximal refers to something which is near to being mastered; therefore, the zone of proximal development is the difference between what a learner can do without help and what they can achieve or master with guidance and encouragement from a more knowledgeable other (a teacher, classroom assistant, other adult in the learning situation or a more competent peer) and how a learning activity is designed and scaffolded. Thus, pupils progress by being supported to complete a learning activity within their zone of proximal development. Support is tapered off and eventually withdrawn when it is no longer needed, that is, when the learner is able to complete the task on their own. A task may be returned to later – adding, for example, more difficulty, complexity or challenge.

Explaining

Explaining relates to how new knowledge is presented and communicated. For example, it may be explained to pupils through verbal instructions or modelled through the use of demonstrations (visual), or both, for example, through a narrated demonstration highlighting the key aspects that pupils need to do to be successful.

The way in which information is explained will impact how pupils access the information and therefore how they are able to use this to learn new knowledge or make connections

Table 9.2 Activating hard thinking in physical education

Strategy	Summary	Example in physical education
Structuring	How activities are structured and sequenced. Appropriate scaffolds need to be put in place to support pupils to develop the knowledge needed.	Clear learning outcomes are provided and explained at the start of the lesson. Activities within the lesson build on the knowledge that is needed to meet the learning outcomes with regular review of progress undertaken throughout the lesson.
Explaining	How information is presented and modelled for pupils. Prior learning also needs to be activated.	Specific learning is modelled. During modelling, verbal description provides an explanation of what pupils need to do, with reference made to similar activities pupils may have experienced, which can be used to support new learning.
Questioning	How thinking is elicited. The way in which questions are asked will impact on the quality and depth of pupils' thinking.	Throughout the lesson, pupils are posed questions linked to the activities they are undertaking. The questions asked require pupils to provide explanations for the responses they provide.
Interacting	How pupils are supported to build their capacity to learn. This includes how pupils receive feedback in relation to how they are interacting with the information they are working with.	Regular review and focused feedback against the learning outcomes provide opportunities for pupils to reflect on the progress they are making.
Embedding	The use of activities to allow for the reinforcement of learning.	Time is given within lessons for pupils to practice/rehearse specific skills or concepts, resulting in them enhancing their learning and becoming more fluent in the activities they are undertaking.
Activating	How pupils are supported to develop metacognitively with regard to development of self-regulation and learning to learn.	Over time, pupils are given increased levels of responsibility to direct their own learning, for example, they are expected to design and complete their own warm-up or devise a specific practice to develop a specific skill.

to what they already know (hence are able to recall, retrieve, activate prior knowledge) to support what they are now being asked to learn. Consideration needs to be given to the amount of information being given at any one time to ensure that pupils do not become overloaded and unable to identify the key points they need to learn. This is referred to as cognitive overload (see, for example, Sweller, 1988 and Chapter 2) and can be avoided by breaking explanations into small steps (see, for example, Rosenshine, 2012).

Within this theme is the use of modelling to show pupils what it is they are expected to do. Most teachers of physical education are confident in the skill of modelling (in essence demonstrations), but are they making connections to what the pupils might already know (activating prior learning) and are the principles of scaffolding identified above being thought about and applied, to ensure that all pupils are able access the information being explained and/or modelled?

Questioning

Questioning is an effective way of drawing out what pupils are thinking and as such is a way of eliciting what they have learned and their current level of understanding. Whilst asking questions is possibly one of the key aspects of teaching, it is also possibly one that is not always considered in sufficient depth or effectively implemented in lessons. Effective questioning needs to be planned and embedded within the lesson planning process. For the Bell Foundation (2024), "Asking the right questions at the right time, to the right people, in the right way, can often transform any ordinary lesson into something truly inspiring".

To achieve this, when questioning, it is important to consider:

- why a question is being asked – how does it align to the learning outcomes?/what specific questions will be asked?
- when in the lesson will the question be asked?
- who is going to be asked questions?
- how will pupils be supported to respond to the question?
- how will pupils' responses be built on – how will pupils' knowledge be stretched and challenged?

These are now considered in turn:

- why a question is being asked
    - how does it align to the learning outcomes?
    - what specific questions will be asked?

Earlier in the chapter, the work of Bloom and colleagues (1956) was considered in relation to the specific processes involved in cognitive development. However, their work also focused on the creation of learning objectives (or learning outcomes). Thus, it is important to identify the purpose of the questions being asked; what knowledge pupils should be able to demonstrate and how this relates to the learning outcomes. To achieve this, pupils need to be asked different questions. For example, if they are being asked to recall prior knowledge, the question will be framed/worded differently than if they are being asked to demonstrate their ability to apply their knowledge. Thus, questions need to be identified in the planning phase so that they teacher knows what question they are going to ask.

- When in the lesson will the question be asked?
  Within the planning phase, it is also important to consider when the question will be asked. Many pupils struggle to answer questions, not necessarily because they do not know the answer, but because they have not had time to process the information to be able to respond to the question. Thus, when asking a question, it is not just what the question is and when it is asked, but also when a response is going to be expected. For example, a question might be posed at the start of a lesson, and during the remainder of the lesson, opportunities are provided for pupils to develop the knowledge to be able

to respond to the question at the end of the lesson. The provision of time to think about and formulate a response is an important aspect of questioning. Thinking time or wait time (the time pupils are given to consider a response to the question before being asked to give the answer) is important.

- Who is going to be asked questions?

Choosing who is going to answer the question is a further consideration. For example, is targeted questioning going to be used based on current understanding of the progress that pupils have made or is a pupil going to be selected randomly to respond? Whilst a teacher might identify a specific individual to focus a question towards, an increasingly common approach is the use of cold calling (refer to the following section) or random name generators, techniques which have the potential to ensure that any pupil might be asked at any point in the lesson.

- How will pupils be supported to respond to the question?

How pupils are supported to respond to questions is also important. Care needs to be given in preparing pupils to be able to respond to questions. Ideally, at any one time within a lesson, all pupils will be able to respond to a question asked of them. How this is achieved requires careful consideration. For example, if a pupil is struggling to answer a question, what prompts might be given to direct them towards an answer? Might they be able to seek support from another pupil in the class whom they think might know the answer? Might the question be reframed so that it becomes a little clearer to the pupil what is being asked (this links to the section above looking at the strategies for activating hard thinking, specifically in relation to the strategy of explaining)?

Scaffolding of questions might also be used. For example, do questions build on prior learning from earlier in the lesson; can the pupil responding be directed to some source within the learning environment (for example, a wall display) on which to base their response?

- How will pupils' responses be built on – how will pupils' knowledge be stretched and challenged?

Once a response has been received, it is important to consider how the response will be built on. For example, will pupils be encouraged to add more depth to their response? This might mean, for example, that rather than just describing what is happening or how a skill is performed, they are able to explain why they are performing a skill in that way. In this way, questions should allow pupils to make connections or apply their answers to a different context. This links to the cognitive processes identified previously.

Whilst identifying what effective questioning might look like, not all pupils may be willing to respond. Chiles (2023) identified some reasons why pupils might not wish to respond to questions.

1. Peer pressure – in this context, peer pressure reflects how a pupil might see themselves in relation to others. For example, a pupil might be reluctant to engage because they are shy and do not want to become the focus of attention. Alternatively, they may not want to engage in the learning process.

2. Fear of failure – here, a pupil's focus is on what happens if they get the question wrong. For example, how does the class as a whole respond when a pupil gives an incorrect answer? How does the teacher respond when the answer is incorrect?
3. They already know the answer – here, the pupil becomes passive in the learning process. They are reluctant to engage as they are not motivated or do not see the value in what is taking place.

In developing pupils' knowledge and thinking within the cognitive domain, the application of effective questioning, and ensuring that pupils feel supported to respond effectively, can be achieved through the adoption of specific thinking routines and questioning approaches. Whilst a range of thinking routines and questioning approaches can be adopted (see, for example, Project Zero (Harvard Graduate School of Education, 2025)), four key approaches are explored below:

1. Think, Pair, Share

    This approach encourages pupils to consider what they already know (think), work with others (pair) to discuss ideas and their thinking and then share (share) a practiced response. For example, during a warm-up, pupils may be asked to think about what is happening to their body as they are warming up. They are then placed with a partner to discuss as a pair their thoughts. As a class, they are then asked to share their answers.

    By setting the question as part of the warm-up, the pupils will be experiencing what is happening to their body as they exercise. Therefore, whilst they might not have been able to recall this as a direct question, because they are experiencing the changes they are provided with knowledge they can then use to support their response to the question. By pairing with someone else, they have an additional source of information on which to build their response. This means that if they have not been able to come up with a response themselves, they are able to work with a partner to formulate one. The teacher can then be confident that any pupil in the class can be asked a question, and they will be able to provide a response.

2. Cold calling

    Cold calling, put simply, is randomly selecting someone to answer a question. Consequently, pupils do not volunteer an answer by raising their hand, they are asked directly. Similar to Think, Pair, Share, a routine is established, whereby: a question is posed, pupils have thinking time to compose a response, and then a pupil is chosen randomly to respond. Following the response, the question might be redirected for another pupil to expand on it or offer an alternative response.

3. Say it again, better

    This routine encourages pupils to expand on the initial response to a given question. The focus is on developing the depth of response, encouraging pupils to provide more detail, strengthen the language they are using, or provide explanations. For example, in response to the question 'what is happening to our body as we exercise?', an initial response might be 'We get warm, we breathe more, we change colour'. By asking pupils to 'say it again, better', in essence, they are asked to expand on the first response. A second response might be 'we get warm because our muscles are moving and this creates heat energy'.

Such an approach not only allows pupils to demonstrate the depth of their knowledge, it also provides opportunities for them to develop their literacy skills in relation to how they communicate a response as well as the subject-specific language they might use. This aligns closely with the role of all teachers as teachers of literacy (DfE, 2024).

4. Teaching games for understanding

If an aim is to develop pupils' knowledge, skills and understanding to support their learning through making thinking visible, in the context of physical education, a teaching games for understanding (TGFU) approach may be appropriate. This pedagogical approach, developed by Bunker and Thorpe in the 1980s (Bunker and Thorpe, 1982), focused on allowing "every child to participate in decision-making based upon tactical awareness thereby maintaining an interest and involvement in the game" (Thorpe, Bunker and Almond, 1986, p.8). It has relevance even today. Central to the approach is a focus on 'games-based' activities in contrast to a more didactic, skills-based teaching approach. Through the use of open-ended questions, the teacher facilitates pupils to use their cognitive processes by, for example, remembering or recalling existing knowledge; understanding; application; analysis; evaluation; creation/synthesis (Bloom et al., 1956) to solve problems and to support the development of existing and new knowledge.

The second part of the case study revisits Sam, to look at what she implemented to support pupils' learning and the impact this had on their progress.

Case study (part 2)

Following a review of the literature supporting high-quality teaching and learning and reviewing a range of strategies that could be implemented in relation to developing knowledge and thinking in the cognitive domain, Sam decided to start each lesson with a 'recall-based' activity to check what pupils could remember from the previous lesson. This was undertaken in the changing rooms so that learning started as pupils prepared for the lesson. Sam provided 'hook' activities (small thinking activities that were placed on the hooks where pupils changed) that pupils read and were asked to think about as they changed. These activities focused on the recall, retrieval and 'activation of prior knowledge' and included providing key teaching points for a skill they had previously learnt.

As pupils arrived in the sports hall, they were given a starter activity, which required them to demonstrate an aspect of learning they had completed in the previous lesson. This provided a second opportunity to 'retrieve' and 'activate prior knowledge', as well as providing a link between what pupils had already learned and what they would be focusing on in the lesson.

Once all pupils were in the sports hall, Sam shared the learning outcomes for the lesson. The learning outcomes were framed as a key question that pupils needed to explore during the lesson. This laid the foundation for Sam to adopt a 'cold calling' approach later in the lesson. Throughout the lesson, pupils were refocused back to the key question and asked to consider how what they were doing was going to support them to answer the question. In this way, all pupils were being provided with opportunities to 'think' about their own progress.

As Sam was keen to provide multiple opportunities for pupils to rehearse potential responses to the question, she looked to embed a TGFU approach in lessons. This was achieved by structuring lessons so that pupils worked in small groups to consider the key question set at the start of the lesson by practicing specific skills in isolation and in small game situations. This resulted in increased practice time, in reduced pressure situations and provided all pupils with the opportunity to 'share' their ideas and discuss what they could do to be more successful. Opportunities for peer feedback (see Chapter 5) were embedded, allowing all pupils to develop their understanding and application of the specific skills/concepts they were exploring. This allowed them to demonstrate increased declarative knowledge.

As part of the plenary at the end of the lesson, Sam returned to the key question set at the start of the lesson. As a result of the structure of the lesson and support provided, Sam was able to 'cold call' pupils to provide responses to the learning outcomes and ask more probing questions requiring pupils to expand on their initial responses ('say it again, better').

Throughout the teaching of the unit of work, Sam reflected on the impact of this approach in relation to the progress being made by the pupils in developing their declarative knowledge and thinking in the cognitive domain. She sought feedback from a sample of pupils at the end of each lesson to establish how they felt about the changes that were being implemented. Responses indicated that when the routines were first introduced, pupils took time to adjust to the change in expectations. However, by sustaining the routines throughout the unit of work, pupils became clearer about what was expected of them. They became more confident in responding to questions, and more willing to share ideas. They also felt that they were making more progress in learning declarative knowledge and in developing their thinking as they were spending more time practicing and applying their learning in games.

From Sam's perspective, she felt that, overall, pupils made better progress and were able to respond in more depth to the questions they were being asked. At the start of the unit of work, Sam felt she needed to spend more time in the planning phase to ensure that each lesson had a clear structure and that questions were formed in a way that supported pupils to recall prior knowledge and apply this in different contexts. However, over time, this became easier as both Sam and the pupils became more comfortable with the routines that were being learned, practiced and embedded, and how these were supporting the development of their declarative knowledge and ability to think.

Summary and key points

Cognitive development focuses on building knowledge and the ability of an individual to think. Within the context of physical education, having knowledge and understanding of cognitive processes underpins the planning and structuring of lessons that enable pupils to develop both their declarative knowledge and their ability to think.

This chapter sought to identify cognitive skills and process that can be developed through physical education. Drawing on the concept of 'Making thinking visible' (Ritchhart and Church,

2020; Ritchhart, Church and Morrison, 2011), it identified how teachers can support pupils to develop their cognitive abilities through the use of effective questioning to allow pupils to demonstrate their declarative knowledge and thinking. Whilst not looked at in specific detail within the chapter, over time, this enables pupils to be supported to develop their ability to make connections between the activities in which they engage and to take responsibility for their own learning, as reflected in Table 9.1.

References

Anderson, L.W. and Krathwohl, D.R. (eds) (2001) *A Taxonomy for Learning, Teaching and Assessment: A Revision of Bloom's Taxonomy of Educational Objectives*, Boston, MA: Allyn and Bacon (Pearson Education Group).

Bates, B. (2019) *Learning Theories Simplified* (2nd edition), London: SAGE.

Bell Foundation (2024) *Great Ideas: Questioning Strategies*, available at: https://www.bell-foundation.org.uk/resources/great-ideas/questioning-strategies/ (accessed 7 December 2024).

Bloom, B.S., Engelhart, M.D., Furst, E.J., Hill, W.H. and Krathwohl, D.R. (eds) (1956) *Taxonomy of Educational Objectives, Handbook I: Cognitive Domain*, New York: David McKay.

Bruner, J.S. (1966) *Towards a Theory of Instruction*, New York: W.W. Norton.

Bunker, R. and Thorpe, R. (1982) 'Model for the teaching games in secondary school', *Bulletin of Physical Education*, 18 (1), 5-8.

Capel, S., Whitehead, M. and Lawrence, J. (2025) *Progression and Progress in Physical Education*, Abingdon: Routledge.

Chiles, C. (2023) *Powerful Questioning: Strategies for Improving Learning and Retention in the Classroom*, Carmarthen: Crown House Publishing.

Coe, R., Rauch, C.J., Kime, S. and Singleton, D. (2020) *Great Teaching Toolkit: Evidence Review*, Evidence Based Education, available at: https://evidencebased.education/great-teaching-toolkit-evidence-review/ (accessed 16 June 2025).

DfE (Department for Education) (2013) *The National Curriculum in England Framework Document, December 2014*, available at: https://www.gov.uk/government/publications/national-curriculum-in-england-physical-education-programmes-of-study (accessed 7 December 2024).

DfE (Department for Education) (2024) *Initial Teacher Training and Early Career Framework*, available at: https://www.gov.uk/government/publications/initial-teacher-training-and-early-career-framework (accessed 16 June 2025).

Education Endowment Foundation (2021) *Special Educational Needs in Mainstream Schools: Guidance Report*, available at: https://educationendowmentfoundation.org.uk/education-evidence/guidance-reports/send (accessed 7 December 2024).

Harvard Graduate School of Education (2025) *Project Zero*, available at: https://pz.harvard.edu (accessed 6 January 2025).

Ofsted (Office for Standards in Education, Children's Services and Skills) (2022) *Research and Analysis: Research Review Series: PE*, published 18 March 2022, available at: https://www.gov.uk/government/publications/research-review-series-pe/research-review-series-pe (accessed 7 December 2024).

Ofsted (Office for Standards in Education, Children's Services and Skills) (2023) *Levelling the Playing Field: The Physical Education Subject Review*, published 20 September 2023, available at: https://www.gov.uk/government/publications/subject-report-series-pe (accessed 7 December 2024).

Piaget, J. (1962) *Judgement and Reasoning in the Child*, London: Routledge and Keegan Paul.

Ritchhart, R. and Church, M. (2020) *The Power of Making Thinking Visible: Practices to Engage and Empower All Learner*, San Francisco, CA: Jossey-Bass.

Ritchhart, R., Church, M. and Morrison, K. (2011) *Making Thinking Visible: How to Promote Engagement, Understanding and Independence of All Learners*, San Francisco, CA: Jossey-Bass.

Rosenshine, B. (2012) 'Principles of instruction: research based strategies that all teachers should know', *American Educator*, 36 (1, Spring), 12-19, 39.

Sweller, J. (1988) 'Cognitive load during problem solving: effects on learning', *Cognitive Science*, 12, 257-285.

Tan, S.H. (2022) 'Knowing students as individuals and understanding their needs', in S. Capel, J. Lawrence, M. Martens and H. Abdul Rahman (eds) *CPD for Teaching and Learning in Physical Education; Global Lessons from Singapore*, Abingdon: Routledge, pp.27–44.

Thorpe, R.D., Bunker, D. and Almond, L. (eds) (1986) *Rethinking Games Teaching*, Loughborough: University of Technology.

Vygotsky, L. (1978) *Mind in Society: The Development of Higher Psychological Processes* (translated and edited by M. Cole, V. John-Steiner, S. Scribner and E. Souberman), Cambridge, MA: Harvard University Press.

Wood, D., Bruner, J.S. and Ross, G. (1976) 'The role of tutoring in problem solving', *Journal of Child Psychology, Psychiatry, and Applied Disciplines*, 17, 89–100.

Chapter 10 Challenges related to promoting learning in the affective domain

Meeting the emotional needs of pupils

Kate Bancroft and George Kinkead

Introduction

In physical education, teachers have a strong influence on pupils' learning and play a key role in shaping how pupils see themselves as learners in the subject (Hemingway et al., 2023). Whether intentionally or not, physical education teachers can influence pupils' feelings, attitudes, motivation and emotions about the subject and physical activity more generally. The development of feelings, motivation, emotions and attitudes is associated with learning in the affective domain.

This chapter highlights the importance of the affective domain in learning in physical education. It considers how teaching goes beyond just imparting knowledge by recognising how it can influence the way pupils approach learning, not only in physical education but also in participating in physical activity in the future (Vankúš, 2021), as well as the impact it may have on pupils' attitudes towards physical activity and overall life satisfaction (Moral-Garcia et al., 2021). The influence of physical education teachers can be positive, sparking a love of physical education and a passion for being active and learning about physical activity, which can lead to improved mental health and well-being throughout life. However, it can also be negative, generating a dislike for the subject and for physical activity altogether.

The affective domain is one part of Bloom's Taxonomy (Bloom et al., 1956), which provides a broad framework that includes the cognitive, affective and psychomotor (physical) domains. While this chapter focuses on the affective domain, it is important to recognise the interconnected nature of the different learning domains (Dudley et al., 2022). For example, Piaget (1932) proposed that the cognitive and affective dimensions are closely linked throughout a child's development, suggesting that moral reasoning, including understanding rules and emotional engagement, evolves alongside their cognitive growth. Further, research (Bloom et al., 1956), focusing on the holistic development of individuals identifies how the affective, cognitive and psychomotor (physical) domains work together. Capel, Whitehead and Lawrence (2025, p.39) argued that "In any learning situation in physical education, the physical, the cognitive and the affective aspects of being human need to be considered and planned for".

This chapter invites reflection on the role of the affective domain in teaching and learning in physical education. It starts with the first part of a case study that highlights challenges identified by physical education teachers, specifically in relation to the engagement and enthusiasm of pupils in lessons. The chapter then defines the affective domain. It then considers the self-determination theory of Deci and Ryan (1985), which underpins key aspects that need to be considered in relation to learning in the affective domain. The affective domain is then examined through the social-emotional dimensions of learning in physical education, exploring how these can inform effective teaching approaches. How to assess affective learning is addressed by discussing tools and methods available for evaluating changes in social-emotional learning. Strategies for supporting social-emotional learning through targeted teaching approaches are also explored. The chapter concludes with the second part of the case study, which illustrates how challenges identified in the first part of the case study were addressed and how they impacted on pupil learning outcomes. The chapter therefore aims to provide both theoretical insights and actionable strategies to assist pupils' learning in the affective domain in physical education lessons.

Case study (part 1)

Sewerby School prides itself on inclusivity and the highest levels of academic excellence. It also has a strong focus on pupil well-being. Recently, physical education teachers noticed some pupils were being less engaged and enthusiastic in physical education lessons. This was particularly evident in year 9, where both boys and girls appeared more reluctant to participate fully in lessons as reflected in:

1. A decline in effort:
   - effort rates have decreased in some lessons, with some pupils expressing less interest than previously and a reluctance to engage in physical activity.

2. Limited positive emotional connection with lessons:
   - pupils do not appear to value the subject in the way they have previously, with many now expressing negative views towards lessons
   - many pupils seem to view physical education solely as a mandatory lesson rather than an opportunity for personal growth, self-care and well-being.

3. Social dynamics:
   - some pupils report feeling excluded or discouraged when working in groups. This affects their overall enjoyment of lessons, which has raised the risk of forming a negative perception of engaging in physical activity for life.

In order to try and address these changes in engagement and enthusiasm and encourage a more positive and holistic learning environment for pupils, the physical education department identified the need to consider how they could integrate learning in the affective domain in lessons.

Definitions

The affective domain refers to learning that involves feelings, attitudes, motivation, and emotions (Adijaya et al., 2023). It prompts the values and beliefs attached to the learning with which pupils are actively engaging. It plays a role in shaping pupils' willingness to embrace new learning experiences, and their ability to make thoughtful decisions about their behaviour and actions in various situations.

The affective domain includes social-emotional learning, which is defined as

> the process through which all young people and adults acquire and apply the knowledge, skills and attitudes to develop healthy identities, manage emotions and achieve personal and collective goals, feel and show empathy for others, establish and maintain supportive relationships, and make responsible and caring decisions.
> (Collaborative for Academic, Social and Emotional Learning (CASEL), 2020, para. 1)

In support of this, five key social-emotional competencies were identified, these being:

1. Self-awareness
2. Self-management
3. Social awareness
4. Relationship skills
5. Responsible decision-making.

(See Abdul-Rahman, 2022; CASEL, 2020 for more details)

To support learning within the affective domain, these competencies require careful consideration of positive teacher-pupil relationships, alongside the development of taught activities that promote pupil motivation and collaborative work. For teachers to effectively support learning within the affective domain, a prerequisite is their comprehensive grasp of key theories and practices related to motivation and social-emotional learning. This is essential because positive relationship development directly contributes to pupils' improved self-awareness, self-management, and ultimately, their decision-making capabilities.

Self-determination theory

Research over the past three decades has indicated that the cognitive, physical and affective aspects of learning are often intertwined and difficult to separate (Cai & Demmans Epp, 2024; Faella, Albano and Conson, 2025). Focusing predominantly on the affective domain, Deci and Ryan's (1985) self-determination theory emphasises the importance of meeting three fundamental psychological needs: autonomy (making independent decisions), competence (feeling capable), and relatedness (building connections with others). As such, links can be made between these psychological needs and the five social and emotional competencies introduced above (CASEL, 2020). For example, autonomy can be linked with self-awareness and responsible decision-making (Abdul-Rahman, 2022); competence can be linked with self-management; and relatedness can be linked to social awareness and relationship skills.

As pupils develop their self-determination, they become more intrinsically motivated (Deci and Ryan, 1985, 2017; Ryan, Huta and Deci, 2019), increasing the likelihood of them persisting with the activity in which they are participating.

In its broadest sense, autonomy relates to the right of an individual to make choices from a range of options. Giving pupils options in the physical education curriculum helps fulfil this need and can bring about positive experiences (Lewis, 2014). Options can range from, for example, choosing specific activities, allowing pupils to decide how certain activities are structured or selecting from different assessment options. It also involves supporting pupils in setting personal goals that align with their interests and abilities within the physical education curriculum, which in turn contribute to healthy lifestyles (Alexandr, Sergij and Olena, 2016).

When pupils have a voice in shaping their learning in physical education and are given the agency to make decisions and set personal goals, they feel a greater sense of ownership and responsibility for their learning (Low, 2022). This increased agency can positively influence pupils' motivation – boosting intrinsic motivation, self-esteem and emotional management. It can improve emotional well-being by reducing feelings of external control, enhancing satisfaction and generating deeper engagement in activities (Deci and Ryan, 2008).

Competence can be seen as an individual's ability to perform a specific aspect of learning. The visual nature of physical education means that pupils will regularly perform in front of their peers. How this is managed can impact on their motivation and willingness to participate. Where pupils feel less capable, they are likely to withdraw from the activity or look to limit their engagement. Consideration, therefore, needs to be given to the intended learning outcomes, the tasks that are set, how feedback is provided (see Chapter 5 for more on feedback) and how pupils are supported to make progress.

How pupils relate to the activities is also important. Pupils need to value the activities they undertake. If this is not the case, again they might become withdrawn or disengaged. Research by Hemingway et al. (2023) has suggested that during the early stages of secondary education (ages of 11–13, or key stage 3), there is a decline in engagement levels of pupils; however, this decline is somewhat reversed as pupils enter the later stages of their secondary education (ages 14–16 or key stage 4). They concluded that one reason for this is the value pupils place on physical education (or the relatedness), with older pupils seeing it as supporting their mental health and well-being, whilst younger pupils feel that it is more about social comparisons (linked to competence). Further, older pupils see themselves as having more choice (autonomy) over the activities in which they participate. This has the potential to create a more meaningful connection, allowing them to better relate to the subject and to physical activity in general, with pupils approaching physical activities with greater enthusiasm, personal investment and emotional resilience. Emotional resilience in this case refers to a pupil being able to adapt to a confronting situation (del Carmen Torres-Gázquez, López-García and Granero-Gallegos, 2023).

By incorporating aspects of self-determination (autonomy, competence and relatedness), teachers can empower pupils to take control of their learning by developing a sense of ownership and emotional well-being.

The importance of focusing on the affective domain in physical education

Researchers have examined the connections between emotions and learning. For example, Pekrun et al. (2002) discussed how emotions influence academic performance, while Immordino-Yang and Damasio (2007) explored the neurobiological aspects of emotions and their role in cognition. More recently, studies looking at emotional and psychological aspects of pupils' experiences in physical education have focused on the negative impact of imposed activities and didactic teaching on feelings of empowerment and engagement (Curtin, 2022; Hemingway et al., 2023). However, planning for emotional and psychological needs can be challenging for physical education teachers.

Some teaching approaches for learning in the affective domain

Research in physical education highlighting the importance of learning in the affective domain has showcased various interventions that emphasise specific teaching approaches. The Framework of a Quality Physical Education (QPE) programme (McLennan and Thompson, 2015), emphasised the importance of using a range of different instructional designs and interventions – or teaching approaches in order for pupils to learn. Mosston and Ashworth's (2002) spectrum of teaching styles is a commonly used approach in physical education, identifying teaching approaches which give pupils more autonomy (productive styles, such as inclusion, convergent or divergent discovery and learner-designed or -initiated) and connectedness (reciprocal).

Other approaches include, for example, Task, Authority, Recognition, Grouping, Evaluation and Time (TARGET)/mastery teaching, which enhances motivation by prioritising skill mastery and recognising effort; games-based approaches which focus on developing tactical skills and boosting engagement through gameplay; and Sport Education, which aims to create a genuine sports experience that encourages competition, teamwork and responsibility (Arufe-Giráldez, 2023; Ramires et al., 2023; Simonton, Garn and Mercier, 2023). Further, more holistic approaches are proving to be effective in achieving meaningful outcomes in the affective domain (Fletcher et al., 2021; Jennings and DiPrete, 2010; Jess and Gray, 2016; Kraft and Grace, 2016).

Teaching and learning in the affective domain have evolved over time. Given its unique role as a practical subject, physical education provides clear opportunities to support pupils' learning in the affective domain. For example, opportunities occur through aspects such as communication, teamwork, relationship-building, cooperation challenges, empathy and emotional resilience, as well as teachers providing inclusive learning environments (Penney, 2001). In addition, being respectful of different cultures (Benn, 2000) which contribute to motivational learning environments (Ames, 1992) can assist pupils' social-emotional learning.

Thus, when focusing on learning in the affective domain, the teaching approach to be adopted needs careful consideration as this may well impact on how pupils view the subject (Hemingway et al., 2023).

Assessing learning in the affective domain

Assessing learning in the affective domain remains relatively underexplored. One reason for this might be that assessing learning in the affective domain poses significant challenges as compared to assessing pupils' learning in the cognitive and physical domains (see Chapters 8 and 9, as well as Capel, Whitehead and Lawrence (2025), for more assessing in the three domains). One reason for this is that affective learning often occurs internally; therefore, it can be challenging to observe and for changes to be measured.

Whilst emotions are valid in their own right, it is not always feasible to try and measure a pupil's emotions. However, the way individuals express these emotions (for example, through their levels of engagement, social awareness and interactions – in general, the attitudes towards physical education) can be assessed. Thus, emotions (as reflected in pupils' attitudes) are typically inferred from behaviours like verbal responses or visible actions (Bednar and Levie, 1993).

According to CASEL (2018; 2019), assessing pupils' affective learning should prioritise:

1. Focusing on social, emotional and learning skills and competencies, such as self-awareness, self-management, social awareness, relationship skills and responsible decision-making.
2. Using formative assessments to provide insights into pupils' growth in these areas throughout the curriculum, observations, check-ins and feedback, rather than relying on a single summative assessment.
3. Encouraging peer and self-assessments to prioritise a culture of reflection in lessons, prompting pupils to think critically about their social interactions and emotional responses.
4. Implementing performance-based assessments, where pupils demonstrate their ability to apply social-emotional learning skills in real-life scenarios.
5. Integrating social-emotional learning with cognitive and physical learning to highlight the connection between physical activity and emotional well-being.
6. Enhancing pupil voice in the assessment process, allowing pupils to share their perspectives and contribute to their evaluation.

Recent practices reflect a narrowing of what is considered an 'outstanding' physical education lesson, one characterised by activity, enthusiasm and engagement, yet one which moves towards practices that prioritise more able pupils' progress over others. This is reflected in the use of ability grouping, which tends to focus on pupils on the cusp of achieving higher grades, creating an 'intervention culture' (Bradbury, Braun, and Quick, 2021, p.148; Prior et al., 2021). However, emphasising performance indicators over the affective domain is a false dichotomy. The relationship between feelings, attitudes, motivation, emotions and success appears to be bidirectional; positive feelings, attitudes motivation and emotions can lead to success, while achieving success (or competence) can enhance positive feelings, attitudes motivation and emotions (Guay, Marsh and Boivin, 2003; Zimmerman, 2000). Chi, Glazer and Rees (1981) argued that effective learning depends on domain-specific knowledge, which in turn boosts competence in those areas. Therefore, if competence promotes motivation and positive social-emotional learning, and cognitive or physical learning in specific subjects results in feelings of accomplishment, then cognitive or physical learning might be a necessary precursor to affective learning in physical education.

Case study (part 2)

Following a review of practice with evidence collected from both pupils and teachers, the physical education department at Sewerby School identified the following challenges that they needed to address to revise the decline in engagement and enthusiasm towards physical education as evidenced by year 9 in the first part of the case study:

- the changes they needed to make to the teaching of physical education to ensure that pupils saw and better understood the value of, and the benefits associated with, the subject
- how they could better support pupils to become more motivated by focusing on increasing their levels of autonomy.

Recognising the importance of a holistic educational experience, whilst focusing on the affective domain (Adijaya *et al.*, 2023), the head of physical education initiated a professional development programme aimed at deepening teachers' understanding and application of social-emotional learning (CASEL, 2020). Through regular workshops drawing heavily on the work of CASEL (2020), teachers explored theories behind social-emotional learning, the latest research and practical strategies, ensuring they were equipped to support pupils' social-emotional learning alongside their learning in the cognitive and physical domains.

They then took a thoughtful approach to revising the curriculum for year 9 to include activities that target the affective domain. By integrating social-emotional learning components into existing lessons, for example, providing pupils with opportunities to develop their understanding of healthy lifestyles (Alexandr, Sergij and Olena, 2016) and providing opportunities for pupils to lead and create their own training plans, opportunities to build essential social and emotional skills alongside their physical and cognitive learning and progress became embedded. This intentional curriculum design, providing a clear focus around specific learning outcomes, teaching approaches and methods of assessment, aimed to develop skills such as resilience (del Carmen Torres-Gázquez, López-García and Granero-Gallegos, 2023) and teamwork, preparing pupils not only for success in physical education but also for a lifetime of meaningful engagement in physical activities and the various challenges life presents (Moral-Garcia *et al.*, 2021; Vankúš, 2021).

By recognising pupils as active partners in their educational journey, the department actively involved them in responsible decision-making (Abdul-Rahman, 2022). Pupils had a say in selecting activities, suggesting topics for discussion, and contributing ideas to shape their physical education learning environment (Low, 2022). This resulted in the department creating options in the physical education curriculum (Lewis, 2014), whereby pupils were allowed to choose an activity each term to participate in alongside a core activity that all pupils had to do. By valuing and incorporating pupil perspectives, the physical education department prioritised pupils having a sense of ownership and belonging, helping generate a positive motivational climate (Ames, 1992) and inclusive culture in physical education lessons.

At Sewerby School, inclusivity is a core principle that underpins all aspects of physical education (Penney, 2001). The department actively worked to create an environment in which every pupil felt a sense of belonging, through culturally relevant activities that celebrated diverse cultures (Benn, 2000), mixed-ability groups (Bradbury, Braun and Quick, 2021; Prior et al., 2021) that helped all pupils to feel included and able to make progress and mentorship programmes between year groups and skill sets, allowing pupils to take on a greater level of responsibility and become more socially aware. This resulted in higher levels of engagement. The physical education department also developed a suite of assessment tools designed specifically to measure affective outcomes.

Each term, pupils were asked to report on how the changes adopted were impacting their social-emotional learning, attitudes and overall well-being through a short questionnaire survey (CASEL, 2018) and termly reflections. These showed that pupils felt more listened to and were keen to take more responsibility. This valuable feedback was then used to inform the department's next steps, enabling teachers to tailor their approaches based on the social-emotional learning needs of their pupils. By systematically evaluating affective outcomes, the department ensured that pupils' emotional and social learning was prioritised alongside their learning in the cognitive and physical domains.

In summary, the physical education department at Sewerby School focused on three key priorities that brought about meaningful changes in pupil learning outcomes. First, improving pupil engagement was achieved by providing pupils with greater choice in some of the activities they participated in. This increased level of autonomy – alongside other changes embedded in relation to learning outcomes, teaching approaches and assessment – provided opportunities for pupils to develop a better understanding of the value and benefits of physical education. This led to noticeable increase in participation, where pupils who had previously been disengaged or hesitant became more involved as the focus shifted from performance alone to creating a sense of belonging and enjoyment.

Second, cultivating positive attitudes (Moral-Garcia et al., 2021) encouraged pupils to see physical activity, teamwork and well-being as opportunities for personal growth. Many pupils reported a stronger sense of purpose and fulfilment in their activities, along with a newfound appreciation for collaboration that extended beyond physical education lessons. Lastly, enhancing social skills promoted inclusivity and improved peer interactions, encouraging confidence, empathy and stronger relationships among pupils.

By prioritising engagement, attitudes and social skills, Sewerby School's physical education programme demonstrated that integrating learning in the affective domain alongside learning in the cognitive and physical domains can lead to real, tangible benefits. Indeed, by grounding the affective domain in self-determination theory (Deci and Ryan, 1985), these efforts not only enriched pupils' experiences in physical education but also equipped them with teamwork skills and the sense of well-being necessary to thrive in the future as a result of emphasis placed on their social-emotional learning.

Summary and key points

This chapter has explored the importance of the affective domain, which encompasses emotional and social learning and attitudes in physical education. One of the main hurdles teachers face is assessing this domain. Unlike cognitive and physical skills, measuring social-emotional learning and attitudes is inherently more complex. The lack of effective methodologies, combined with the subtlety of emotions, complicates the process of conducting meaningful assessments. Assessing the affective domain often relies on observable behaviours, which can make accurately measuring pupils' emotions and experiences more challenging.

Recent changes in education policy, such as increased accountability measures, have led to a narrow focus that often overshadows the holistic development of pupils, especially in physical education. Amid these challenges, the chapter has emphasised the importance of giving pupils autonomy and choice in their physical education experiences, which aligns with self-determination theory. When pupils have opportunities to make decisions about their activities, it positively influences their emotional well-being, developing intrinsic motivation and engagement.

References

Abdul-Rahman, H. (2022) 'Intentionality: the key to effective affective learning', in S. Capel, J. Lawrence, M. Martens and H. Abdul Rahman (eds) *CPD for Teaching and Learning in Physical Education: Global Lessons from Singapore*, Abingdon: Routledge, pp.130–146.

Adijaya, M.A., Widiana, I.W., Agung Parwata, I. and Suwela Antara, I. (2023) 'Bloom's taxonomy revision-oriented learning activities to improve procedural capabilities and learning outcomes', *International Journal of Educational Methodology*, 9 (1), 261-270.

Alexandr, A., Sergij, T. and Olena, O. (2016) 'Role of physical education on the formation of a healthy lifestyle outside of school hours', *Journal of Physical Education and Sport*, 16 (2), 335-339.

Ames, C. (1992) 'Classrooms: goals, structures, and student motivation', *Journal of Educational Psychology*, 84, 261-271.

Arufe-Giráldez, V., Sanmiguel-Rodríguez, A., Ramos-Álvarez, O. and Navarro-Patón, R. (2023) 'News of the pedagogical models in physical education–a quick review', *International Journal of Environmental Research and Public Health*, 20 (3), 2586.

Bednar, A. & Levie, W.H. (1993) 'Attitude-change principles', in M. Fleming & W.H. Levie (eds.) *Instructional message design: Principles from the behavioral and cognitive sciences*. 2nd edn. Englewood Cliffs, NJ: Educational Technology Publications, pp. 283-304.

Benn, T. (2000) 'Valuing cultural diversity: the challenge for physical education', in S. Capel and S. Piotrowski (eds) *Issues in Physical Education*, Abingdon: Routledge, pp.64-78.

Bloom, B.S., Englehart, M.D., Furst, E.J., Hill, W.H. & Krathwohl, D.R. (1956) *Taxonomy of Educational Objectives: The Classification of Educational Goals. Handbook I: Cognitive Domain*. New York: David McKay.

Bradbury, A., Braun, A. and Quick, L. (2021) 'Intervention culture, grouping and triage: high-stakes tests and practices of division in English primary schools', *British Journal of Sociology of Education*, 42 (2), 1-17, https://doi.org/10.1080/01425692.2021.1878873.

Cai, M. and Denmans Epp, C.D. (2024) Exploring the optimal time window for predicting cognitive load using physiological sensor data. https://doi.org/10.48550/arXiv.2406.13793

Capel, S., Whitehead, M. and Lawrence, J. (2025) *Progression and Progress in Physical Education*, Abingdon: Routledge.

CASEL (Collaborative for Academic, Social, and Emotional Learning) (n.d.) *Fundamentals of SEL*, available at: https://casel.org/fundamentals-of-sel/ (accessed 1 February 2025).

CASEL (Collaborative for Academic, Social, and Emotional Learning) (2018) *Choosing and Using SEL Competency Assessments: What Schools and Districts Need to Know*, Chicago, IL: Collaborative for Academic, Social, and Emotional Learning, available at: https://measuringsel.casel.org/pdf/Choosing-and-Using-SEL-Competency-Assessments_What-Schools-and-Districts-Need-to-Know.pdf (accessed 2 February 2025).

CASEL (Collaborative for Academic, Social, and Emotional Learning) (2019) *Student Social and Emotional Competence Assessment: The Current State of the Field and a Vision for Its Future*,

Chicago, IL: Collaborative for Academic, Social, and Emotional Learning, available at: casel.org/casel-gateway-student-sel-competence-assessment/?view=true (accessed 1 February 2025).

CASEL (Collaborative for Academic, Social, and Emotional Learning) (2020) *What Is the CASEL Framework?* available at: https://casel.org/fundamentals-of-sel/what-is-the-casel-framework/ (accessed 1 February 2025).

Chi, M., Glaser, R. and Rees, E. (1981) 'Expertise in problem solving', *Semantic Scholar*, available at: https://www.semanticscholar.org/paper/Expertise-in-Problem-Solving.-Chi-Glaser/58c368ff407a5c055b82a91389fd6780f412156a (accessed 20 December 2024).

Curtin, D. (2022) 'The possibilities of SEL in physical education', *Edutopia*, available at: https://www.edutopia.org/article/sel-possibilities-physical-education/ (accessed 26 September 2024).

Deci, E.L. and Ryan, R.M. (1985) 'The general causality orientations scale: self-determination in personality', *Journal of Research in Personality*, 19 (2), 109-134.

Deci, E.L. and Ryan, R.M. (2008) 'Self-determination theory: a macrotheory of human motivation, development, and health', *Canadian Psychology*, 49 (3), 182-185, https://doi.org/10.1037/a0012801

del Carmen Torres-Gázquez, S., López-García, G.D. and Granero-Gallegos, A. (2023) 'Emotional intelligence and resilience in secondary school physical education students during the COVID-19 pandemic', *Espiral. Cuadernos del Profesorado*, 16 (32), 51-63.

Dudley, D., Mackenzie, E., Van Bergen, P., Cairney, J. and Barnett, L. (2022) 'What drives quality physical education? a systematic review and meta-analysis of learning and development effects from physical education-based interventions', *Frontiers in Psychology*, 13, 799330.

Faella, A., Albano, G., and Conson, M. (2025) 'Embodied cognition in primary education: A systematic review of effects on learning and engagement', *Contemporary Educational Psychology*, 70, 102204. https://doi.org/10.1016/j.cedpsych.2024.102204

Fletcher, T., Ní Chróinín, D., Gleddie, D. and Beni, S. (2021) *Meaningful Physical Education: An Approach for Teaching and Learning*, Abingdon: Routledge.

Guay, F., Marsh, H.W. and Boivin, M. (2003) 'Academic self-concept and academic achievement: developmental perspectives on their causal ordering', *Journal of Educational Psychology*, 95 (1), 124-136, https://doi.org/10.1037/0022-0663.95.1.124

Hemingway, K., Butt, J., Spray, C., Olusoga, P. and Beretta De Azevedo, L. (2023) 'Exploring students experiences of secondary school physical education in England', *Physical Education and Sport Pedagogy*, 1-16. https://doi.org/10.1080/17408989.2023.2256771

Immordino-Yang, M.H. and Damasio, A. (2007) 'We feel, therefore we learn: the relevance of affective and social neuroscience to education', *Mind, Brain, and Education*, 1 (1), 3-10.

Jennings, J.L. and DiPrete, T.A. (2010) 'Teacher effects on social and behavioral skills in early elementary school', *Sociology of Education*, 83 (2), 135-159, https://doi.org/10.1177/0038040710368011

Jess, M. and Gray, S. (2016) 'Curriculum reform and policy cohesion in physical education', in C. Ennis (ed.) *Routledge Handbook of Physical Education Pedagogies* (Routledge international handbooks), Abingdon: Routledge, pp.143-156.

Kraft, M.A. and Grace, S. (2016) 'Teaching for tomorrow's demands: the role of instructional practice in improving social-emotional outcomes', *Educational Researcher*, 45 (8), 473-483, https://doi.org/10.1080/17408989.2023.2256771

Lewis, K. (2014) 'Pupils' and teachers' experiences of school-based physical education: a qualitative study', *BMJ Open*, 4 (9), 005277.

Low, K. (2022) 'Continuity and progression: what do my students need to know and understand to make progress?' in S. Capel, J. Lawrence, M. Martens and H. Abdul Rahman (eds) *CPD for Teaching and Learning in Physical Education: Global Lessons from Singapore*, Abingdon: Routledge, pp.9-26.

McLennan, N. and Thompson, J. (2015) *Quality Physical Education (QPE): Guidelines for Policy Makers*, Paris: UNESCO.

Moral-Garcia, J.E., Jiménez, A., Cabaco, A.S. and Jiménez-Eguizabal, A. (2021) 'The role of physical activity and school physical education in enhancing school satisfaction and life satisfaction', *International Journal of Environmental Research and Public Health*, 18 (4), 1689.

Mosston, M. and Ashworth, S. (2002) *Teaching Physical Education* (5th edition), London: Pearson.

Pekrun, R., Goetz, T., Titz, W. and Perry, R.P. (2002) 'Academic emotions in students' self-regulated learning and achievement: a program of qualitative and quantitative research', *Educational Psychologist*, 37 (2), 91-105.

Penney, D. (2001) 'Equality, equity and inclusion in physical education and school sport', in A. Laker (ed.) *Sociology of Sport and Physical Education: An Introduction*, Abingdon: Routledge, pp.110-128.

Piaget, J. (1932) *The Moral Judgment of the Child*, London: Kegan Paul, Trench, Trubner & Co.

Ramires, V.V., Dos Santos, P.C., Barbosa Filho, V.C., da Silva Bandeira, A., Tenório, M.C.M., de Camargo, E.M., de Paula Ravagnani, F.C., Sandreschi, P., de Oliveira, V.J.M., Hallal, P.C. and Silva, K.S. (2023) 'Physical education for health among school-aged children and adolescents: a scoping review of reviews', *Journal of Physical Activity and Health*, 20 (7), 586–599.

Ryan, R.M., Huta, V. & Deci, E.L. (2019) 'Motivational processes in physical education and objectively measured physical activity among adolescents', *Journal of Sport and Exercise Psychology*, 41(6), 407–419. https://doi.org/10.1123/jsep.2019-0163.

Simonton, K.L., Garn, A.C. and Mercier, K.J. (2023) 'Expanding the discrete emotions in physical education scale (DEPES): a framework for understanding students' emotional experiences', *Physical Education and Sport Pedagogy*, 28 (5), 528–548.

Zimmerman, B.J. (2000) Attaining Self-Regulation A Social Cognitive Perspective. In M. Boekaerts, P. R. Pintrich, & M. Zeidner (Eds.), *Handbook of Self-Regulation*. San Diego, CA: Academic Press, pp. 13–39.

Chapter 11 Challenges related to inclusion, special educational needs and disabilities

Supporting hard-of-hearing pupils in a mainstream specifically resourced provision in their physical education lessons

Rebecca Foster and Alice Smyth

Introduction and context

According to the Consortium for Research in Deaf Education (CRIDE, 2023) there are over 45,000 deaf children in England. Of these, 77% are schooled in a mainstream environment, 6% are in a mainstream school that has an attached specifically resourced provision (SRP) for the deaf, 3% are in a deaf special school, 14% attend a special school that has no specific provision for deaf pupils, whilst 1% of deaf children are homeschooled (Department for Education (DfE), 2015). The statistics provided by CRIDE (2023) are approximate numbers due to the difficulties in gathering such data from local authorities. However, looking at the data, it can be assumed that most teachers will come across at least one deaf pupil in their career.

This chapter presents a case study from an 11-18-year-old mainstream academy in England. The academy has an SRP for pupils who are hard of hearing (HoH). There are approximately 1,400 pupils on roll and 83 members of teaching staff; it is part of a large multi-academy trust with 10+ other secondary academies and 20+ other primary academies. The physical education department is a large department of 10 teachers with a range of different specialisms and experience across the teaching, coaching and technical workforce. None of the teachers have a disability, and all are hearing.

Explanation of terminology

Before continuing, it is important to clarify the authors' stance on deafness and choice of terminology. Within this chapter, people with hearing loss/those who are deaf are referred to as HoH. This term covers a wide range of hearing loss and currently is the recommended term when discussing people with hearing loss as outlined by DfE (2023). The term Deaf

DOI: 10.4324/9781032662978-12

awareness is used to identify how hearing people can become more Deaf-aware. Examples of being Deaf-aware include:

- that there are different communication styles for each HoH person
- not all HoH people use sign language
- not all HoH people lip read
- not all HoH people link or identify with Deaf culture
- from a HoH person's point of view, it is frowned upon when hearing people stop communicating and say 'it doesn't matter' if the HoH person does not follow the conversation.

Acknowledging these examples can go some way in making the reader more Deaf-aware. Thus, it is beneficial to recognise, respect and understand the contested nature of such terms 'as just being Deaf' as the situation is more complex.

To further explain, the umbrella term of HoH is used; however, it is also important to introduce the notion of 'Deaf' and 'deaf' (as in capital D and lowercase d) which sit within the HoH term. Capital Deaf refers to people who are more likely to have been born Deaf, are aware of Deaf history, Deaf identity and are active members in the Deaf community, who may well use the British Sign Language (BSL) as their main form of communication. Those with lowercase deaf are likely to have acquired deafness and are potentially born to a predominantly hearing family, who may lip read, are oral speakers and may not be as aware of the Deaf community, where deafness is a medical diagnosis (Lee, 2016). It is important to highlight this difference as it links to Deaf awareness and how interaction between the two communities can be problematic. This will be discussed later in the chapter.

Many HoH people feel more accepted in a Deaf community as they feel they do not have to explain themselves, and Deaf awareness is accepted and practiced (Foster, 2016). HoH people identity or rather embracing deafness can be challenging for some due to the complexity of our society and how it views deafness. Often, it is the HoH person that has to adapt to fit into a hearing world, rather than the hearing world seeking what they can do to support the HoH person (Foster, 2013). By appreciating the value and importance of encouraging a person to explore their HoH people identity could benefit their personal growth and belonging. HoH people could discover that the HoH community is as rich as a hearing community.

Case study (part 1)

There are 12 HoH pupils in the school who attend the SRP and have moderate, severe, profound or permanent bilateral (both ears) hearing loss. There is a strong infrastructure around the HoH pupils, such as a Special Education Needs Coordinator (SENCO), a qualified teacher of the deaf (ToD) and a teaching assistant (TA). The pupils attend more than 50% of their timetable in mainstream classes, including physical education as part of core physical education lessons or as an examination option at key stage (KS) 4 or 5. Six of the pupils also have an Education Health Care Plan (EHCP). An EHCP is a combined document from three providers (education, health and care) that collectively supports pupils who require more assistance than is available (DfE and Department of Health (DoH) 2015). The pupils in the SRP are granted individual support to develop or learn a specific skill (such as lip reading, speech and language support) or to access specialist equipment such as radio microphones (RMs) (DfE, 2015).

Within the context of this case study, teachers had undertaken continuous professional development (CPD) to facilitate an inclusive curriculum and delivery, with a focus on the STEP (Space, Task, Equipment, People) principle (Haskins, 2005) and Inclusion Spectrum (Stevenson, 2009). However, the physical education department had not undertaken any CPD to specifically support HoH pupils in their physical education lessons. Teachers had felt that they had used the STEP and Inclusion frameworks successfully to the benefit of all pupils, but nothing specifically for pupils who were HoH. In fact, the teachers confirmed that the delivery of physical education had not been adapted specifically to support HoH pupils.

The issue

Teachers were concerned that HoH pupils may be missing out on high-quality physical education. They were aware that no HoH pupil had opted to study GCSE/BTEC in sport as a KS4 option for at least 10 years. The teachers were keen to include the pupils in their lessons but were concerned that as pupils received no extra support in physical education (from TAs), the lack of support may restrict the pupils' development. In core physical education lessons, teachers had noticed that HoH pupils relied on friends to give an extra explanation if there is confusion. The teachers were aware that the HoH pupils were missing key information, such as the receiving and understanding all the teaching points to perform a skill effectively. The teachers acknowledge that they had allowed this to happen as they themselves have not been given any Deaf awareness training nor felt confident to offer further advice to the peer group so were reluctant to intervene.

Feedback from some of the HoH pupils reported that they struggled to understand instructions and were concerned about misunderstanding and getting the instructions wrong (which can be very public in physical education). This issue was amplified when lessons were outside as the weather conditions often disrupted hearing aids. Pupils also mentioned that they benefitted from demonstrations from the teacher but reported that this did not always occur, which put them at a disadvantage. As a result, they felt they could not perform the practice properly.

The interventions

A reluctance to intervene is a common trait. In fact, the National Deaf Children's Society (NDCS) (2019) research stated that 52% of Britons do not feel confident about communicating with HoH people, with such a resistance from some hearing people to engaging with HoH people referred to as Surdophobia (Shropshire (D)deaf and Hard of Hearing Forum, 2015). For instance, Dovidio, Gaertner and Kawakami (2003) proposed that recognising the intergroup contact theory (in this example, consider HoH and hearing as two 'groups') is a factor when discussing prejudice because there is a lack of intergroup contact. This means that because the HoH community is small compared to the hearing community, the 'groups' seldom meet so no myths or appreciation of different culture are ever challenged. As a result, prejudice often remains. Siah et al. (2023) explained that discrimination perceived by HoH people may also effect social interaction with the hearing community, whilst Dunn (2021) considered non-disabled people and how they often fear they may cause offence or 'get things wrong' by behaving awkwardly due to not necessarily being socialised into a HoH world.

Based on the authors' experiences, there are a number of interventions that can be used to support HoH pupils in physical education. Whilst not an exhaustive list (gentle disclaimer – these are some ideas, not all ideas!), Table 11.1 provides a range of interventions, in addition to those used in the case study school, that may benefit you as a teacher.

As with any such interventions, there could be benefits and constraints for schools, and it is appreciated that all schools and teachers within them are different. Therefore, discretion should be used when selecting which interventions to use, so that (hopefully) interventions suit the school and its circumstances, allowing HoH pupils to demonstrate progress.

The next section explains the specific interventions used by the authors to help address the issues reported by the physical education teachers and HoH pupils.

To address the teacher and pupils' concerns, it was felt that several areas needed to be explored. Specifically, from the point of view of the physical education department, the HoH pupils and for the ToD, a transparent approach was needed and therefore adopted. To facilitate this, the Trust Wide Subject Lead for Physical Education (TWSL), who was known to the school and only taught one of the HoH pupils, ensured a level of impartiality in what was discussed and reflected, and acted as the lead. All parties were aware of the desire to improve provision and inclusion for HoH pupils in the school and that if they worked together, aspects may improve. The three intervention areas identified and adopted are discussed below.

Intervention 1: start purposeful communication between physical education teachers and HoH pupils

Over a 16-week period, across the summer term, the TWSL was tasked to talk to the ToD to seek permission to approach the HoH pupils. The aim was to seek honest and focused feedback from the HoH pupils regarding their experiences of physical education. The initial informal discussions would centre around what the pupils may like in physical education, whether there could be any improvements in their physical education lessons and whether the physical education teachers could do anything to support them that they currently do not do. It was important that the ToD was present to reassure and clarify any questions the pupils had whilst in conversation with the TWSL. As the physical education teachers had already been consulted about their concerns related to the HoH pupils, the TWSL role became that of a conduit regarding feeding back information from the HoH pupils.

Intervention 2: promotion of Deaf awareness

The second approach was for the TWSL to work with the physical education teachers for them to become more Deaf-aware. Specific training was offered via free and/or paid online courses. The TWSL and main author co-created a Deaf-aware presentation that included her initial feedback from the HoH pupils and a true or false slide that created an interactive quiz about what the physical education teachers knew and did not know about deafness. A short YouTube clip on what it is like to be 'Deaf in a hearing world' (https://www.youtube.com/watch?v=d7m6HEZ6auE&t=26s) was shared, whilst other slides included knowledge surrounding Big D and little d, ableism, statistics on educational outcomes of HoH children in England and top tips for teachers to instantly use. These included, for example, speak clearly and naturally (rather than shout) and always try to face the pupil (rather than

Supporting hard-of-hearing pupils 145

Table 11.1 Interventions that might be considered when teaching HoH pupils

Potential intervention	Potential benefits	Potential constraints
Provide HoH pupils with an outline of the physical education lesson (something they can refer to) before class starts (preferably 24 h ahead).	The pupil can follow the lesson and check clarity of teaching points.	Lack of available time for the teacher to provide the plan. Lessons may change at the very last minute.
Seek the preferred communication style from the HoH pupil, ask them for some top tips that can be shared with classmates.	All pupils will have elements of Deaf awareness and a way to communicate.	The HoH pupil may not wish to share or know their preferred style. The pupil may feel singled out if handled inconsiderately.
Use more facial expressions, gestures when explaining points, demonstrate everything.	A more engaged pupil as they may follow and copy the visual stimuli more.	A teacher may feel conscious and over-exaggerate movement when it is not necessary.
Use visual commands (hand up to stop play, wave a bib to gain attention).	All pupils benefit due to using periphery vision. HoH pupil is not disadvantaged as no sound is being used.	Teacher may use their voice instead.
Avoid standing in front of a bright light (as your face may be in the shadow), avoid covering your mouth, turning your back whilst speaking.	Better communication and understanding from the HoH pupil as they can watch the lip pattern.	Teacher may forget to be Deaf-aware.

turning and walking away). Further information regarding the Deaflympics, which is an international pathway for talented HoH people to be engaged with, provided teachers with a view that this might be aspirational for some pupils.

Intervention 3: to develop a sense of Deaf identity

The key aim of the project was to encourage the HoH pupils to feel empowered and be involved in decision-making. The TWSL asked the HoH pupils if they wanted to deliver a Deaf-awareness session for their classmates/year group. Further suggestions made were to create an informative bulletin board to raise the profile of Deaf awareness or Deaf sport in the community within the school and the celebration of Deaf Awareness Week or even a sponsored BSL event.

Case study part 2 – The outcomes

Due to the new communication channel between teachers and pupils, the TWSL was able to feed back the issues directly between the groups for quick results. The impact of the interventions is explained below. Some direct quotes from the HoH pupils and physical education teachers have been used.

Intervention 1: start purposeful communication between physical education teachers and HoH pupils

It was important for the TWSL to seek approval from the ToD and the pupils themselves before working together to initiate potential changes. By having pupil-centred discussions, the TWSL was able to draw the positives and concerns the HoH pupils felt in their physical education lessons. Initially, the HoH pupils were rather cautious about attending a meeting and being asked direct questions about their physical education lessons, but due to the ToD being present they soon realised it was a safe space that the department had created. The HoH pupils voiced their concerns over the teachers' use of RMs, that teachers often shouted whilst using them, which amplified sound even more, that over 20m away the RM would not be effective for the pupil to hear, teachers not being aware that the RM often cut in and out, so instructions may not have been fully understood and for teachers to avoid running whilst wearing an RM due to the impact of the RM on the teacher and the banging of keys. Borg, Neovius and Kjellander (2001) stated that whilst wearing RM the direction of sound plays a significant role in contributing to selective attention, listening in noise and speech reading. Hearing teachers are likely to be unaware of the RM requirements, so should consider their placement when giving instructions and volume as well as other external noises (such as cars/lorries driving past or a strong wind that would interfere with the RMs).

By sharing information, a strong relationship was created between the TWSL, the ToD and the HoH pupils because the pupils felt valued and validated. Beyond the initial meeting, two HoH pupils sought out the TWSL to expand on more information, advice and experiences. This bond grew as the TWSL was able to successfully share the pupils' concerns with the physical education teachers, who instantly put into practice the adaptations. This relationship became so powerful because the pupils noticed that the physical education teachers were more aware of their specific needs by being more cautious with the RM usage, meaning communication between the TWSL and the physical education teachers was successful. This positivity made the interaction sustainable because the physical education teachers started to 'check in' on pupils' understanding of instructions more, and teachers demonstrated rather than spoke instructions and ensured they were facing pupils when delivering instructions.

The HoH pupils felt 'cared for' and 'important' in physical education as they felt 'listened to' by teachers. This echoes MacConville's (2006) work on listening to the voice of disabled youngsters if non-disabled adults want young people to feel valued. Physical education teachers also noted that the pupils 'seem more confident to ask if they haven't heard or need more clarification'. The physical education teachers expressed that they can 'better understand and are more confident in meeting the needs of the pupils' and that the pupils seemed 'more engaged' in lessons because of their adaptations. Teachers also reported that they 'feel more confident to discuss individual needs with a pupil directly'. These comments underline how positive and happy the HoH pupils felt to be able to speak up and out and how much more open physical education teachers are to approach pupils. The intervention gave both groups the opportunity to communicate effectively and to build a sustainable, healthy dialogue between the groups.

Intervention 2: promotion of Deaf awareness

Most of the HoH pupils did initially express a feeling of isolation within physical education lessons. Physical education teachers had observed other pupils assisting HoH pupils to understand. Isolation is a common trait that HoH and disabled individuals feel in as they are often overlooked (Dixon, Braye and Gibbons, 2022; NDCS, 2019). The isolation could be due to not comprehending what is taking place in class – HoH people find it difficult to follow conversation as there is often 'overlay' of words (Coates and Sutton-Spence, 2001). BSL could be another way teachers could help HoH pupils gain further clarity, but accredited BSL training comes at a substantial cost (£275) and dedication of time to learn the language, up to 20 weeks of guided learning hours (Signature, 2023). Learning BSL is not mandatory at school as it is not part of the National Curriculum, but in 2019 a petition was presented to government calling for BSL to be taught in more schools (NDCS, 2019). BSL is not offered at many university teacher training courses, which could be a place to grasp basic sign language.

Nevertheless, some of the HoH pupils did request that the physical education teachers learn some basic sign language. The pupils even wrote specific words for the teachers to learn, such as goal, pass and shoot. As conversations developed, the HoH pupils started to request more knowledge in BSL and suggested teachers have aspects of the language. HoH pupils suggested a gesture hybrid, meaning that it was unlikely that BSL would be taught, so to share a common gesture for some actions and signs that all can understand. This method has proved successful (Venugopalan and Reghunadhan, 2021) because employing sign language interpreters is not a pragmatic solution to such communication problems. Research has suggested the need to develop a reliable system for automatic sign language recognition. This could be a suitable compromise in the short term as the HoH pupils are selecting the terms that would be most useful for them. The physical education teachers were willing to learn basic signs but recognised this skill needs to happen over a longer period of time and could be part of whole-school development in order to raise the whole profile of the SRP unit in the school.

As part of the Deaf awareness intervention, the TWSL created a noticeboard that was placed on the physical education corridor. Pupils reported that this made them 'feel more included in the Sports Enrichment and physical education programme'. She also invited a Deaflympian to school to speak with the HoH pupils. The Bronze medal Deaflympic footballer spent time discussing her journey and her love of sport as well as the merits of learning sign language. She came to BSL once she had been selected for the Deaflympics and she realised she was in the minority as she could not sign. Because she wanted to communicate, she learnt BSL, and it enriched her life, reflecting other Deaflympians who also felt inspired to learn BSL to communicate whilst competing at the Deaflympics (Foster, 2013; Kelly, 2022). By being able to communicate in both spheres is an asset despite the Deaflympian not having had the opportunity to learn BSL whilst at school. The TWSL reported how interested the HoH pupils were about BSL and that they became motivated to learn BSL. The CPD given to the physical education teachers enabled them to empathise and understand the HoH pupils' physical education experiences in their lessons and that being Deaf-aware was helpful for engaging in conversations by checking the HoH pupils' understanding, which is culturally accepted in the Deaf community (Foster and Barber, 2021).

Intervention 3: to develop a sense of Deaf identity

All except one of the HoH pupils said they enjoyed physical education lessons more since the intervention with the TWSL (the other pupil said they 'always loved PE'). They all spoke about 'feeling more confident' in physical education lessons and 'I enjoy [PE] more as I am not as nervous of being left out', 'if I am not sure I feel braver asking questions', 'I have started to go to an after-school club'. These comments emphasise how empowered the HoH pupils feel in speaking up to teachers, something they did not do prior the intervention. At least one of the HoH pupils plans to opt for GCSE physical education, which will end the physical education department's 10-year drought, with another saying 'maybe, as I like it, but not sure'. The remainder appreciate the improvements in their physical education experience but felt comfortable saying they 'prefer other subjects' and 'I don't like physical education *that* much'.

The improvement in communication and the growth of relationship building between the teachers and pupils are evident as it has affected the pupil's confidence, 'if I see Miss in school, I always say hello', with physical education teachers saying, 'the pupils are more vocal in corridors saying hello to physical education teachers more regularly'. This is something that did not happen before the interventions. This positivity was duplicated with the physical education teachers who no longer felt they needed a TA to work alongside the HoH pupils as their relationship had developed and the teachers expressed more confidence and Deaf awareness.

The ToD reported that she saw a change in the pupils, they 'seem to be really motivated about improving their experiences in physical education, while they weren't having negative experiences, they didn't have the same buzz around physical education which they have now. The pupils are very good at adapting but with the teachers considering their needs more it means they can focus more on learning the skills and reduce cognitive load". It is valuable that the ToD draws attention to the cognitive load that HoH people have in engaging in or following conversation and the amount of concentration it takes to engage, a term titled 'concentration fatigue' which does affect academic performance (Bess and Hornsby, 2014).

As previously mentioned, the Deaflympian inspired the HoH pupils when she spoke about her journey. After the visit, the HoH pupils asked if they could fundraise for the GB Deaflympic football team as the squad do not receive government funding. The pupils were motivated to organise a girl's football tournament. This leads the authors to feel the HoH pupils felt empowered to do something for other HoH people and to raise awareness of Deaf sport.

Summary and key points

To summarise, the authors focused on developing Deaf awareness within a school that had an SRP for deaf provision. The physical education teachers recognised that meeting and listening to comments made by the HoH pupils meant they could put pupil requests into their own practice immediately, such as standing closer to the HoH pupils and facing them when they were speaking. It was positive that the HoH pupils were willing to discuss issues with the TWSL about their physical education experiences, which highlights a good teacher–pupil relationship. The HoH pupils expressed concerns about the use of RMs and how, when outside, the weather can interrupt the effective functioning of hearing aids. Had the HoH pupils not expressed their concerns to the TWSL, little to no progress would be made, and the cycle of communication would remain a barrier. Had all parties not been motivated to work together, be open to discussion and address the concerns, interventions may not have worked. The HoH pupils suggested that teachers learn some basic sign language to help them understand and that from time to time, the teacher would check their understanding. These ideas from the HoH pupils became a focus and were included in the project, which took place in the summer term. The time of year may have been a factor in its success as the intensity of the year was ending. Three key interventions were suggested:

1. Start purposeful communication between physical education teachers and HoH pupils.
2. Promote Deaf awareness.
3. Develop a sense of Deaf identity.

A healthy, transparent conversation worked between teachers and pupils, which enabled a huge amount of progress in a short time. The openness and willingness of teachers to speak with people outside their department was beneficial as no teacher was left out of the process and, therefore, all had the HoH pupils' benefit at the centre. As part of the multi-academy trust, the TWSL offered CPD surrounding the HoH provision trust wide and then more specifically to heads of physical education. Although the knowledge transfer was beneficial to all teachers, the specific nature of focusing on just HoH pupils lost some impact as the other academies had no HoH pupils; therefore, the TWSL broadened the title to 'Inclusive physical education' in order to make the content relevant and to encapsulate wider disabilities. This decision was valuable as one school decided to follow a similar set of interventions but for autistic pupils. Inspiration from the interventions was given to teachers to approach and ask certain pupils what might benefit them more in physical education, particularly around sensory overload. This approach proved successful in their school as pupils felt empowered to talk about triggers (that could be avoided), such as autistic pupils allowed to watch the activity first and then become involved. Due to schools' competing agendas for professional development, teachers felt the largest barrier for delivery of information and the execution of it was time. The pupils as well as teachers and then to feedback to others when the agenda of CPD is often crowded. In order to combat the issue of time, teachers were able to reflect and spoke about the 'success' stories because of the interventions and felt it was worth finding the time as the HoH pupils had benefitted greatly.

The promotion of Deaf awareness was also a positive change due to teachers learning what changes they could adopt and to apply them instantly, such as standing closer to the pupil, making sure the teacher did not turn their back whilst they were talking, asking open-ended questions to the HoH pupil to check understanding of the task. Teachers felt they were no longer 'getting it wrong' and felt less awkward (Lyra, Koullapi and Kalogeropoulou, 2023) because the HoH pupils knew any questions and comments from the teachers were coming from a place of support for the pupils themselves felt more confident expressing their needs.

For the HoH pupils, developing a sense of Deaf identity was crucial. Part of Deaf identity is knowing and using aspects of BSL. There still remains a controversial debate on why Deaf people have been discouraged from learning BSL and the promotion of oralism (Kelly, 2022). This could be a reason why trainee teachers do not have the opportunity to learn BSL as part of their training. Historically, the use of sign language was banned as a form of communication to force Deaf people to learn to lip read and/or talk (Anglin-Jaffe, 2013). This method supports the medical model of disability (Bingham et al., 2013; Johnston, 1996; Marks, 2000; Nind, Flewitt and Payler, 2010), meaning deafness is the responsibility of and owned by the Deaf person, it is up to the Deaf person to 'learn' how to communicate with the hearing. This attitude has, over time, shifted to a more social model of disability approach (Barney, 2012; Hutchison, 1995; Purdue, 2009), whereby society itself is the barrier. To explain, a HoH person cannot hear but hearing people could learn BSL, people could be more Deaf-aware, BSL should be taught on the school curriculum as an additional language. Rather than the HoH person having to adjust to a potentially hostile hearing world, society could challenge how the narrative surrounding deafness could be changed to make access more equal. HoH people often do not view themselves as disabled but as a linguistic minority (World Federation of the Deaf, position paper, 2018). Offering opportunity can only enhance a richer population, who are celebrated for their diversity using any communication method they choose.

Reflection

Due to such positive outcomes from the interventions, the TWSL recognises the benefits of targeting and supporting marginalised groups. This was developed by the TWSL broadening training to include other disabilities rather than focusing on one in particular. This highlighted the value of pupil voice and by simply asking, listening and acting upon information shared, quick, positive gains were made. These changes could be the difference between keeping a pupil happy in school, or not. Moving forward, the academy does intend to induct new teachers into its CPD programme and use pupil voices (in the guise of a talking head pre-recorded videos) as to how beneficial it is for HoH pupils to be asked what their needs are by teachers. The TWSL feels it is vital that all teachers are exposed to this training. It must be acknowledged that all parties within this case study were willing participants, all ready to share and support a positive change.

References

Anglin-Jaffe, H. (2013) 'Signs of resistance: peer learning of sign languages within "oral" schools for the deaf', *Studies in Philosophy and Education*, 32 (3), 261-271.

Barney, K.W. (2012) 'Disability simulations: using the social model of disability to update an experiential educational practice', *SCHOLE: A Journal of Leisure Studies and Recreation Education*, 27 (1), 1-11.

Bess, F.H. and Hornsby, B.W. (2014) 'Commentary: listening can be exhausting—fatigue in children and adults with hearing loss', *Ear and Hearing*, 35 (6), 592.

Bingham, C., Clarke, L., Michielsens, E. and Van de Meer, M. (2013) 'Towards a social model approach? British and Dutch disability policies in the health sector compared', *Personnel Review*, 42 (5), 613-637.

Borg, E., Neovius, L. and Kjellander, M. (2001) 'A three-microphone system for real-time directional analysis: toward a device for environmental monitoring in deaf-blind', *Journal of Rehabilitation Research and Development*, 38 (2), 265-272.

Coates, J. and Sutton-Spence, R. (2001) 'Turn-taking patterns in deaf conversation', *Journal of Sociolinguistics*, 5 (4), 507-529.

CRIDE (Consortium for Research in Deaf Education) (2023) *2022 Report for England Education Provision for Deaf Children in England in 2021/22*, available at: https://www.batod.org.uk/wp-content/uploads/2022/11/CRIDE-2022-England-report-FINAL.pdf (accessed 10 January 2025).

DfE (Department for Education) (2015) *Area Guidelines for SEND and Alternative Provision Including Special Schools, Alternative Provision, Specially Resourced Provision and Units*, available at: https://assets.publishing.service.gov.uk/government/uploads/system/uploads/attachment_data/file/905693/BB104.pdf (accessed 10 January 2025)

DfE (Department for Education) (2023) *Inclusive Language: Words to Use and Avoid When Writing about Disability*, available at: https://www.gov.uk/government/publications/inclusive-communication/inclusive-language-words-to-use-and-avoid-when-writing-about-disability (accessed 17 July 2025).

DfE (Department for Education and Department of Health) (2015) *SEND Code of Practice: 0-25 years*, available at: https://www.gov.uk/government/publications/send-code-of-practice-0-to-25 (accessed 5 June 2025).

Dixon, K., Braye, S. and Gibbons, T. (2022) 'Still outsiders: the inclusion of disabled children and young people in physical education in England', *Disability & Society*, 37 (10), 1549-1567.

Dovidio, J.F., Gaertner, S.L. and Kawakami, K. (2003) 'Intergroup contact: The past, present, and the future', *Group Processes and Intergroup Relations*, 6 (1), 5-21.

Dunn, D. (2021) *Understanding Ableism and Negative Reaction to Disability, Engaging in Critical Thinking Can Be Helpful in Altering Beliefs and Avoiding Ableist Conclusions*, American Psychology Association, available at: https://www.apa.org/ed/precollege/psychology-teacher-network/introductory-psychology/ableism-negative-reactions-disability#:~:text=Ableism%2C%20either%20subtly%20or%20directly,behave%20awkwardly%20around%20disabled%20people (accessed 10 January 2025).

Foster, R. (2013) 'Is there an Olympic legacy for deaf athletes?' *Physical Education Matters*, 8 (2), 16-18.

Foster, R. (2016) '"Hearing" the deaf perspective of physical education', *Physical Education Matters*, 11 (1), 34-37.

Foster, R. and Barber, L. (eds) (2021) *Physical Education for Young People with Disabilities: A Handbook of Practical Ideas Created by Practitioners for Practitioners*, Abingdon: Routledge.

Haskins, D. (2005) *TOP Play and TOP Sport Handbook*, Loughborough: YST.

Hutchison, T. (1995) 'The classification of disability', *Archives of Disease in Childhood*, 73 (2), 91.

Johnston, M. (1996) 'Models of disability', *Physiotherapy Theory and Practice*, 12 (3), 131-141.

Kelly, L. (2022) 'Oralism, ableism and counter culture', *PN Review*, 48 (4), 8-9.

Lee, A. (2016) 'The culture of a silent minority', *The Review: A Journal of Undergraduate Student Research*, 17, 1-4, available at: https://fisherpub.sjf.edu/cgi/viewcontent.cgi?article=1196&context=ur (accessed 10 January 2025).

Lyra, O., Koullapi, K. and Kalogeropoulou, E. (2023) 'Fears towards disability and their impact on teaching practices in inclusive classrooms: An empirical study with teachers in Greece', *Heliyon*, 9 (5), available at: https://www.cell.com/heliyon/fulltext/S2405-8440(23)03539-9 (accessed 5 June 2025).

MacConville, R.M. (2006) *Looking at Inclusion: Listening to the Voices of Young People*, London: Sage.

MacConville, R. and Palmer, J. (2007) 'Including pupils with hearing impairments', in R. MacConville (ed.) *Looking at Inclusion: Listening to the Voices of Young People*, London: SAGE, pp.99-126.

Marks, B.A. (2000) 'Jumping through hoops and walking on egg shells or discrimination, hazing, and abuse of students with disabilities?', *Journal of Nursing Education*, 39 (5), 205-210.

National Deaf Children's Society (2019) *More Than Half of Adults Don't Feel Confident Talking to Deaf People*, available at: https://www.ndcs.org.uk/about-us/news-and-media/latest-news/more-than-half-of-adults-don-t-feel-confident-talking-to-deaf-people/ (accessed 5 June 2025).

Nind, M., Flewitt, R. and Payler, J. (2010) 'The social experience of early childhood for children with learning disabilities: inclusion, competence and agency', *British Journal of Sociology of Education*, 31 (6), 653-670.

Purdue, K. (2009) 'Barriers to and facilitators of inclusion for children with disabilities in early childhood education', *Contemporary Issues in Early Childhood*, 10 (2), 133-143.

Shropshire Deaf and Hard of Hearing Forum (2015) *Did you Know? – Surdophobia*, available at: https://www.facebook.com/339961526033495/posts/did-you-know surdophobia-is-the-hostility-intolerance-or-fear-against-deaf people/1090436590985981/ (accessed 17 March 2023).

Siah, P.C., Tan, C.S., Lee, W.Y. and Lee, M.N. (2023) 'An intergroup contact approach for understanding attitudes and behaviours towards deaf students among hearing students in Malaysia', *Equality, Diversity and Inclusion: An International Journal*, 42 (7), 927–942.

Signature (2023) *British Sign Language Level 1 Award*, available at: https://www.signature.org.uk/british-sign-language-level-1-award/ (accessed 10 January 2025).

Stevenson, P. (2009) 'The pedagogy of inclusive youth sport. Working towards real solutions', in H. Fitzgerald (ed.) *Disability and Youth Sport*, Abingdon: Routledge, pp. 119–131

Venugopalan, A. and Reghunadhan, R. (2021) 'Applying deep neutral networks for the automatic recognition of sign language words: a communication aid to deaf agriculturalists', *Expert Systems with Application*, 185, 115601, 1–9.

World Federation of the Deaf (2018) *Complementary or Diametrically Opposed: Situating Deaf Communities within 'Disability' vs 'Cultural and Linguistic Minority' Constructs: Position Paper*, available at: https://wfdeaf.org/wp-content/uploads/2018/07/LM-and-D-Discussion-Paper-FINAL-11-May-2018.pdf (accessed 10 January 2025).

Chapter 12 Challenges related to enacting trauma-informed practice

supporting trauma-affected pupils

Oliver Hooper, Vincent Coleman, Rachel Sandford, Thomas Quarmby and Shirley Gray

Introduction

Within this chapter, we seek to explore how teachers can support trauma-affected pupils in physical education. Initially, we examine the impacts of trauma on children and young people broadly, before outlining the impacts it can have on learning and development within the school context. Next, we consider how the impacts of trauma might 'play out' within the subject of physical education specifically, taking into account some of the particularities of this context. Subsequently, we present a reflective contribution from one of the authors – Vincent (Vince) – around which this chapter is structured. Within this, Vince reflects on a specific experience of working with a trauma-affected pupil – James[1] – within his physical education lessons. Following this, we explore how Vince's practice aligned with the principles for trauma-aware pedagogies in physical education, developed by Quarmby and colleagues (2022). In doing so, we identify the various strategies that Vince used within his practice to support this pupil – and, indeed, all pupils – within his classes, before offering some concluding thoughts around enacting trauma-aware pedagogies within physical education.

Case study

Before we begin to examine the impacts of trauma on children and young people, we wish to share a little more about James (14 years old). James was a pupil that Vince formerly worked with during his time as a physical education teacher at a secondary school in Scotland, before he embarked on doctoral study. James was a pupil who – over the course of his time at the school – Vince came to know well and a young person who might be considered to be trauma-affected. As Vince reflects:

> I had taught James for a number of years. In that time, I learned about his background, his family and the community he lives in. Without probing too much, I would regularly

DOI: 10.4324/9781032662978-13

engage him in conversation about his interests and hobbies, and what he had been doing the previous weekend. Often, he would complain about moving between his own home with his mother, and his auntie's house across town. He didn't usually have PE kit, so I would keep his and wash it at the end of each week. The Learning Support Team informed me his father was in prison, and social workers were involved in custody disputes. On his pupil record, James had diagnoses for attention deficit hyperactivity disorder (ADHD) and post-traumatic stress disorder (PTSD). In lessons, James would sometimes zone out, become unresponsive and withdrawn, whereas other times he would be hyperactive, noisy, disruptive and energetic.

Vince's reflection may well resonate with many practising physical education teachers, given the growing prevalence of trauma within schools. We now turn our attention to examining the impacts of trauma on children and young people broadly within the school context, before considering further how the impacts of trauma might 'play out' specifically within the subject of physical education.

Examining the impacts of trauma on children and young people

Children and young people are increasingly encountering 'adverse childhood experiences' (ACEs). These refer to persistent, frequent and intense sources of stress that children and young people may experience from birth, up to the age of 18 years (Felitti et al., 1998). Felitti and colleagues (1998) originally outlined ten distinct adversities that may be encountered during childhood. These include exposure to physical, verbal or sexual abuse and physical or emotional neglect, as well as forms of household dysfunction that affect the environment in which a child grows up – for instance, parental separation, domestic violence, substance misuse, mental illness and incarceration of a family member. Smith (2018) has more recently, however, called for recognition of forms of adversity that extend beyond the context of the home. For example, he suggested that ACEs can include facing racism, witnessing community violence, residing in an unsafe neighbourhood, being bullied, entering foster care or suffering the death of a parent, as well as having a lack of food, being exposed to consistent parental arguments, holding low socioeconomic status, poor academic performance, having limited social capital or being rejected by peers.

Adversities such as these are often associated with resultant stress responses. While stress in small doses can be manageable – and is, in fact, an important part of healthy child development – it can become harmful and have detrimental impacts on young people's health and well-being in larger doses. There are three kinds of responses to stress: positive, tolerable and toxic. A positive stress response is associated with brief increases in heart rate and mild elevations in stress hormone levels (for example, starting a new school), whereas a tolerable stress response includes more serious but temporary stress responses (for example, experiencing the death of a relative). With positive and tolerable stress responses, the impact of the associated biological processes (for example, increased heart rate, elevated blood pressure and the release of cortisol) can be moderated by the attention of a loving caregiver, who can comfort and reassure the child. However, a toxic stress response involves prolonged activation of the stress response system and – in the absence of protective relationships – the body can fail to recover fully (for example, when a child experiences repeated abuse or neglect)

(Franke, 2014). As such, toxic stress is more likely to occur for certain groups of children and young people who, for instance, lack the care and support of close, trusted adults. Such groups of young people include those who are care-experienced (Sandford et al., 2021) and those who are refugees and asylum-seekers (Wood et al., 2020) – with both groups known to be at risk of experiencing multiple ACEs.

It is important to note that children and young people's responses to ACEs will vary – even when a similar situation is experienced – and that it is an individual's response to ACEs that determines whether they are considered traumatic or not. When stress arising from ACEs becomes toxic, it engulfs the internal and external coping resources available to children and young people, resulting in trauma. Trauma, therefore, occurs when an individual is exposed to an experience that overwhelms them, creating a sense of extreme threat that has lasting negative effects on their functioning and overall well-being (Substance Abuse and Mental Health Services Administration (SAMHSA), 2014). Importantly, trauma has negative impacts on multiple facets of a child's development, including: *neurological impacts* – limiting neural connections in regions of the brain involved in reasoning, learning, memory, decision-making, behaviour regulation and impulse control while also interfering with the hormonal systems that regulate stress and thus an individual's ability to regulate behaviour in response to subsequent stressors; *physiological impacts* – making those who have experienced trauma more susceptible to chronic diseases, obesity, diabetes, high blood pressure and sleeping problems; and *psychological impacts* – leading to depression, anxiety, anger and aggression, difficulty trusting others and, hence, unstable relationships, as well as a variety of disorders (including ADHD, personality disorders and eating disorders).

Childhood trauma is now considered a global health epidemic, with ACEs becoming increasingly prominent (United Nations, Educational, Scientific and Cultural Organization (UNESCO), 2019). In England, specifically, a survey of 3,885 individuals aged 18–69 years revealed that nearly half of the respondents (47%) had experienced at least one type of adversity prior to the age of 18, while 9% had experienced multiple (four or more) ACEs (Bellis et al., 2014). Meanwhile, the Scottish Health Survey highlighted that 15% of adults had experienced four or more ACEs (Scottish Government, 2020). Hence, with potentially traumatic experiences increasing, the effect on children and young people's outcomes with respect to health, well-being and education has become of particular concern (UNESCO, 2019). Trauma and the impacts it can have on young people are therefore highly relevant for teachers and schools. Indeed, understanding the impact of trauma and the responses it might evoke is becoming increasingly important for those working in schools so as to help them comprehend underlying reasons why some pupils have difficulties with learning, building relationships and managing behaviour. While the impacts of trauma can be seen to 'play out' across the school context, it has been argued that these might be more visible in certain contexts than others, with physical education being one such space (Quarmby et al., 2022).

Exploring trauma within the context of physical education

Physical education is rather uniquely placed within the school curriculum in relation to not only the content it covers, but also the environments in which learning takes place, and the interactions that occur within these environments (Hooper, Sandford and Jarvis, 2020;

Sandford, Quarmby and Hooper, 2024). On this, Ciotto and Gagnon (2018, p.28) noted how "the activities that take place in [PE] may elicit different emotions and feelings than those in the academic classroom". There are various reasons for this, but the public nature of participation and the centrality of the body within the learning process are certainly significant. Teachers within the subject are likely to be well-aware that some pupils might struggle with issues associated with body image and putting their physical self 'on display'; however, the depth of vulnerability felt by pupils who have been exposed to trauma is unlikely to be fully recognised. Moreover, the interactions that take place in physical education – such as those involving physical contact – may also serve to further exacerbate the anxieties of pupils who have experienced trauma.

Caldeborg, Maivorsdotter and Öhman (2019) noted that physical contact between pupils and teachers – while sometimes necessary in physical education – can be problematic. Although physical contact is frequently used as means of supporting pupils during activities (for example, during a balance in gymnastics) or providing reassurance (for example, after losing a race), there may be instances where it is unwelcome. For instance, children and young people might have concerns with physical contact if they have experienced physical abuse and may unknowingly be subject to further (unintentional) distress by a teacher (innocently) giving them reassurance if they were to get upset within a lesson. Moreover, wider spaces associated with the subject can also be challenging for those who have experienced trauma. Changing rooms were identified by O'Donovan, Sandford and Kirk (2015) as 'highly charged' spaces, whereby pupils are subject to the 'gaze' of others. This may be particularly difficult for certain groups, who may have visible remnants of the abuse they encountered during childhood, such as care-experienced young people (Quarmby, Sandford and Elliot, 2019). Evidently, experiencing childhood trauma has a number of specific implications for pupils' engagement in physical education.

The effects of trauma negatively impact pupils' learning, behaviour and relationships and can present pupils with challenges around processing information, being able to distinguish between threatening and non-threatening situations, forming trusting relationships with peers and/or adults and being able to regulate their emotions (Cole et al., 2005). Consequently, this can result in trauma-affected pupils adopting behavioural coping mechanisms (for example, defiance, aggressiveness, social withdrawal) that can be difficult for teachers to manage – both generally, and within physical education, specifically. Within the physical education context, the effects of trauma may manifest in a multitude of ways. For example, pupils may display an inability to form connections with peers or refuse to be part of a team, they may struggle to adhere to the rules or be unable to handle pressure situations in competition (Bergholz, Stafford and D'Andrea, 2016). Pupils may also respond in ways that seem disproportionate, such as a small foul escalating into physical conflict within a game. However, as noted above, it is possible for individuals with similar experiences – in terms of the nature of trauma – to have very different responses, due to the individualistic nature of traumatic experiences. As such, it can be difficult for teachers to know how a pupil might respond to particular circumstances or events within the context of physical education.

Given the increasing prominence of trauma, there have been growing calls within the subject of physical education for teachers to adopt a 'trauma-aware lens', which enables them to better understand the reasons underlying pupils' potentially challenging presentations (Quarmby et al., 2022; Quarmby et al., 2025). Without this, pupils' behaviours can be misinterpreted as intentional and within their control, rather than as a result of pain-based or survival responses triggered by the environment. Misinterpretation of the intent of the behaviour and what the pupil is communicating – for example, regarding behaviour as 'off-task' or wilful disobedience – can result in disciplinary actions more likely to exacerbate the behaviour than to ameliorate it. However, if teachers view challenging behaviours through a trauma-aware lens, they are less likely to regard trauma-related behaviours as intentional or due to a pupil being 'unmotivated' or 'disobedient'. In turn, this can reduce – or even avoid – punitive responses that may only serve to exacerbate the problem or to re-traumatise the pupil (Cole et al., 2005).

By adopting a trauma-aware lens, teachers can not only better understand why pupils might be reacting in particular ways which might be deemed challenging, but also begin to predict triggering situations. Moreover, teachers can work with pupils in this endeavour and, in doing so, can enhance pupils' self-awareness and their self-regulation over time. This serves to build trusting and caring pupil-teacher relationships and helps pupils to recognise the physical education context as a 'safe space'. It is important to note, however, that it is not uncommon for teachers to experience uncertainty and apprehension when working with trauma-affected pupils, often having limited training and knowledge to draw on in their practice (Alisic et al., 2012; Gray et al., 2023). As such, there have been efforts made to support teachers in this regard, such as through the development of evidence-informed principles for trauma-aware pedagogies in physical education (see Quarmby et al., 2022).

Reflecting on experiences of supporting trauma-affected pupils within physical education

The importance of being – or perhaps rather, becoming – 'trauma-aware' is evidently receiving increased attention within physical education. However, this can be challenging for teachers – both those who are experienced and those who are newer to the profession (Gray et al., 2023). There is, therefore, a need to consider how teachers become trauma-aware, with reflection being recognised as key in this regard. We take this point as stimulus and, in this section, focus attention on Vince's experiences during his time as a physical education teacher at a Scottish secondary school. Here, Vince reflects on a particular experience of working with the trauma-affected pupil (James) – who was introduced earlier in the chapter – within physical education:

> It is five or six months into the 'point system', a manifestation of the cooperative learning model I have been incorporating into my teaching practice. In each lesson, teams work together to achieve the learning objective and earn points across the significant aspects of learning (Personal Qualities, Physical Fitness, Physical Competencies, and Cognitive Skills).[2] Within each team, pupils uphold a role (captain/coach/counsellor) and, in today's lesson, the lesson objective is to bring together a sequence of movements to execute a table tennis shot of the group's choosing.
>
> The class filter in each passing the 'mood board', tapping which smiley face corresponds to how they are feeling today. I watch closely as the pupils do so, trying to gauge if I need to check in with anyone. I share this responsibility with each group's counsellor, who is available to chat when necessary.

Pupils immediately begin activity on the tables, playing games or rallying with a partner. This 'soft start' to the lesson was agreed by pupils as a good way to allow those with different changing needs the time to get ready and enter the lesson without missing the learning objective during introductory discussions.

The last pupils arrive, including James, who taps the 'sad face' as he brushes past me. 'James' I remark, 'what's going on today, how come you are feeling down?'. James responds with a despondent shrug of the shoulders. I ask if we should put up the traffic lights around the room, he suggests it would be a good idea. 'Okay James, I'll pop the red one over there in that side of the room, and you place the amber and green ones where you like.' 'Okay sir, no probs' he replies.

I have taught James for a number of years, and the traffic light system has been effective in monitoring and regulating his mood. It is a simple strategy for him to identify when he is overwhelmed, off-task, or doing great. James will point to or go and stand next to the traffic light that reflects how he is feeling, where I will meet him to engage in discussion.

Following the class discussion about the learning objective, pupils follow their captain to a table to begin team teaching a selected table tennis shot. The equipment manager, iPad in hand, scans a QR code placed on the table, leading to an instructional video to give pupils hints and tips about the shot. The coach then explains the practice to the rest of the group, who begin practising.

I keep an eye on James, who, after some encouragement from his captain, begins practising the forehand drive. He manages 10 or 15 repetitions, taking on feedback from the group's coach. Following his turn, I quickly head towards his table. 'James...where are we right now?' I ask. 'Green sir, feeling good'. He responds. 'You really applied yourself there James and your coach was buzzing with your progress even in just a few shots - great work!' I exclaim. 'I am going to add 2 points to your personal qualities for showing determination in the task even though you weren't feeling great to begin with - go tell your group.' James permits himself a grin before returning to the group with the good news.

It's not always so straightforward with James. Depending on his mood, often determined by his medication, he can be hyperactive, aggressive, or the opposite, showing reluctance and refusal to engage in lessons. Small routines, such as the mood board and the traffic light system, have shown promise, allowing him to acknowledge if he is in danger of 'blowing up' (red) or if he is 'working well' (green). At either amber or red, it is agreed that he can step outside if the hall becomes too overwhelming, sometimes accompanied by his group's counsellor. It has not always worked, and we have had heated exchanges in the past, but having these strategies in place has allowed for a greater deal of agency and responsibility for James to recognise and respond to his emotions before things boil over.

As the pupils conclude the practice, having had time to give each other feedback on their progress, the lesson draws to a close, and I am heartened to see James place his hand over the smiley face when exiting the hall.

Whilst Vince might not have been wholly aware of it at the time, his practice, as recounted here, resonates strongly with the evidence-informed principles for trauma-aware pedagogies proposed by Quarmby and colleagues (2022). These principles include: ensuring safety and well-being; establishing routines and structures; developing and sustaining positive relationships that foster a sense of belonging; facilitating and responding to youth voice, and; promoting strengths and self-belief (Quarmby et al., 2022). We now consider each of these principles in turn, examining how they are evidenced within Vince's reflection. However, it is important to bear in mind that, reflecting the complex nature of teaching practice, these principles are inter-related, and there are connections across and between principles.

Ensuring safety and well-being: Pupils who have experienced trauma often perceive the world as 'unsafe', which can manifest in hypersensitivity to anything that they feel threatens their safety. Safe environments should be considered from both a physical and emotional perspective and account for pupils' thoughts and feelings on what this means – not just those of the teacher. Vince endeavours to facilitate this by having a 'soft start' to the lesson, whereby pupils can come in, and begin activity, in their own time. He highlights how this was agreed 'by pupils' and was done in an effort to accommodate different needs with regard to changing for lessons. Teachers can also ensure safety and well-being by demonstrating sensitivity, empathy and compassion, and they should allow pupils to speak freely, without fear of being judged. 'Check-ins' have been identified as being useful in this regard (Ellison and Walton-Fisette, 2022; Quarmby et al., 2025) and are clearly a strategy that Vince uses within his practice. He also describes using a 'mood board' to provide a simple means by which pupils can share (non-verbally) how they are feeling as they enter and exit lessons. He can subsequently use this to identify any pupils who are not feeling particularly positive and who might need additional encouragement and support, as was the case with James. Additionally, Vince employed 'traffic light cards', which gave James a means by which to demonstrate how he was feeling during the lesson. If James were to be feeling overwhelmed, he could stand by the red card, which acted as a designated space within the class where he could stop and reflect and discuss how he was feeling with Vince. Ellison and Walton-Fisette (2022) have noted the value of such spaces within physical education, particularly for those pupils who have experienced trauma.

Establishing routines and structures: Routines and structures are particularly important for trauma-affected pupils as they can help to provide a sense of control. It is important, therefore, for pupils to know what is expected in advance, to reduce the likelihood of stress responses and support pupils' self-regulation. Vince endeavours to do this, as discussed above, by having a 'soft start' to the lesson, so pupils know what to expect when they arrive. There are also clearly established routines and structures that Vince has in place to support James within lessons. For example, the 'traffic light cards', discussed above, provide James with a designated space within the class that he can go to should he be feeling overwhelmed. This allows James to take himself away from the lessons – for some 'time out' – and enables Vince to identify that James needs some additional support. Strategies such as this may well be particularly useful for trauma-affected pupils, enabling them to manage their emotions with relevant support from teachers (Quarmby et al., 2025). Physical education teachers can also support trauma-affected pupils by identifying how and when an activity will end – ensuring pupils are aware of this – and signposting any potential changes so that pupils are forewarned.

Developing and sustaining positive relationships that foster a sense of belonging: Trauma-affected pupils can have difficulty trusting adults and forming relationships with peers, which can have significant implications for their engagement in physical education. Teachers should focus on getting to know the pupils in their class by, for example, greeting them, using their names and sitting on their level when speaking. Vince identifies that he has 'taught James for a number of years', and it is clear that he has developed strategies to positively support him within physical education lessons. To do this, he has evidently 'got to know' James – and the adversity he has faced – which Sutherland and Parker (2020) argued is key to supporting pupils. Indeed, communicating relational concepts, such as trust, empathy, kindness, caring and support, can help physical education teachers to develop positive relationships and become trusted adults that pupils can relate to. Vince also tried to do this by 'checking in' with James when he tapped the sad face on the 'mood board' at the beginning of the lesson. In doing so, Vince demonstrated an ethic of care which has been highlighted as being influential in helping to develop and sustain positive relationships (Mordal Moen et al., 2020). That said, Vince also describes how 'it has not always worked', and that there have been 'heated exchanges' in the past. However, by implementing various strategies, Vince has endeavoured to promote and enhance James' self-awareness and self-regulation. As such, he has been able to avoid – or at least, reduce – the need for more punitive disciplinary measures, which Lynch and Curtner-Smith (2019) also caution against.

Facilitating and responding to youth voice: Youth voice can support physical education teachers in understanding pupils' thoughts, feelings and experiences and so consideration needs to be given to how this can be both facilitated and responded to. As Quarmby et al. (2022) noted, this is particularly important for those pupils who have experienced trauma, as it enables them to recognise that an adult is interested in and cares about them. There are various means by which voice might be facilitated (see Quarmby et al., 2025), but Vince does this through both his 'mood board' and the 'traffic light cards' discussed above. These more inadvertent forms of voice enable pupils to share how they are feeling within the lesson without putting them under pressure or necessarily requiring them to discuss this in front of their peers. Vince has also evidently sought out and responded to youth voice with regard to the routines he adopts within his lesson and the 'soft start' which was agreed 'by pupils'. Enabling pupils to participate in decision-making in such ways not only serves to ensure that their needs are taken into account but can also further enhance feelings of safety and promote positive relationships between teacher and pupils.

Promoting strengths and self-belief: Pupils who have experienced trauma are more likely to view themselves negatively, and so promoting their strengths within the context of physical education can help to build self-esteem and self-efficacy. A focus on skill development can allow pupils to develop competencies in a variety of different areas and can serve as a platform for identifying their strengths – something which Vince endeavours to do by recognising attainment across different learning areas. Focusing on what pupils *have* achieved within physical education – even the simple fact that they attended the lesson – represents a shift from traditional deficit approaches. Indeed, by acknowledging effort and perseverance, and demonstrating belief in a pupil's potential to succeed, teachers can signify that success is about extending their own abilities rather than making comparisons with their peers. Vince endeavours to do this with James by positively reinforcing the success that he had within the lesson – which he was not really 'feeling' at the start – and rewarding him with points for determination. Vince also assigns roles to pupils within his lesson, and this act of providing pupils with responsibility could also be seen to be a means by which their strengths and self-belief could be promoted, somewhat akin to the notion of supporting pupils to be model performers, proposed by Quarmby and colleagues (2025).

Summary and key points

We argue that Vince's approach to teaching physical education – as demonstrated through this reflection – was evidently 'trauma-aware'. Indeed, his teaching practice – and the strategies he employed – align closely with the principles for trauma-aware pedagogies in physical education (see Quarmby et al., 2022). This perhaps demonstrates their utility as a framework for teachers endeavouring to be more 'trauma-aware' in their own practice. It is important to note, however, that Vince's intention at the time was not necessarily to be 'trauma-aware'; rather, he was simply trying to meet the needs of his pupils. This is akin to how Quarmby and colleagues (2022) envisaged these being taken up by teachers as they note that the principles for trauma-aware pedagogies largely just reflect what might be termed 'good pedagogy'. It is also noteworthy that Vince enacted this trauma-aware approach in a rather organic and unobtrusive manner, with the rest of the class likely just regarding this as a 'normal' lesson. This means that James was not 'singled out' as a trauma-affected pupil and would not necessarily have been deemed to be getting treated 'differently' by his peers.

Importantly, Vince acknowledged that he did not always 'get it right' and that he had encountered difficulties in the past in seeking to support trauma-affected pupils – such as James – within his lessons. This demonstrates that becoming trauma-aware takes time and is not an easy endeavour for teachers who are likely to face challenges along the way (Gray et al., 2023). However, getting to know his pupils was evidently key in enabling Vince to understand their needs and to implement strategies that work for them (most of the time) within physical education lessons. It is notable, though, that we do not know a great deal about the trauma that James encountered – but we do not necessarily need to. While a pupil's background and context are important, the focus within trauma-aware pedagogy is on working with the pupil with where they are at now. Indeed, trauma-aware pedagogies are very much premised on adopting a strengths-based approach, as opposed to a deficit one (which might often be associated with the notion of trauma). Vince's reflection demonstrates the positive impact that adopting trauma-aware pedagogies can have on young people like James and evidences why it is something that all teachers – especially those within physical education – should be seeking to embrace.

We hope that this chapter encourages teachers to reflect on how they might enact a trauma-aware approach to teaching physical education within their own contexts. To support this, they might consider the five principles for trauma-aware pedagogies proposed by Quarmby and colleagues (2022) and consider: a) the ways in which they might already employ these within their practice and b) other ways in which they might further align with a trauma-aware approach. The strategies for enacting trauma-aware pedagogies outlined by Quarmby and colleagues (2025) might provide useful insight in this respect, to supplement teachers' own ideas.

Notes

1 James is a pseudonym for the pupil referred to within Vince's reflection.
2 The significant aspects of learning represent the broad areas of learning that should be covered within physical education as part of the Scottish curriculum (Education Scotland, 2014).

References

Alisic, E., Bus, M., Dulack, W., Pennings, L. and Splinter, J. (2012) 'Teachers' experiences supporting children after traumatic exposure', *Journal of Traumatic Stress*, 25 (1), 98-101, https://doi.org/10.1002/jts.20709

Bellis, M., Hughes, K., Leckenby, N., Perkins, C. and Lowey, H. (2014) 'National household survey of adverse childhood experiences and their relationship with resilience to health-harming behaviors in England', *BMC Medicine*, 12, 72, https://doi.org/10.1186/1741-7015-12-72

Bergholz, L., Stafford, E. and D'Andrea, W. (2016) 'Creating trauma-informed sports programming for traumatized youth: core principles for an adjunctive therapy approach', *Journal of Infant, Child and Adolescent Psychotherapy*, 15 (3), 244-253, https://doi.org/10.1080/15289168.2016.1211836

Caldeborg, A., Maivorsdotter, N. and Öhman, M. (2019) 'Touching the didactic contract – a student perspective on intergenerational touch in PE', *Sport, Education and Society*, 24 (3), 256-268, https://doi.org/10.1080/13573322.2017.1346600

Ciotto, C. and Gagnon, A. (2018) 'Promoting social and emotional learning in physical education', *Journal of Physical Education, Recreation and Dance*, 89 (4), 27-33, https://doi.org/10.1080/07303084.2018.1430625

Cole, S., O'Brien, J., Gadd, M., Ristuccia, J., Wallace, D. and Gregory, M. (2005) *Helping Traumatized Children Learn: Supportive School Environments for Children Traumatized by Family Violence*, Boston, MA: Massachusetts Advocates for Children.

Education Scotland (2014) *Significant Aspects of Learning in Physical Education*, Livingston: Education Scotland.

Ellison, D.W. and Walton-Fisette, J. (2022) '"It's more about building trust": physical education teachers' experiences with trauma-informed practices', *European Physical Education Review*, 28 (4), 906-922, https://doi.org/10.1177/1356336X221096603

Felitti, V., Anda, R., Nordenberg, D., Williamson, D., Spitz, A., Edwards, V., Koss, M. and Marks, J. (1998) 'Relationship of childhood abuse and household dysfunction to many of the ceading causes of death in adults: the adverse childhood experiences (ACE) Study', *American Journal of Preventative Medicine*, 14 (4), 245-258.

Franke, H. (2014) 'Toxic stress: effects, prevention and treatment', *Children*, 1 (3), 390-402, https://doi.org/10.3390/children1030390

Gray, S., Sandford, R., Quarmby, T. and Hooper, O. (2023) 'Exploring pre-service physical education teachers' trauma-related learning experiences in schools', *Teaching and Teacher Education*, 132, 104212, https://doi.org/10.1016/j.tate.2023.104212

Hooper, O., Sandford, R. and Jarvis, H. (2020) 'Thinking and feeling within/through physical education: What place for social and emotional learning?' in F. Chambers, A. Bryant and D. Aldous (eds) *Threshold Concepts in Physical Education: A Design Thinking Approach*, Abingdon: Routledge, pp. 137-148.

Lynch, S. and Curtner-Smith, M. (2019) '"You have to find your slant, your groove": one physical education teacher's efforts to employ transformative pedagogy', *Physical Education and Sport Pedagogy*, 24 (4), 359-372, https://doi.org/10.1080/17408989.2019.1592146.

Mordal Moen, K., Westlie, K., Gerdin, G., Smith, W., Linnér, S., Philpot, R., Schenker, K. and Larsson, L. (2020) 'Caring teaching and the complexity of building good relationships as pedagogies for social justice in health and physical education', *Sport, Education and Society*, 25 (9), 1015-1028, https://doi.org/10.1080/13573322.2019.1683535

O'Donovan, T., Sandford, R. and Kirk, D. (2015) 'Bourdieu in the changing room', in lisahunter, W. Smith and E. Emerald (eds) *Pierre Bourdieu and Physical Culture*, Abingdon: Routledge, pp. 57-64.

Quarmby, T., Sandford, R. and Elliot, E. (2019) '"I actually used to like PE but not now": understanding care-experienced young people's (dis)engagement with physical education', *Sport, Education and Society*, 24 (7), 714-726, https://doi.org/10.1080/13573322.2018.1456418.

Quarmby, T., Sandford, R., Green, R., Hooper, O. and Avery, J. (2022) 'Developing evidence-informed principles for trauma-aware pedagogies in physical education', *Physical Education and Sport Pedagogy*, 27 (4), 440-454, https://doi.org/10.1080/17408989.2021.1891214.

Quarmby, T., Sandford, R., Hooper, O. and Gray, S. (2025) 'Co-creating strategies for enacting trauma-aware pedagogies with pre-service physical education teachers', *Physical Education and Sport Pedagogy*, 30 (2), 109-122, https://doi.org/10.1080/17408989.2023.2194905.

SAMHSA (Substance Abuse and Mental Health Services Administration) (2014) *SAMHSA's Concept of Trauma and Guidance for a Trauma-Informed Approach*, Rockville, MD: Substance Abuse and Mental Health Services Administration.

Sandford, R., Quarmby, T. and Hooper, O. (2024) 'Theorising the potential of physical education and school sport to support the educational engagement, transitions, and outcomes of care-experienced young people', *British Educational Research Journal*, 50 (2), 580-598. https://doi.org/10.1002/berj.3907

Sandford, R., Quarmby, T., Hooper, O. and Duncombe, R. (2021) 'Navigating complex social landscapes: examining care experienced young people's engagements with sport and physical activity', *Sport, Education and Society*, 26 (1), 15-28, https://doi.org/10.1080/13573322.2019.1699523

Scottish Government (2020) *Scottish Health Survey 2019*, Edinburgh: Scottish Government Health Directorates.

Smith, M. (2018) 'Capability and adversity: reframing the "causes of the causes" for mental health', *Palgrave Communications*, 4 (13), 1-5.

Sutherland, S. and Parker, M. (2020) 'Responding to trauma in and through physical education', *Journal of Physical Education, Recreation and Dance*, 91 (9), 16-21, https://doi.org/10.1080/07303084.2020.1811621

UNESCO (United Nations, Educational, Scientific and Cultural Organization) (2019) *Education as Healing: Addressing the Trauma of Displacement through Social and Emotional Learning (Global Education Monitoring Report No. 38)*, Paris: UNESCO.

Wood, S., Ford, K., Hardcastle, K., Hopkins, J., Hughes, K. and Bellis, M. (2020) *Adverse Childhood Experiences in Child Refugee and Asylum-seeking Populations*, Cardiff: Public Health Wales NHS Trust.

Chapter 13 Challenges related to pupil participation in physical activity and sport outside lessons

What can be done in physical education that might increase young people's participation in physical activity and sport beyond school

Ken Green, Daragh O'Hare, Suzy Twist and Hannah Vecchione

Introduction

What, if anything, can school physical education do to increase the likelihood of young people doing more physical activity (PA) and sport both now and in the future. More specifically, what can physical education teachers, in particular, do in terms of the content, organisation and delivery - of both curricular and extra-curricular physical education - that might increase young people's participation beyond the school day and into the rest of their lives? After all, it seems intuitively plausible that the ultimate goal of school physical education should be laying the foundations for lifelong participation in PA and sport. Which school subject would not aim to make a difference to young people's propensity to utilise and act upon what they have learned beyond their years of compulsory schooling and into adult life, whatever else it might hope to achieve in the meantime?

In order to answer this rhetorical question, the chapter begins by sketching an ideal-typical secondary school physical education scenario. This is followed by a brief summary of what is known about PA and sports participation in England - in terms of rates and forms as well as trends over time - before an examination of what locks young people into PA and sport *per se* and how that is best achieved. A further summary of what is known about lifelong engagement with PA and sport concludes with what might be termed a recipe for lifelong participation. Finally, and in light of the extant research, we discuss just what an ideal-typical school - Marlott Academy - might need to do in order for physical education to contribute to lifelong participation in PA and sport.

In what follows, sport is conceptualised broadly to incorporate more informal and recreational physical activities of the kind often referred to as 'lifestyle sports'. This broader conception of sport is increasingly implicit in studies such as the Youth Sport Trust's (YST) *PE and School Sport* (2023a) report. PA is defined as bodily movement produced by skeletal muscles that results in energy expenditure above basal metabolic rate (Caspersen, Powell and Christenson, 1985; Marshall and Welk, 2008). This, too, is a definition adopted by YST (2023a). Sport is, then, a particular sub-set of PA. Although, in recent years, Sport England have broadened the scope of their young people and adult surveys to incorporate PA beyond sport, much of the research into participation (especially lifelong participation) has focused upon sport, defined broadly (see below). It is worth pointing out in passing, however, that there are additional reasons for concentrating on sport: first, although the ideal-typical Marlott Academy strives to increase pupils' levels of PA and sport, the main vehicle for achieving this goal continues – as with many government policies, such as National Curriculum for Physical Education (NCPE) (see, for example, Sprake and Walker, 2015; Stride et al., 2022), the work of the YST (see, for example, YST, 2024) and the pronouncements of various interested parties (see, for example, Sport and Recreation Alliance, 2024) – to be *sport*; second, it is our contention that sport is more likely to deliver adherence to health-related PA over both the shorter and longer terms.

Scenario part 1 – Marlott Academy as an ideal-type

The concept of 'ideal types' is associated with the sociologist Max Weber (1964-1920) and is used in the social sciences as a kind of conceptual shorthand that brings together key features of a more complex social phenomena or process, such as school physical education, in order to make sense of it. In the 'ideal-typical' school, Marlott Academy, we assemble a number of important features of physical education commonly found in different secondary schools in England but rarely or never found in one school in such an ideal-typical form. Rather than being an exact replication of any one physical education department at any one school, physical education at Marlott represents an intentionally one-sided accentuation of particular features of the subject intended simply to enable us to answer the question, 'What can be done in physical education that might increase young people's participation in physical activity and sport beyond school?'

Physical education at the ideal-typical Marlott Academy consists of boys' and girls' departments that deliver largely gender-stereotypical curricula to single-sex groups. The stated aim of what was once simply referred to as physical education at Marlott, then Physical Education and School Sport (PESS) and, more recently, as PESSPA (Physical Education, School Sport and Physical Activity) is the development of young people's enjoyment of PA and sport, ostensibly in the service of health and well-being. In pursuit of this aim, the department endeavours to develop pupils' 'skills, knowledge and understanding' of a range of PA and sports in a 'well-balanced curriculum' that covers the original six activity areas of the NCPE (Department of Education and Science (DES), 1991), even though, as an academy,[1] the school is technically exempt from the national curriculum. Despite the school's claim to deliver a 'well-balanced' physical education curriculum, the bulk of curricular physical education is given over to sporting activities and, in particular, individual and team games. The girls' curriculum is dominated by netball, hockey and dance while the boys' consists predominantly of football, rugby and basketball. While striving for a minimum of 2 h of 'high-quality physical education and PA and sporting activities' each week, in key stage (KS) 3, pupils receive around 1.5 hours per week over two lessons. Physical education lessons tend to be teacher-led, albeit less so in girls' physical education. Pupils are assessed every half-term following each block of practical activity. At KS4, Marlott offers GCSE physical education, resulting in an additional two lessons per week for pupils on top of their 'core' physical education. All-in-all, as things stand, the content of curricular physical education at Marlott reflects a good deal of continuity revolving, as it does, around the kinds of traditional sporting activities – and sporting techniques – deeply rooted in the history of physical education (see, for example, Kirk, 1992; Stolz and Kirk, 2015) and underscored by NCPE (see, for example, Department for Education (DfE), 2013) as well as the Office for Standards in Education, Children's Services and Skill (Ofsted) (see, for example, Ofsted, 2022).

When it comes to extra-curricular provision, Marlott Academy offers extra-curricular physical education 'clubs' after school on 4 days in a typical week, as well as during lunch time and before school ('breakfast clubs') on 3 days. The focus of after-school extra-curricular physical education is on competitive team games and inter-school sporting competition. The breakfast clubs are more recreational in orientation while the lunch time clubs are a mixture of formal (for example, team practices) and informal sporting activities. Inevitably, the diet of competitive sport that dominates after-school extra-curricular physical education restricts involvement to a relatively small number of pupils (often involved in several different team sports). These pupils are disproportionately drawn from the minority of middle-class pupils enrolled at Marlott; that is to say, the very pupils who are already more likely to have opportunities to participate in PA and sport beyond school. There is a large degree of overlap between these extra-curricular activities and those that dominate curricular physical education (for example, football, rugby, netball and hockey). Consequently, while more activities are delivered in a recreational format (for example, fitness, badminton, dance, yoga), there is relatively little available in extra-curricular physical education that might entice the very many pupils marginalised, even alienated, by conventional physical education (and sport and team games, in particular), whatever their socio-economic background. While Penney and Harris (1997) would discover some changes in the content of extra-curricular physical education (in the direction of more recreational activities) at Marlott from a quarter of a century ago – when they described extra-curricular physical education as 'more of the same, for the more able' (that is, dominated by team games and sporting competition, for those 'good' at sport) – they would also find a great deal of continuity in that bastion of competitive sport. When, at the beginning of the school year, the physical education department organises its extra-curricular programme, inter-school sporting competition continues to be prioritised.

Against this backdrop, attention turns to what is known about the very thing that physical education at Marlott Academy seeks to deliver: participation in PA and sport both now and in the future.

Participation in PA and sport among young people in England

Rates of participation in both PA and sport tend to follow a bell-shaped curve: minorities at each end (doing a little or a lot) and a majority in the middle (doing something on a 'regular' basis), albeit, with a skew towards inactivity. In broad terms, while over half do little or nothing, almost one-half of adults take part in PA and sport monthly, more than one-third weekly, a quarter twice a week and just over one-sixth three times a week or more (Sport England, 2016-2023). Increases in sports participation (if not PA) since the 1970s notwithstanding, it remains the case that participation in both PA and sport declines with age from around 12-14 years (the early secondary school years) (see, for example, Eime et al., 2016) and markedly around the minimum school-leaving age (16/18 years), then around the mid-40s and retirement age (mid- to late-60s). As indicated below, it is the early age at which drop-off and dropout begin that physical education departments, such as Marlott, need to address, *if* they can.

When it comes to forms of sports participation, a marked feature, internationally, since the 1970s, has been a shift from outdoor team sports towards indoor sports, lifestyle sports (see below) and individual recreational exercise[2] (Borgers, Seghers and Scheerder, 2018; Roberts, 2020; Sport England, 2005-2016; Sport England, 2016-2023; Sport England, 2017-2023). This amounts to a broadening and diversification in the kinds of PA and sport undertaken by both adults and young people. Lifestyle sports are characterised as being non- or, at least, less-competitive (than 'traditional' sports), more recreational in nature, flexible, individual or small group activities (that can, in effect, be undertaken in the ways that people want, where they want, with whom they want and when they want), often with a health and fitness orientation.

Despite the fact that only a small minority go on to play competitive sport in their adult lives, the substantial move towards lifestyle sports should not, however, be taken to indicate that more formal sports – and especially competitive games – are in terminal decline among young people. The trends in leisure-time sport among the young reflect a broadening and diversification of participation rather than a wholesale rejection of competitive sport *per se*. Indeed, while it is true to say that, overall, team games have become less popular in participatory terms in England since the latter decades of the twentieth century – especially among secondary-age youngsters – there have been several 'good news' stories; most notably in the popularity of girls' and young women's football and, to a lesser extent rugby (see, for example, Sport England surveys 2016-2023, 2017-2023). This is illustrative of a trend towards greater involvement by girls and young women in historically male-dominated activities. Even though lifestyle sports have become an increasingly prominent feature of the participation profiles of young people and adults, it is evident that a number of sports – such as golf, badminton and martial arts – are not only popular among secondary-age young people (see, for example, Sport England, 2016-2023) in their leisure time but also track into youth and through to adulthood for significant numbers of people (UK Sport/Sport England, 2001).

Lifelong participation: a recipe

The relative increase in participation in sport over the last 50 years notwithstanding, there is no escaping the fact that age has a deleterious effect on involvement (see, for example, Sport England, 2023a). Lessons from studies of adherence to sport, in particular, throughout the life course are pretty clear: it is much easier to keep people in sport – in other words, to stop them dropping out in the first place – than to bring them back. Given the increased survival rates of sports careers[3] once individuals are in their 20s, adult participation rates would rise considerably if more young people could be retained in sport (Roberts and Brodie, 1992). So, what encourages those who remain in sport to do so? Despite the scarcity of longitudinal studies, a fair amount is, in fact, known about the pre-conditions for adherence to sport. There is persuasive evidence that the foundations for sports careers are laid in childhood (see, for example, Engström, 2008; Haycock and Smith, 2014; Knoester and Allison, 2021; Roberts and Brodie, 1992; Roberts, Kovacheva and Kabaivanov, 2020) – in the family, in particular (see, for example, Haycock and Smith, 2014; Johansen and Green, 2019; Qunito Romani, 2020; Strandbu, Bakken and Stefansen, 2020; Wheeler and Green, 2019) – and that later-life involvement in any leisure activity depends largely on the skills and tastes that people carry with them from earlier life stages (Roberts, 2016). In short, young people must develop a proclivity to participate based not only on habit (or what sociologists would call 'habitus') and enjoyment but also on the acquisition of sporting capital (in effect, what young people know and can do) and sporting repertoires. The point about wide sporting repertoires is that – whatever reasons young people have for dropping out of particular sports – if they are typically engaged in several activities, their entire sporting careers tend to be considerably less vulnerable (Roberts and Brodie, 1992) as they progress from childhood through youth to adulthood. The point is this: while it is an open question whether a focus on sport in order to promote health and well-being (as Marlott Academy seeks to do) is likely to bind young people into a lifelong commitment to engaging in health-related PA and sport, it strikes us as highly unlikely, given their well-established preference for fun and enjoyment in physical education (see below). Indeed, it is argued that a more indirect approach, focusing on participation in PA and sport for its own sake (that is, for the intrinsic pleasures that it brings), is far more likely to deliver some of the health benefits those preoccupied with health-related PA seek than a focus upon activity for largely extrinsic reasons (that is, health promotion) (see, for example, Rindler, Luiggi and Griffet, 2022). After all, encouraging healthier lifestyles requires young people to be not only recruited but also retained, not just throughout youth, but for their entire subsequent adult lives.

Scenario part 2 – the implications for Marlott Academy

Having reflected upon what is known about sports participation in England as well as what we think we know about lifelong participation, we now turn to what seem to us to be the take-home lessons for physical education at Marlott Academy in terms of the content, organisation and delivery of the subject.

Physical education at Marlott Academy

If we allow ourselves to put to one side the potential significance of primary physical education for embedding PA and sporting habits during the early years – and in the absence of a substantial and significant improvement in the resources (time, equipment, teachers/coaches, facilities) available for physical education in feeder primary schools – we inevitably return to the question 'What role might the physical education department at Marlott Academy have in locking its pupils into PA and sport?' The obvious place to begin is with the content of physical education, both curricular and extra-curricular.

The content of physical education at Marlott Academy

In order to encourage PA and sporting habits and the acquisition of PA and sporting capital (relevant PA and sporting skills, knowledge and understanding), the content of curricular physical education needs to be more cognisant of, and in tune with, the broader trends in young people's lives and, in particular, their leisure lifestyles. This would require the introduction of lifestyle sports wherever feasible (from relatively easy-to-deliver activities such as fitness, yoga and contemporary dance through to more logistically problematic activities involving types of blading, boarding and biking) *alongside* "traditional" sports and games. In addition, the 'activity area' of games would need to include those that not only track into adulthood (for example, golf) but also those that have cultural traction with ethnic minorities (for example, kabaddi) and contemporary appeal among girls (for example, football, rugby and basketball). At the same time, the physical education department needs to embrace the small-sided and more recreational variants (such as kwik-cricket, tag and touch rugby and futsal) of the team games that continue to form such a staple of their physical education offer if they are to retain many pupils' interest, let alone encourage new participants from among those pupils currently disengaged from PA and sport or on the margins of participation. Overall, while there are clear indications of change alongside the undoubted continuity in the make-up of physical education at Marlott, perhaps inevitably changes to the content of curricular physical education have occurred considerably more slowly than young people's leisure-sport lifestyles. Facilitated by the relative freedom in the NCPE for schools to design physical education curricula around the 'needs' of pupils, Marlott has slowly but steadily broadened its array of individual (for example, badminton and table tennis) and team (for example, basketball for boys and football and rugby for girls) games on offer. However, newer, lifestyle (in effect, more recreational) sports and activities need to be introduced if the physical education curriculum is to be more closely aligned with young people's preferred leisure-sport lives. One area of the physical education curriculum that currently enables the creative introduction of alternative lifestyle activities – such as yoga, boxercise, walking or even spinning at the local gym as one-off 'taster' sessions – is the health-related exercise unit.

The slow but sure broadening and diversification of the content of physical education should not be taken to imply, however, that sport-based physical education curricula are devoid of merit in relation to the goal of lifelong participation and should, therefore, be sidelined. As hinted at above, the physical education teachers at Marlott are correct when they insist that sport and team games continue to hold a place in both the tastes and participatory repertoires of many young people. While many may not like physical education programmes dominated by traditional sports, it seems that they want such activities supplemented by other, more recreational, activities in broader curricula rather than simply expunged. In this regard, Marlott's physical education department is equally justified in their belief that, at the secondary level especially, multi-activity physical education programmes can provide a broad base of experiences (and familiarisation with the requisite skills) while encouraging pupils to be discriminating, in order that they can pick their own mixes from the opportunities that are available. In the promotion of lifelong participation, it seems that what matters is not so much what physical education teachers might anticipate young people doing as adults or even what activities they do in the present – whether young people experience precisely the same activities at school as those they appear likely to engage in as adults does not appear to be crucial. What seems to matter more is enabling them to develop a repertoire or portfolio of PA and sporting interests and skills. Some of these will endure whilst others will be replaced, supplemented or even dropped as their lives unfold.

Perhaps the most obvious aspect of their provision that the physical education department at Marlott needs to tailor more to the tastes of the pupils is extra-curricular physical education. If it is to have any chance of serving as a 'fundamental link' (Penney and Harris, 1997) between curricular physical education and young people's leisure-sport lifestyles, let alone as a vehicle for reaching young people who are generally inactive in leisure sport (De Meester et al., 2014), then extra-curricular physical education needs to change quite dramatically. As things stand, the emphasis upon inter- (and intra-) school competitive sport in conventional games (especially football and netball), means that extra-curricular physical education amounts to Penney and Harris' (1997) 'more of the same for the more able'. Very few extra-curricular activities encourage those pupils on the margins of PA and sport, let alone those inactive, to attend extra-curricular clubs. There are indications of change – in the case of the more recreational 'breakfast clubs', including drop-in badminton and basketball, for example. However, the balance between clubs focused upon training for, and competition in, conventional sports and more recreational, lifestyle sports, as well as the aforementioned 'sport light' versions of team games (Borgers, Seghers and Scheerder, 2018), such as touch and tag rugby and futsal, needs redrawing towards the latter.

This issue of content is intimately related to the organisation and delivery of curricular and extra-curricular physical education at Marlott.

The organisation and delivery of physical education at Marlott Academy

As previously indicated, when it comes to how physical education is organised and taught, we need to keep in mind that the three main perceived drivers for, and benefits of, PA and sports participation are enjoyment (having fun), socialising (spending time with friends) and health and fitness (YST, 2023a). Beyond being an inherent aspect of games, competition should not, we suggest, be a central focus of the subject at Marlott, if physical education is to draw more pupils in and retain them throughout their secondary school careers. The evidence is overwhelming that young people respond better to fun and collaborative approaches (see, for example, Department for Education, Department for Digital, Culture, Media and Sport, and Department of Health and Social Care (DfE, DCMS and DHSC), 2023). However, as important as a pedagogical approach that prioritises enjoyment of the task at hand and the development of a basic level of competence is (Parry, 2013), pupils also desire a say in shaping their own experiences (MacPhail, 2010; Mitchell, Gray and Inchley, 2015). On the face of it, Marlott's physical education department recognises the importance of giving pupils a choice of activities in order to improve engagement – enabling pupils to do the things they choose with the people they choose, when, where and how they choose. As things stand, however, 'activity choice' is restricted solely to core physical education at KS4 (that is, years 10 and 11). All-in-all, the physical education teachers at Marlott need to recognise that there has been a real shift in what contemporary young people are interested in and want to experience in curricular and extra-curricular physical education. There needs to be something of a democratisation of physical education in both primary and secondary schools, in terms of pupil consultation on the content of physical education, alongside an element of activity choice throughout the secondary years but especially as pupils get older. This applies especially to girls' physical education. It is worth noting, however, that any latent inclination to democratise the content, organisation and delivery of physical education that the physical education department at Marlott may have harboured has been given some impetus by the impact of COVID on young people's involvement in PA and sport and concomitant levels of (health-related) PA.

All that said, curricular as well as extra-curricular physical education at Marlott continues to be organised around what might be termed a 'privileging' of sport and team games which, in their delivery, emphasise performance over participation, thereby exacerbating the already existing differences in participation – rather than reducing inequalities – and further diminishing the enjoyment of those pupils who were already less likely to be active (see Parry, 2013). Any shift in the direction of facilitating participation for its own sake is not indicative, however, of a fundamental shift in philosophy among the physical education teachers at Marlott (see Green, 2000, 2002). On the whole, they remain steadfast in their desire to highlight the ostensibly educational dimension of physical education and somewhat resistant to the idea of physical education as physical *recreation*. This is perfectly understandable, even inevitable, given (a) the deep-seated and long-standing conviction among very many physical educationalists that there is considerably more to physical education than merely sports participation for its own sake; and (b) the pressure on physical education departments to contribute to wider school success in the contemporary educational market (see, for example, Green, 2005, 2008). Thus, physical education at Marlott tends to reflect not only the wider demands of the school and the requirements of NCPE and Ofsted but also the preferences of staff and their deeply socialised tastes and habits (their predispositions or habitus). Consequently, sport continues to dominate much of the physical education provision (and boys' physical education, in particular). Some activities are, of course, taught more not only because of staff tastes and habits but also because of their skills and expertise. When planning curricula and extra-curricular physical education, the head of department inevitably finds herself catering for teachers as well as pupils. That said, there is a perception that female physical education teachers are more likely to embrace – and be prepared to deliver – a broader physical education curriculum. There is also evidence to suggest that the teachers in the department recognise the need to "upskill" themselves in order to feel more comfortable teaching some of the newer lifestyle activities, such as dance, yoga and parkour. While the physical education teachers may be very reluctant to make physical education more recreational – not least for fear of making the position of the subject vulnerable on the school curriculum, let alone contravening the strictures of NCPE and Ofsted – if it is to impact pupils' propensity to participate in PA and sport both now and in the future, this is what needs to happen; at the very least in extra-curricular physical education. It is worth reminding ourselves not only that fun appears to be a critical factor in making physical education enjoyable (Dismore and Bailey, 2011) but also, that for many pupils, physical education and sport were last seen as fun in primary school (Parry, 2013). The intrinsic enjoyment of PA and sport often gets lost in secondary school as it starts to be perceived as a more serious, competitive pursuit for those who are 'good' at it – pupils who enjoyed playing PA and sports at primary school often find, later on, that they are unwanted in PA and sports teams and clubs that are interested in recruiting and retaining only those players who will strengthen them (Parry, 2013; Roberts, 2016).

Caveats

Notwithstanding our observations regarding what would need to change at Marlott for physical education to impact pupils' participation in PA and sport, it is important to acknowledge some of the constraints that would complicate matters. In the first instance, it is important to bear in mind that physical education at Marlott does not occur in a vacuum. It is not simply that the school's physical education department has a history – the pupils it teaches also have a history! One potentially vital aspect of that history is primary physical education. It is clear from the growing body of research into sporting careers that early intervention is crucial if young people are to begin to develop the necessary PA and sporting habits, PA and sporting capital and PA and sporting repertoires that – if sustained through the secondary school years – would significantly increase their chances of becoming locked-in to PA and sport over the life course. Primary physical education may be decisive in two ways: first, in going some way to making good any deficiencies in PA and sport among those pupils not fortunate enough to experience PA and sports socialisation in the family (Wheeler and Green, 2019) while, at the same time, building upon the PA and sporting skills and repertoires of those pupils who have, indeed, been fortunate enough to have such exposure to PA and sport in the family; second, in preparing pupils for secondary school physical education. In this regard, although the content of both primary and secondary physical education has broadened in recent decades, the continued prioritisation of games has indirectly been boosted by the impact of the [primary] physical education and PA and sport premium (PESP) in Marlott's feeder primary schools. Despite some having physical education specialists as curriculum 'leads', very many have tended to enter into contracts (and/or a 'pay-as-you-go' arrangement) with sports coaching companies. As we know, these businesses tend to be populated by young sportsmen and women inclined, unsurprisingly, to deliver games at every opportunity (Jones and Green, 2017; Smith, 2015; Sperka and Enright, 2018). Either way, whether delivered by external sports coaches, generalist class teachers or physical education specialists, physical education programmes dominated by sport, and team games in particular, cannot be justified in terms of trends in participation among young people. Such physical education programmes inevitably alienate many pupils on the margins of participation who dabble in PA and sport and may be biddable with a more appealing physical education diet.

Evidence of some change alongside continuity notwithstanding, the stubbornly conservative character of curricular and extra-curricular physical education tends to be reinforced by wider school demands. While some headteachers doubtless value physical education and school sport in its own right, many may see sport as a marketing tool for reputation and pupil recruitment. Yet, while inter-school sporting competition and sporting success may have reputational benefits, it is also likely to have unintended consequences for the ostensible role of extra-curricular physical education as a catalyst for wider PA and sports participation among young people. On the one hand, there is an opportunity cost in relation to the provision of other, potentially more widely appealing, extra-curricular clubs. On the other hand, successful sports teams inevitably tend to make increasing demands on physical education teachers' time, not least in terms of the organisation and staffing of fixtures. While it may be extremely difficult to challenge the dominance of sport and team games, it is our contention that it must be challenged if extra-curricular physical education is to play the role that is claimed for it in providing a link between curricular physical education and young people's involvement in leisure-time PA and sport.

When it comes to the academicisation of physical education (see, for example, Brown and Penney, 2018; Green, 2005, 2008; Stidder, 2022), it would seem churlish – especially in the context of the contemporary educational marketplace – to challenge the view among the physical education teachers at Marlott that examinable physical education can play a part in promoting ongoing participation in PA and sport; nonetheless, we must. The relatively rapid expansion of examinable physical education and its apparent significance for the status and influence of physical education departments – as physical education redefines itself as an academic subject – is well-established (see, for example, Brown and Penney, 2018; Green, 2005, 2008). However, in relation to lifelong participation, the demands of examinable physical education inevitably tend to compromise the range of activities and degree of choice available to pupils in KS4 physical education at Marlott. Physical education departments have always to keep in mind the need to prepare pupils for examinable physical education, whether GCSE or BTEC or even A level at KS5. Indeed, recent changes in both the theoretical and practical expectations for BTEC – in terms of what the pupils and their schools need to demonstrate in order to evidence performance – mean that more demands are made of physical education departments in both curricular and extra-curricular physical education. Anecdotal instances abound of the content of physical education at KS4 (and even KS3) being shaped by the perceived need to prepare pupils to meet exam board expectations. In addition, the demands of examinable physical education continue to limit the ability of physical education teachers to contribute to extra-curricular physical education, in particular. Similar issues arise with regard to assessment in physical education more broadly – not so much in terms of its utility for physical education teachers in establishing what pupils can and cannot do but, rather, in terms of the unintended consequence of assessment for pupils' enjoyment of and engagement with school physical education, let alone the impact upon the already limited amount of time available to the subject. The demands of assessment (and Ofsted scrutiny thereof) mean that primary and secondary schools can find themselves needing to 'evidence learning' and, in effect, 'teaching to the test' – preparing their pupils for the inevitable 'end of block' assessment (on skill, knowledge and leadership, for example). Once again, however, many physical education teachers' genuine commitment to so-called formative assessment or 'assessment for learning' should not be downplayed (see, for example, Hay, 2006; López-Pastor et al., 2013).

All-in-all, it would be too easy to point the finger at the physical education teachers and suggest that they are distracted by the desire to improve their subject's educational status, whether through examinable physical education or school sporting success. Nonetheless, it is Ofsted that constrain teachers to formally assess physical education, with all the implications that has for pupils enjoyment of and engagement with the subject. The more Ofsted intervene in such a manner, the more the potential for physical education to act as an enclave in which youngsters can escape an increasingly pressure-laden and stressful academically oriented curriculum is jeopardised. This is, perhaps, the ultimate irony. If, as is typically assumed, the over-arching goal of physical education is the encouragement of lifelong participation in PA and sport, and if "being with friends and peers while engaging in joyful activities are generally the most often reported reasons for taking part in PA and sports" (Persson et al., 2020, p.853), then assessment in physical education seems likely to prove counter-productive with the very pupils on the margins of PA and sports participation that the subject seeks to recruit.

Summary and key points

Improving the participation rates and levels of adults is not simply a problem of introducing young people to PA and sport – they already do a lot during the primary and early secondary years both in and out of school. The problem is the likelihood that young people will drop out of sport and physically active recreational pursuits at key periods of transition in their lives: for example, when they transfer from primary to secondary school and when they leave compulsory education. It is simply less convenient to play PA and sport at times in people's lives when they are developing alternative interests and are constrained by a variety of contextual pressures. But the difficulties or barriers to participation are not insuperable. If people can survive these key transitions – and particularly that from childhood to youth (in effect, from primary to secondary school and on into the early post-school years) – then they may well be locked-in to PA and sport for a long time and possibly for life. Getting young people involved early then reducing dropout during the early teenage years is likely to be the best strategy for boosting participation. Herein lies the potential role of physical education; that is to say, in introducing pupils to PA and sport for their own sake (that is, the intrinsic pleasures to be found therein, especially in the company of friends) and helping them develop a mix or repertoire of activities (and relevant skills) that they engage with habitually (therefore, regularly). Because it is easier to keep people in PA and sport than bring them back, the wider the PA and sporting repertoires young people carry with them the more likely their PA and sports careers are to survive the transitions from childhood through youth into adulthood (Roberts, Kovacheva and Kabaivanov, 2020). In this regard, simply promoting existing PA and sports among young people more vigorously and extensively through schools and sports clubs will not yield lifelong changes. There needs to be a significant shift in not only content but also organisation and delivery.

UK government policy does not help much here, if at all. The claim that "Where schools provide high quality physical education and young people play sport, they equip young people to continue that participation into their later lives" (DfE, DCMS and DHSC, 2023, p.7) is simplistic in the extreme. There is far more to lifelong participation than physical education in the form that the NCPE and Ofsted champion. However, this narrative has run for years, and there is no sign of a significant shift in government thinking, vis-à-vis physical education, away from competitive PA and sport towards physically active recreation in the form of lifestyle sports. The centrality of sport and competition to extra-curricular physical education tends to be bolstered by individual school as well government policies. Under the heading 'Extra-curricular sport and competition', the DfE, DCMS and DHSC (2023, p.13), for example, highlighted an expectation that NCPE will "introduce young people to competitive sport in their timetabled PE lessons" and make "[F]urther competitive opportunities … available through intra school competitions and competitions against other schools". In the context of the demands made by NCPE and Ofsted, it is very difficult for those physical education teachers at Marlott Academy who may harbour an inclination to adopt a different, more recreational approach to extra-curricular physical education to gain traction for their ideas.

As if to compound matters, it must be acknowledged that physical education cannot easily over-ride tastes and habits that have their roots in family cultures and the social dynamics (such as social class) that more-or-less shape these. This does not mean, however, that physical education interventions cannot be effective. As noted above, PA and sport attract young people independently of their socio-economic origins. Suitable physical education might, therefore, modify the PA and sporting repertoires that pupils develop and enable all to explore the leisure-sport opportunities their circumstances allow. Nor should it be taken to downplay or diminish the significance of enthusiastic physical education teachers for sparking interest among pupils on the margins of involvement in PA and sport.

We conclude by reflecting on the fact that a focus on competitive sport (and team games in particular) and health-related exercise has clearly not delivered either the kinds of health benefits – nor increases in PA and sports participation among the young– hoped for and even expected by government, YST and physical educationalists, including the physical education staff at Marlott Academy. With more than half of young people in England failing to meet national guidelines on levels of health-related PA – and sedentariness growing with rates of obesity among the young higher than before the pandemic (YST, 2023b) – perhaps it is time for the kind of re-imagination and re-design of school physical education (see, for example, Lawson, 2018) that YST (2023b) hinted at when they argued that "If we want an active and healthier nation, physical education must be focused on helping young people firstly develop a positive relationship with – and then enjoyment of – one or more PA and sports and activities". It is high time, therefore, that we sought to discover whether a greater focus on physical *recreation* rather than physical *education* and the development of pupils' PA and sporting tastes and repertoires – by populating curricular and extra-curricular physical education with more of the relatively new lifestyle sports and giving pupils more say in what they do – can make a difference in terms of locking more young people into PA and sport (and, by extension, PA) both now and in the future. It must be said, however, that this proposal may well amount to a flight of fancy, given (a) the perfectly understandable perceived need among physical education teachers to play-up the supposedly educational aspects of physical education and, within that, competitive sport, and (b) successive governments' determination to treat physical education as tantamount to sport in schools.

Notes

1. Academies are self-governing schools in England that receive funding direct from central government rather than being local-authority-maintained. Approximately 80% of secondary schools are academies or free schools (new state schools that operate as academies) and account for a similar percentage of secondary school pupils.
2. What Sport England tends to refer to as PA.

3 The term sporting career refers to the sequence of sporting forms (formal and informal) and individual sports that characterise young people's sporting repertoires (the stock or blend of sports that a person regularly and habitually engages in and, more specifically, the number and differing forms of activity involved) during a particular period. Thus, young people's sporting careers are typically built upon and enabled by previous experiences, leading to what are referred to, below, as a PA and sporting habitus. The significance of the concept of a PA and sporting career lies in what it may tell us about the mix of structural and agentic influences during their school lives; that is, the ways in which the structural influences of PESSPA and formal sporting organisations begin to lose hold as young people reflexively exercise degrees of agency in constructing their sporting repertoires in the company, typically, of their friends and peers as they get older.

References

AfPE (Association for Physical Education) (2023) *Concrete Crisis: Advice for the PESSPA Workforce 04/09/2023*, available at: https://www.afpe.org.uk/physical-education/concrete-crisis-advice-for-the-pesspa-workforce/ (accessed 20 September 2023).

Borgers, J., Seghers, J. and Scheerder, J. (2018) 'Dropping out from clubs, dropping into PA and sport light? organizational settings for young people PA and sports', in K. Green and A. Smith (eds.) *Routledge Handbook of Youth Sport*, Abingdon: Routledge, pp.158–174.

Brown, T.D. and Penney, D. (2018) *Examination Physical Education. Policy, Practice and Possibilities*, Abingdon: Routledge.

Caspersen, C.J., Powell, K.E. and Christenson, G.M. (1985) 'Physical activity, exercise, and physical fitness: definitions and distinctions for health-related research', *Public Healt Report*, 100 (2), 126–131.

DCMS/NAO (Department for Digital, Culture, Media and sport) and the National Audit Office (2022) *Grassroots Participation in Sport and Physical Activity*, London: NAO.

De Meester, A., Aelterman, N., Cardon, G., De Bourdeaudhuij, L. and Haerens, L. (2014) 'Extracurricular school-based sports as a motivating vehicle for sports participation in youth: a cross-sectional study', *International Journal of Behavioral Nutrition and Physical Activity*, 11 (48), 1–15.

Department of Education and Science (DES) (1991) *Physical Education for Ages 5 to 16*, London: DES.

DfE (Department for Education) (2013) *National Curriculum in England: PE Programmes of Study*, London: DfE.

DfE (Department for Education) (2014) *Physical Activity and Sport Premium for Primary Schools*, London: DfE.

DfE, DCMS and DHSC (Department for Education, Department for Digital, Culture, Media and Sport and Department of Health and Social Care) (2023) *School Sport and Activity Action Plan 2023 Update*, London: DfE, DCMS, DHSC.

Dismore, H. and Bailey, R. (2011) 'Fun and enjoyment in physical education: young people's attitudes', *Research Papers in Education*, 26 (4), 499–516.

Eime, R.M., Harvey, J.T., Charity, M.J., Casey, M.M., Westerbeek, H. and Payne, W.R. (2016) 'Age profiles of sports participants', *BMC Sports Science, Medicine and Rehabilitation*, 8 (6), 1–10.

Engström, L.-M. (2008) 'Who is physically active? cultural capital and PA and sports participation from adolescence to middle age – a 38-year follow-up study', *Physical Education and Sport Pedagogy*, 13 (4), 319–343.

Green, K. (2000) 'Exploring physical education teachers' everyday "philosophies" from a sociological perspective', *Sport, Education and Society*, 5 (2), 109–129, pp.1–37.

Green, K. (2002) 'Physical education teachers in their figurations: a sociological analysis of everyday "philosophies" in physical education', *Sport, Education and Society*, 7 (1), 65–83.

Green, K. (2005) 'Examinations: the "new orthodoxy" in physical education', in K. Green and K. Hardman (eds) *Physical Education: Essential Issues*, London: Sage Publications, pp.143–160.

Green, K. (2008) *Understanding Physical Education*, London: Sage.

Green, K. (2014) 'Mission impossible? reflections on the relationship between physical education, young people, sport and lifelong participation', *Sport, Education and Society*, 19 (4), 357–375.

Hay, P.J. (2006) 'Assessment for learning in physical education', in D. Kirk, D. Macdonald and M. O'Sullivan (eds) *Handbook of Physical Education*, London: Sage Publications, pp.312–325.

Haycock, D. and Smith, A. (2014) 'A family affair? exploring the influence of childhood sports socialisation on young adults' leisure-sport careers in north-west England', *Leisure Studies*, 33 (3), 285-304.

Johansen, P.F. and Green, K. (2019) '"It's alpha omega for succeeding and thriving": parents, young people and PA and sporting cultivation in Norway', *Sport, Education and Society*, 24 (4), 427-440.

Jones, L. and Green, K. (2017) 'Who teaches primary physical education? change and transformation through the eyes of subject leaders', *Sport, Education and Society*, 22 (6), 759-771.

Kirk, D. (1992) *Defining Physical Education: The Social Construction of a School Subject in Post-war Britain*, London: Routledge.

Knoester, C. and Allison, R. (2021) 'U.S. family cultures of sport and physical activity and 15-year-olds' physical activity, sport, and subjective health', *Leisure Studies*, 41 (4), 517-530.

Lawson, H. (ed.) (2018) *Redesigning Physical Education: An Equity Agenda in Which Every Child Matters*, Abingdon: Routledge.

López-Pastor, V.M., Kirk, D., Lorente-Catalán, E., MacPhail, A. and Macdonald, D. (2013) 'Alternative assessment in physical education: a review of international literature', *Sport, Education and Society*, 18 (1), 57-76.

MacPhail, A. (2010) 'Listening to young people' voices', in R. Bailey (ed.) *Physical Education for Learning: A Guide for Secondary Schools*, London: Bloomsbury, pp.228-238.

Marshall, S.J. and Welk, G.J. (2008) 'Definitions and measurement', in A.L. Smith and S.J.H. Biddle (eds) *Youth Physical Activity and Sedentary Behavior*, Champaign, IL: Human Kinetics, pp.3-29.

Mitchell, F., Gray, S. and Inchley, J. (2015) '"This choice thing really works…". changes in experiences and engagement of adolescent girls in physical education classes, during a school-based physical activity programme', *Physical Education and Sport Pedagogy*, 20 (6), 593-611.

Ofsted (Office for Standards in Education, Children's Services and Skills) (2022) *Research Review Series: PE*, London: Ofsted, available at: https://www.gov.uk/government/publications/research-review-series-pe/research-review-series-pe (accessed 12 October 2024).

ONS (Office for National Statistics) (2005-2012) *Taking Part Survey*(s) 2005/06-2011/12, London: DCMS.

Park, C.W. and Curtner-Smith, M. (2018) 'Impact of occupational socialisation on South Korean teachers' reading and delivery of physical education', *Curriculum Studies in Health and Physical Education*, 9, 107-122.

Parry, W. (2013) *Experiences of Physical Activity at Age 10 in the 1970 British Cohort Study*, London: University of London, Working paper 2013/6.

Penney, D. and Harris, J. (1997) 'Extra-curricular physical education: more of the same for the more able?', *Sport, Education and Society*, 2 (1), 41-54.

Persson, M., Espedalen, L.E., Stefansen, K. and Strandbu, Å. (2020) 'Opting out of youth sports: how can we understand the social processes involved?', *Sport, Education and Society*, 25 (7), 842-854.

Qunito Romani, A. (2020) 'Parental behaviour and children's sports participation: evidence from a Danish longitudinal school study', *Sport, Education and Society*, 25 (3), 332-347.

Rindler, V., Luiggi, M. and Griffet, J. (2022) 'Fostering unorganized PA and sport to sustain adolescent participation: empirical evidence from two European countries', *Sport, Education and Society*, 27(7), 862-877.

Roberts, K. (2016) 'Young people leisure as the context for young people PA and sport', in K. Green and A. Smith (eds) *Routledge Handbook of Youth Sport*, Abingdon: Routledge, pp.18-25.

Roberts, K. (2020) 'Locked down leisure in Britain', *Leisure Studies*, 39 (5), 617-628.

Roberts, K. (2023) 'Time use, work and leisure in the UK before, during, between and following the Covid-19 lockdowns', *Leisure Studies*, 42 (1), 56-68.

Roberts, K. and Brodie, D. (1992) *Inner-City Sport: Who Plays and What Are the Benefits?* Culemborg: Giordano Bruno.

Roberts, K., Kovacheva, S. and Kabaivanov, S. (2020) 'Careers in participant PA and sport and other free time activities during young people and young adulthood in south and east Mediterranean countries', *Athens Journal of Sports*, 7, 1-16.

Roberts, K., Minten, J.H., Chadwick, C., Lamb, K.L. and Brodie, D.A. (1991) 'PA and sporting lives: a case study of leisure careers', *Loisir et Societe/Society and Leisure*, 14, 261-84.

Smith, A. (2015) 'Primary school physical education and PA and sports coaches: evidence from a study of school sport partnerships in north-west England', *Sport, Education and Society*, 20 (7), 872–888.

Sperka, L. and Enright, E. (2018) 'The outsourcing of health and physical education: a scoping literature review', *European Physical Education Review*, 24 (3), 349–371.

Sport and Recreation Alliance (2024) *Using Sport to Promote Children's Mental Health and Wellbeing*, available at: https://www.sportandrecreation.org.uk/news/children (accessed 29 February 2024).

Sport England (2005–2016) *Active People Survey(s) 1–11*, 2005/06–2015/16, London: Sport England.

Sport England (2016–2023) *Active Lives Adult Survey(s) 1–7*, 2016/17–2022/23, London: Sport England.

Sport England (2017–2023) *Active Lives Children and Young People Survey(s) 1–6*, 2017/18–2022/23, London: Sport England.

Sport England (2023a) 'Adults' activity levels in England bounce back to pre-pandemic levels', available at: https://www.sportengland.org/news/youngpeoples-activity-levels-recover-pre-pandemiclevels (accessed 26 September 2023)..

Sport England (2023b) 'Young people's activity levels in England bounce back to pre-pandemic levels', available at: https://www.sportengland.org/news/youngpeoples-activity-levels-recover-pre-pandemiclevels (accessed 26 September 2023).

Sport England (2024) *School Game*, available at: https://www.sportengland.org/funds-and-campaigns/children-and-young-people?section=school_games (accessed 20 February 2024).

Sprake, A. and Walker, S. (2015) '"Blurred lines": the duty of physical education to establish a unified rationale', *European Physical Education Review*, 21 (3), 394–406.

Stidder, G. (2022) *Teaching Physical Education*, Abingdon: Routledge.

Stolz, S.A. and Kirk, D. (2015) 'David Kirk on physical education and sport pedagogy: in dialogue with Steven Stolz (part 1)', *Asia-Pacific Journal of Health, Sport and Physical Education*, 6 (1), 77–91.

Strandbu, A., Bakken, A. and Stefansen, K. (2020) 'The continued importance of family PA and sport culture for PA and sport participation during the teenage years', *Sport Education and Society*, 25 (8), 931–945.

Stride, A., Brazier, R., Piggott, S., Staples, M. and Flintoff, A. (2022) 'Gendered power alive and kicking? An analysis of four English secondary school PE departments', *Sport, Education and Society*, 27 (3), 244–258.

UK Sport/Sport England (2001) *Participation in Sport, Past Trends and Future Prospects*, London: Sport England.

Wheeler, S. and Green, K. (2019) '"The fixtures, the kits, the gear, the gum shields, the food, the snacks, the waiting, the rain, the car rides…": social class, parenting and young people's organized leisure', *Sport, Education and Society*, 24 (8), 788–800.

YST (Youth Sport Trust) (2022) *PE and School Sport in England*, Loughborough: YST.

YST (Youth Sport Trust) (2023a) *PE and School Sport. The Annual Report 2023*, Loughborough: YST available at: https://www.youthsporttrust.org/research-listings/research/pe-school-sport-the-annual-report-2023 and https://www.youthsporttrust.org/reimagine-pe (accessed 21 September 2023).

YST (Youth Sport Trust) (2023b) *The Youth Sport Trust Believe It's Time to Re-imagine Why and How we Teach PE*, available at: https://www.youthsporttrust.org/reimagine-pe (accessed 26 September 2023).

YST (Youth Sport Trust) (2024) *National Schools Sports Week 2024*, available at: https://www.youthsporttrust.org/school-support/nssw (accessed 29 February 2024).

Chapter 14 Challenges related to my own context

Identifying and addressing challenges in my own teaching

Julia Lawrence

Introduction

Teachers face a range of challenges each day. These may relate to the activities or to the pupils being taught or to the wider contexts in which they work. How these challenges are identified and acted upon is an important process.

Over recent years, there has been a rise in the use of evidence-based/informed practice to support teachers in identifying where change might be needed in order to improve pupil learning outcomes and the strategies that might be adopted to make this change. In particular, in England, the evolution of research schools and organisations such as the Education Endowment Foundation (EEF) and Evidence Based Education (EBE), coupled with the emergence of 'Walkthru' (see, for example, Sherrington, 2020), provide sources of evidence to support teachers.

This chapter starts by introducing the case study school. It then considers how models of change and implementation can be used to support teachers to explore and use evidence to inform changes to their own practice in order to improve pupil learning outcomes. Drawing heavily on the EEF (2019) *Implementation Guidance*, it looks at key considerations, processes and actions to be put into place to support change, including effective professional development. Throughout, the chapter returns to the case study school to reflect on the actions the school undertook and how they sought to implement change to support pupils' engagement in, and the resulting impact on, their learning.

Case study: part 1

Fortyfoot is a rural secondary school in a large Northern county. The school has recently set up a partnership to support the delivery of an academic qualification alongside a football academy. The pupils who attend this provision travel from across a wide geographical area and have chosen this route as a way of gaining academic qualifications alongside their passion for football.

The provision is different to more tradition methods of delivery, in that it is delivered as a hybrid model – with provision delivered off-site (at a local theme park) and at the school. The academic content of the programme is delivered solely by teachers based at the school.

Whilst the programme has recruited well, there are some difficulties emerging in relation to engagement and retention on the academic programme. Pupils attending do so because they are passionate about football. However, most pupils do not have the same passion towards the academic side of the programme, resulting in poor attendance and engagement in learning. Overall, those attending see the academic aspect of the programme as a means to an end.

The teaching team are conscious that all those attending the academy need to secure their academic as well as their sport-related qualifications. However, they know that the current approach to delivery is not effective and therefore a change is needed to engage pupils and retain more pupils on the programme.

Models of change and how the change process might be implemented are considered next in relation to the case study (above).

Models of change

Models of change are not new, for example, Lewin (1947) proposed a three-step model for making change, that is,

- unfreeze – identifying the need for change
- change – identifying the benefits of change
- refreeze – reinforcing the change.

Kotter (1996) proposed an eight-stage model, structured as follows:

- create – a sense of urgency
- build – a guiding coalition
- form – a strategic vision
- enlist – a volunteer army
- enable – actions to remove barriers
- generate – short-term wins
- sustain – acceleration
- institute – change.

Hiatt's (2006) Awareness, Desire, Knowledge, Ability, and Reinforcement (ADKAR) model identified five key steps to follow when implementing change, that is:

1. Awareness that a change is needed.
2. Desire to support individuals to make a change.
3. Knowledge of what needs to be done to change.
4. Ability to support and implement change.
5. Reinforcement to sustain the change that has been implemented.

Whilst these models reflect structures evident in large organisations, the application of such approaches within school settings (including by individual teachers) is potentially beneficial. Further, whilst a range of models exist, there are common elements embedded within them. For example, each model includes reference to:

- identifying that a change is needed
- identifying what change needs to be made and how this might be achieved

- implementing the change
- reinforcing and sustaining the change.

In identifying the key aspects of change and then considering how the impact of any change can be monitored, individual teachers can start to consider how best to implement changes to their own practice – either individually or as a department.

In 2019, the EEF published *Putting Evidence to Work: A School's Guide to Implementation*. This was designed to support teachers to develop their capacity to identify and manage challenges in their own practice and to enact effective change. Central to the research was the acknowledgement that change is a process and that any change put into place should be actively explored, identified, implemented and monitored. This requires teachers to engage in inquiry and reflection to identify different ways of working. Time is taken to support those enacting the change to develop new skills, practice those skills and then implement and review the impact of these on pupil outcomes (Guskey, 2002). This might require teachers to engage in professional development. When designing effective professional development to support change, consideration must be given to elements such as building knowledge, how teachers motivate themselves and others, how they are supported to develop specific skills and finally how practice is embedded. More recently, the EEF model has been updated with three key elements/behaviours identified that need to be considered when implementing effective change (EEF, 2024). These being:

1. The adoption of behaviours to support and maintain change.
2. The use of evidence to inform the change being made and consideration of the appropriateness of any change to the context in which change is being implemented.
3. The creation of an effective plan based on detailed review embedded through defined phases.

Embedded within the EEF guidance (EEF, 2021; 2024) is the identification of four key phases – these being:

1. Explore
2. Prepare
3. Deliver
4. Sustain.

These marry closely to the steps or stages identified in relation to models of change. These being:

- identifying that a change is needed (explore)
- identifying what needs to change and how this might be achieved (prepare)
- implementing the change (deliver)
- reinforcing and sustaining the change (sustain).

The next section looks at each one of the EEF (2024) phases in a little more detail, starting with the explore phase that helps identify that a change is needed. At the end of the description of each phase, the case study is referred to, in order to demonstrate how the phase might be addressed in practice.

The EEF model (2024)

The explore phase

The explore phase is the first part of any change model, and can be broken down further as follows:

- identifying key priorities, or what specifically needs to change
- systematically exploring approaches/strategies that might support change
- examining the feasibility of making any change.

The starting point is to identify that a change is needed. In so doing, consideration needs to be given to what that change might be. The next step is to be clear as to why that specific change is needed, how it has been identified and therefore on what evidence the need for change is based. In essence, the explore phase encourages the development of an awareness of what change is needed (see also, for example, the ADKAR model, Haitt, 2006) and to identify what the key priorities are to facilitate the change. It could well be that a number of challenges are identified, but it is important to focus on a specific challenge to ensure that any change is targeted.

Having the confidence to question what is happening (or unfreeze-see Lewin's (1947) model of change) allows for more detailed analysis, resulting in identifying aspects that may not have been considered. Therefore, it is important to gain as much insight about the challenge as possible, drawing on a range of sources to do this. Choosing what evidence is needed to support the need for a change is a central part of this exploration phase. For example, seeking feedback from all stakeholders is important. Drawing on a range of stakeholders or audiences (in essence those who will be impacted by any change) is important to ensure all voices are heard. This might include, for example, the following voices:

- pupils – pupils are the consumers of the learning experience. Understanding their experiences of learning, teaching and assessment is an important part of evaluating the impact of teaching. Understanding pupils as wholistic individuals who are able to provide detailed feedback on their learning experiences provides unique opportunities to understand the experience through their own eyes
- teachers – speaking with and learning from those involved in teaching the experience is important. They will have identified reasons why they have planned and taught in that way. Understanding the rationale for their approach provides insight and therefore affords opportunities for sharing their experiences as well as the identification of opportunities for further development.

Part 2 of the case study looks at how this phase was enacted by our case study school.

Case study part 2

Following meetings with pupils, parents, the teaching team and senior leaders in school, the teaching team at Fortyfoot school identified a range of challenges that were being experienced, as detailed in Table 14.1.

Having identified the challenges and therefore where change might need to take place, the focus needs to be tightened in order not to change too much at one time. Once the

Table 14.1 Challenges identified by staff

	Summary of key points
• Health and safety	• Transport of pupils to and from off-site provision • Off-site provision being open to the public as well as providing educational provision • Facilities provided off-site for delivery of the programme
• Timetabling/access to resources	• Constraints of pupil availability in relation to fixtures • Accessibility to specific facilities • Access to teaching resources
• Logistics	• School-based staff needed to deliver on school site and the travel to off-site provision • The extensive catchment area from which the programme draws, with pupils travelling for up to 90 minutes to attend
• Introducing a new programme	• The provision is new, resulting in the need to upskill staff in relation to subject content and assessment protocols • Staff delivering to a new set of pupils, joining the programme from a range of educational establishments
• Methods of delivery	• Provision is a combination of classroom-taught sessions and practical sessions • Practical coaching sessions delivered by qualified coaches • Taught and course work-related sessions delivered by school-based staff
• Pupil intake/engagement	• The programme combines both academic and practical activities – the football academy manages recruitment to the programme • As a post-16 programme, pupils join from a range of other educational establishments, bringing with them different expectations in relation to behaviour and engagement • Minimum entry requirements (both academically and with respect to sport specific ability) mean an inclusive approach to recruitment, resulting in a diverse group (academically) starting the programme • To make the programme viable, there needs to be a balance in relation to pupil numbers to service the football squads. This results in all pupils being male • Pupils view 'playing sport' as their key priority

explore phase of the change has been completed, preparatory work needs to be undertaken in relation to the strategies to be implemented to support change. This is the prepare phase, below.

The prepare phase – getting ready to implement change

During this phase, the focus moves onto developing a clear, logical and specific plan as to how the challenge will be implemented. Teacher engagement in the process of action planning is likely to be embedded as part of the cycle of review and accountability processes evident in, for example, school improvement planning. It is important to remember that action planning requires thought and detail in relation to specific teacher learning that might need to take place prior to implementing any plan, that relevant resources, etc., are in place to support the implementation and understanding how the impact of the change is measured. There is therefore a need to move beyond just developing a plan, to ensuring that those responsible for enacting the plan are fully prepared, that the specific strategies to be implemented are understood and rehearsed and that monitoring systems and processes are appropriate. As such, a period of professional development might be required prior to any plan being implemented.

Once a specific plan has been drawn up, time needs to be taken to ensure that all teachers have an understanding of appropriate strategies they can employ to support the plan. The focus therefore moves towards ensuring that effective professional development is identified and undertaken.

Over recent years, how professional development is viewed has changed somewhat. In particular, the focus of how professional development is accessed has moved away from attending one-off courses to more embedded provision throughout the academic year. However, what has remained at the forefront is the need for any professional development to be seen as having a positive impact on pupil learning outcomes.

When looking at effective professional development, the EEF (2019) identified the following three key factors that need to be taken into account during the prepare phase. Professional development:

1. Must build knowledge.
2. Should motivate staff.
3. Should develop specific teaching approaches.

These are discussed in more detail below.

Professional development to build knowledge

It is likely that teachers given the responsibility for enacting change will have some knowledge around strategies to support the change identified. However, additional support might be needed to build on this. Thus, it is important to gain an insight into teachers' existing knowledge to ensure that this is built upon as needed. This might be achieved by auditing existing knowledge and experience. Where additional learning is identified, consideration needs to be given to how this learning will be structured and supported. For example, as with pupils, consideration needs to be given to ensuring that teachers engaging in any professional development do not become overloaded. This reinforces the need to ensure that there is a tight focus in relation to the change that is being introduced, and that not too many changes take place at any one time. Thinking carefully about sources of information and how this is accessed is also important. For example, is there specific literature that teachers should engage with? How will this be made available to them?

Professional development to motivate staff

Whilst it might be argued that engaging in professional development will impact on pupil learning outcomes, motivating teachers to participate in such activities can be challenging. Consideration needs to be given to any additional time and workload that might arise from engaging in professional development. Further, teachers need to be viewed in the same way as pupils in classes in relation to the strategies used in these contexts to support learning. For example, ensuring that any new knowledge is broken down into small steps, that opportunities for rehearsal are embedded in any development activities and that feedback and support are given (see, for example, Rosenshine, 2012). Therefore, in the context of working with teachers, the following factors need to be taken into account:

1. Teachers need to understand the reason for the change and what specifically they need to do to be ready to implement the change. Engaging teachers early in the process means that they are more likely to see value to the change and 'buy-in' to the change. Setting clear goals and expectations is important so that a clear framework is established.
2. Those leading the change need to be confident in the literature/resources/evidence that is being shared. Consideration can be given to visiting other organisations/departments who might have implemented a similar change so that evidence is collected in relation to potential outcomes.
3. Consideration also needs to be given to how to maintain motivation during the course of any change. Therefore, careful consideration needs to be given to how progress will checked and monitored.

Professional development to develop specific teaching approaches

Where change focuses on changes to or implementation of new teaching approaches, some teachers might see this as a challenge to their professionalism as the suggestion might be viewed as criticising current practice. To be successful, there needs to be 'buy-in' (EEF, 2024), from all those being asked to implement the change, with an emphasis on seeing any change as "ongoing learning and improvement" (p.1).

Thus, when developing specific teaching approaches, consideration needs to be given to the following:

1. Modelling the expected teaching approaches – those tasked with implementing any change need to be confident in what they are implementing. Providing models on which teachers can base their own practice provides a reference point against which progress can be checked. Consideration needs to be given to who will provide the model and whether someone external to the organisation needs to be involved. A note of caution is needed here though – context is important. When using an external expert, they need to understand the context in which the change is being delivered as well as how they will deliver any specific input.
2. Build in opportunities for rehearsal and refinement – any new initiative will take time to embed. Time needs to be given for people to rehearse the approach. They will also need feedback on how they are developing to ensure that there is consistency in the approach. This might include building opportunities for teachers to observe others using the approach. This might bring its own challenges, for example, in relation to time for teachers to plan, observe and reflect on the progress being made.

Returning to the case study, the third part considers how teachers worked through the prepare phase of the implementation of change.

Case study: part 3

The teaching team at Fortyfoot school decided to focus on the key challenge of pupil engagement, creating the action plan detailed in the following section:

Focus: To improve pupil engagement

Actions

- to ensure all those involved (teachers, pupils, coaches, parents) working on the programme have a clear understanding of the expectations in all aspects of the programme
- for staff delivering the programme to develop a deeper knowledge of all aspects of the programme to ensure continuity in the pupil experience
- for all staff to develop a deeper understanding of the needs of the pupils undertaking the programme.

To achieve this, the team identified the following activities:

- establish a behaviour charter detailing expectations of all pupils across the programme-to include expectations of attendance, behaviour, coursework and engagement
- develop a pupil-facing approach to learning to ensure that all pupils are able to develop effective study skills to support independent learning
- create a collaborative culture with all staff working together to identify best practice in relation to approaches to teaching to support effective learning, building in opportunities for teachers to observe each other in practice allowing for reflections on impact on pupil progress and to make amendments to practice as appropriate
- teachers to be given allocated development time to focus on developing their subject knowledge in relation to the content they will be teaching
- all teachers to attend professional development looking at making learning accessible, specifically focusing on the learning environment being created
- to prepare a pupil pen portrait identifying strengths and challenges, allowing all teachers to develop a deeper understanding of the needs of each individual pupil
- undertake regular review of pupil progress through use of pupil and staff feedback to ensure early identification of any areas of concern to ensure these are addressed swiftly.

The team also identified the following criteria on which successful implementation would be reviewed:

- increase in retention rates
- improved pupil outcomes
- pupils demonstrate a positive work ethic, resulting in increased level of confidence and maturity.

Consideration now turns to the delivery phase of implementation of change.

The delivery phase

During this phase, the focus is on how any change is being delivered in practice. Here, the emphasis is on monitoring the enactment of any change and ensuring that the change reflects the intention of the change. Being clear what the conditions for success are, is therefore very important. During this phase, opportunities to be open and honest about the change that is being implemented should be identified. Those involved in making the change need to have the opportunity to feedback on their experiences. There is also the need to ensure that the change becomes embedded in practice, which is considered next.

Embedding into practice

To ensure effective implementation, time is needed to embed the change in practice. Without this period of sustained change, it is not always easy to establish the impact the change is having. During this period, consideration should be given to the following:

1. How those embedding the change receive support and encouragement – it is very easy to withdraw from a change if the feedback being received is not positive. Like any behaviour, there is a learning process taking place and so it is important to understand that impact might not be instant.
2. Ensure that there is frequent review of the change in practice. This should feedback into the action plan that has been drawn up to ensure that all those engaging with the change have opportunities to input their own experiences.
3. Ensure that there is some form of monitoring of the implementation and impact. Earlier in the chapter, reference was made to providing opportunities for modelling to allow participants to understand specifically what is expected of them. Feedback around these specific aspects should ensure that the implementation is effective as it can be.

At this point, it is important to remember that whilst implementation of a specific approach might be backed with relevant research evidence, the specific context in which the research was undertaken will not be exactly the same as the context where it is now being embedded. Thus, a word of warning, a lot of educational research is context-specific and therefore consideration needs to be given to whether the context in which the change was implemented in the research is similar to the context in which it is currently being implemented. Provided time is given for the embedding process, then sometimes it might be that a conclusion is drawn that the change being adopted has not produced the impact expected and therefore is not as effective as originally thought. It is therefore not the approach that is needed. However, should the implementation process be effective, consideration then needs to the final component of the process, that of sustainability.

So how did the team at Fortyfoot school deliver the programme and what was the impact?

Case study part 4

As a result of the explore and prepare phases, changes were made to how the programme was delivered. For example, whilst the teaching programme was scheduled in a 4-hour block, chunking of sessions into 50 minutes with a 10-minute brain break was initiated. This reduced the cognitive overload on the pupils and resulted in increased engagement.

In relation to the delivery of content, a more assessment-focused approach was adopted, with teaching broken down into small steps and then linked to the final assessment piece so that pupils understood how what they were learning linked explicitly to the assessment they would have to submit. This allowed pupils to better understand the purpose of the academic work, and they became more focused on these outputs.

Through adopting a more collaborative approach, teaching and coaching staff worked closely in relation to recording and reviewing their respective lessons/sessions. This approach offered them the opportunity to share ideas and also reflect on what was going well and what they might do differently. Teachers were more confident in their teaching and over time, the approaches adopted became embedded across other lessons and departments within the school. This was important in relation to their own personal and professional identify and resulted in them becoming more reflective and open to new ideas and also to challenge themselves and each other to do things differently.

Over time, changes were seen in the engagement of the pupils. Participation in academic sessions increased with pupils becoming more focused and able to make connections between what they were learning in the classroom and how they were applying this in their sport.

It is clear from part 4 of the case study that the change was having a positive impact. But once change is implemented, it needs to be sustained.

The sustain phase

The final phase in competing any change is ensuring its sustainability. Here, the aim is to ensure that any change that has been implemented remains embedded in the practice of the school. This might result in the change becoming a 'non-negotiable' within the teaching practices of the school (in essence it is expected to be seen in every lesson and monitored as part of focused observation). If the change has been implemented as a pilot or on a small scale, the sustain phase can also focus on rolling out the change across the school, so that it is adopted by others. The initial adopters (those who were involved in the piloting of the change) act as support. For example, if implementation has been successful within the physical education department, then it might be that this success is shared with other departments within the school. However, as has previously been identified, context is key, so even within an organisation, the impact of change might be different across departments; therefore, a degree of flexibility in adoption might be necessary.

Summary and key points

The purpose of this chapter has been to consider carefully how challenges might be identified and addressed through adopting a model of change; for example, the EEF model was described throughout the chapter, although other models are available. Using the four phases of the EEF (2021) model, consideration has been given to how challenges might be identified and explored, the processes that are involved in preparing for change, including considering any professional development that might be needed, the delivery and review of the change and consideration as to how any change might be sustained. Examples of approaches adopted within teaching to support change were introduced, not only focusing on implementing change, but also considering how the impact of this on pupil learning outcomes might be viewed.

Implementing change is not an easy process and requires a collegiate approach if it is to be successful (Ermeling, 2010). It takes time and effort on the part of all those involved with the change. However, when focused and fully supported by those responsible for identifying and enacting the change, the impact on pupil outcomes outweighs the cost (financial and professional).

References

EEF (Education Endowment Foundation) (2019) *Putting Evidence to Work: A School's Guide to Implementation – Guidance report*, EEF, available at: https://dera.ioe.ac.uk/id/eprint/31088/1/EEF-Implementation-Guidance-Report.pdf (accessed 13 January 2025).

EEF (Education Endowment Foundation) (2021) *Effective Professional Development: Guidance Report*, EEF, available at: https://educationendowmentfoundation.org.uk/education-evidence/guidance-reports/effective-professional-development (accessed 12 January 2025).

EEF (Education Endowment Foundation) (2024) *A School's Guide to Implementation: Maximising the Impact of New Approaches and Practices*, available at: https://d2tic4wvo1iusb.cloudfront.net/production/eef-guidance-reports/implementation/a_schools_guide_to_implementation_-_summary_of_recommendations_2024-05-10-074723_lwty.pdf?v=1734266489 (accessed 15 December 2024).

Ermeling, B.A. (2010) 'Tracing the effects of teacher inquiry on classroom practice', *Teaching and Teacher Education*, 26, 377–388.

Guskey, T.R. (2000) *Evaluating Professional Development*, Thousand Oaks, CA: Corwin.

Hiatt, J. (2006) *ADKAR: A Model of Change in Business, Government and Our Community*, Fort Collins, CO: Prosci Learning Center Publications.

Kotter, J.P. (1996) *Leading Change*, Cambridge, MA: Harvard Business Press.

Lewin, K. (1947) 'Frontiers in group dynamics: concept, method and reality in social science; equilibrium and social change', *Human Relations* 1 (1), 5–41.

Rosenshine, B. (2012) 'Principles of instruction: Research-based strategies that all teachers should know', *American Educator*, 36 (1), 12–20.

Sherrington, T. (2020) *Teaching WalkThrus: Five Step Guides to Instructional Coaching*, Melton, Woodbridge: John Catt.

AUTHOR INDEX

Aarskog, E. 53, 57-58, 64, 71
Abdul-Rahman, H. 132, 136, 138
Adijaya, M.A., Widiana, I.W., Agung Parwata, I. and Suwela Antara, I. 132, 136, 138
Aelterman, N., Vansteenkiste, M., Van Keer, H., Van den Berghe, L., De Meyer, J. and Haerens, L. 106, 115
AfPE (Association for Physical Education) 32-33, 36, 40, 43, 49, 58, 176
Alexandr, A., Sergij, T. and Olena, O. 133, 136, 138
Alisic, E., Bus, M., Dulack, W., Pennings, L. and Splinter, J. 157, 162
Allen, G., Milne, B., Velija, P. and Radley, R. 7, 15
Ambrose, S.A., Bridges, M.W., DiPietro, M., Lovett, M.C. and Norman, M.K. 16, 25
Ames, C. 75-76, 81, 83, 134, 136, 138
Anderson, L. W. and Krathwohl, D.R. 117-118, 128
Anglin-Jaffe, H. 150
Araújo, D., Hristovski, R., Seifert, L., Carvalho, J. and Davids, K. 10, 115
Arthur, J. and Golder, G. 53, 57-58, 65, 69-71
Arufe-Giráldez, V., Sanmiguel-Rodríguez, A., Ramos-Álvarez, O. and Navarro-Patón, R. 134, 138
Assessment Reform Group 64, 72
Atkinson, R.C. and Shiffrin, R.M. 20, 22-23, 25
Ausubel, D. 22, 25
Ayvazo, S. and Ward, P. 66, 72

Barney, K.W. 150
Bates, B. 18, 25, 121, 128
BBC Bitesize 53, 58

Bell Foundation 123, 128
Bellis, M., Hughes, K., Leckenby, N., Perkins, C. and Lowey, H. 155, 162
Benn, T. 134, 137-138
Bennett, T. 87-89, 91, 95-96, 98
Benyon, L. 28, 40
Bergholz, L., Stafford, E. and D'Andrea, W. 156, 162
Bernstein, B. 104, 106, 115
Bess, F.H. and Hornsby, B.W. 148, 150
Bingham, C., Clarke, L., Michielsens, E. and Van de Meer, M. 150
Black, P.: Harrison, C., Lee, C., Marshall, B. and Wiliam, D. 64, 72; and Wiliam, D. 42, 59, 61, 64, 69-70, 72, 106, 115
Blair, R. and Capel, S. 100, 103-104, 107-109, 112, 114-115
Bloom, B.S., Engelhart, M.D., Furst, E.J., Hill, W.H. and Krathwohl, D.R. 19, 24-25, 49, 59, 119-120, 123, 126, 128, 130, 138
Borg, E., Neovius, L. and Kjellander, M. 146, 150
Borgers, J., Seghers, J. and Scheerder, J. 167, 170, 176
Bowler, M., Newton, A. Keyworth, S. and Mckeown, J. 103-104, 107, 114-115
Bradbury, A., Braun, A. and Quick, L. 135, 137-138
Bronfenbrenner, U. 93, 98
Brown, T.D. and Penney, D. 173, 176
Brühlmeier, A. 43, 59
Bruner, J.S. 121, 128
Brunsdon, J. 30, 40
Bunker, R. and Thorpe, R. 126, 128
Burnett, P. 93, 98

Author Index

Cai, M. and Denmans Epp, C.D. 132, 138
Caldeborg, A., Maivorsdotter, N. and Öhman, M. 156, 162
Capel, S.: Whitehead, M. and Lawrence, J. 16, 18-21, 25-26, 31-32, 34, 40, 117, 119, 128, 130, 135, 138; Zwozdiak-Myers, P. and Lawrence, J. 36, 40
del Carmen Torres-Gázquez, S., López-García, G.D. and Granero-Gallegos, A. 133, 136, 139
Casbon, C. and Spackman, L. 64, 72
CASEL (Collaborative for Academic, Social, and Emotional Learning) 132, 135-139
Caspersen, C.J., Powell, K.E. and Christenson, G.M. 165, 176
Chan, K., Hay, P. and Tinning, R. 42, 57, 59
Charlton, R., Gravenor, M.B., Rees, A., Knox, G., Hill, R., Rahman, M., Jones, K., Christian, D., Baker, J., Stratton, G. and Brophy, S. 73, 83
Chi, M., Glaser, R. and Rees, E. 135, 139
Chiles, C. 124, 128
Chng, L. and Lund, J. 65, 69, 72
Ciotto, C. and Gagnon, A. 155, 162
Cliffe, J. 65, 70, 72, 103-104, 115
Coates, J.: and Sutton-Spence, R. 147, 150; and Vickerman, P. 7, 9, 15
Coe, R., Aloisi, C., Higgins, S. and Major, L.E. 66, 70, 72; Rauch, C.J., Kime, S. and Singleton, D. 21, 26, 35, 40, 121, 128
Cole, S., O'Brien, J., Gadd, M., Ristuccia, J., Wallace, D. and Gregory, M. 156-157, 162
CRIDE (Consortium for Research in Deaf Education) 141, 151
Curtin, D. 134, 139

Deci, E.L. and Ryan, R.M. 75, 83, 100, 105-106, 112, 115, 131-132, 137, 139
De Meester, A., Aelterman, N., Cardon, G., De Bourdeaudhuij, L. and Haerens, L. 170, 176
DES (Department of Education and Science) 36, 40, 87, 98, 165, 176; and WO (the Welsh Office) 28, 40
DfE (Department for Education) 17, 26, 31-32, 36, 38, 40, 43, 50-51, 59, 86, 89-90, 95-96, 98, 120, 126, 128, 141-142, 151, 166, 176; DCMS and DHSC (Department for Digital, Culture, Media and Sport and Department of Health and Social Care) 170, 174, 176; STA (Standards and Testing Agency) 51, 59

Dismore, H. and Bailey, R. 171, 176
Dix, P. 94, 98
Dixon, K., Braye, S. and Gibbons, T. 147, 151
Dovidio, J.F., Gaertner, S.L. and Kawakami, K. 143, 151
Dudley, D., Mackenzie, E., Van Bergen, P., Cairney, J. and Barnett, L. 139
Dunn, D. 143, 151
Dweck, C.S. 16, 26; and Leggett, E. 105, 115

Education Scotland 31, 40, 162
EEF (Education Endowment Foundation) 35, 40, 121, 179, 181-182, 184-185, 188-189
Eime, R.M., Harvey, J.T., Charity, M.J., Casey, M.M., Westerbeeck, H. and Payne, W.R. 167, 176
Elliot, A.J., Murayama, K. and Pekrun, R. 105-106, 115
Ellis, S. and Tod, J. 92, 98
Ellison, D.W. and Walton-Fisette, J. 159, 162
English Schools Gymnastics 43, 45, 54, 59
Engström, L.-M. 168, 176
Ermeling, B.A. 189
Evidence Based Education 88, 98, 179

Faella, A., Albano, G., & Conson, M. 132, 139
Farrow, D., Baker, J. and MacMahon, C. 105, 115
Felitti, V., Anda, R., Nordenberg, D., Williamson, D., Spitz, A., Edwards, V., Koss, M. and Marks, J. 154, 162
Finlay, L. 7, 15
Fletcher, T., Ní Chróinín, D., Gleddie, D. and Beni, S. 134, 139
Flutter, J. and Rudduck, J. 7, 15
Foster, R. 142, 147, 151; and Barber, L. 147, 151
Franke, H. 154, 162

Gagné, R.M. 16, 18-19, 26
Garner, P. 87, 92-94, 96, 98
Gazibara, S. 49, 57, 59
Gibbons, E. 61, 72
Gibson, J.J. 110, 115
Goleman, D. 94, 98
Gower, C. 53, 57, 59
Gray, S., Sandford, R., Quarmby, T. and Hooper, O. 157, 161-2
Green, K. 171-173, 176; Cale, L. and Harris, J. 31, 40
Guay, F., Marsh, H.W. and Boivin, M. 135, 139
Guskey, T.R. 181, 189

Haerens, L., Aelterman, N., Van den Berghe, L., De Meyer, J., Soenens, B. and Vansteen-kiste, M. 106, 115
Hallam, S., Davies, J. and Ireson, J. 16, 26
Harrow, A.J. 49, 59
Harvard Graduate School of Education 125, 128
Haskins, D. 143, 151
Hastie, P., Sinelnikov, O., Wallhead, T. and Layne, T. 78, 81-83
Hattie, J.A.C. and Donoghue, G.M. 103, 110-112, 114-115
Hay, P. 173, 176; and Penney D. 42, 59, 112, 115
Haycock, D. and Smith, A. 168, 177
Heidorn, B. and Mosier, B. 9-10, 15
Hemingway, K., Butt, J., Spray, C., Olusoga, P. and Beretta De Azevedo, L. 130, 133-134, 139
Hendrick, C. and Macpherson, R. 66, 70, 72
Henninger, M.L. and Coleman, M. 64, 72
Heritage, M. 16, 26
Hiatt, J. 180, 189
Hobbs, V. 6, 15
Hooper, O., Sandford, R. and Jarvis, H. 155, 162
House of Commons Education Committee 50, 56, 59
Howells, K. with Carney. A., Castle, N. and Little, R. 38, 40
Hutchison, T. 150-151

Illeris, K. 17, 26
Immordino-Yang, M.H. and Damasio, A. 134, 139
Islam, M.A., Haji Mat Said, S.B., Umarlebbe, J.H., Sobhani, F.A. and Afrin, S. 49, 59

Jennings, J.L. and DiPrete, T.A. 134, 139
Jensen, A.R. 23, 26
Jess, M.: and Carse, N. 104, 115; and Gray, S. 134, 139
Johansen, P.F. and Green, K. 168, 177
Johnston, M. 150-151
Jones, L. and Green, K. 172, 177
Jones, R.L.: and Kingston, K. 110, 115; Potrac, P., Cushion, C. and Ronglan, L.T. 109, 115
Jowett, S., Warburton, V., Beaumont, L.C. and Felton, L. 105-107, 109-110, 112, 115

Kelly, L. 147, 150-151
Killingbeck, M. and Whitehead, M. 67, 70, 72
Kirk, D. 30, 40, 104, 107, 109, 144-146, 166, 177
Kirschner, P.A. and Hendrick, C. 17, 20, 23, 26

Knoester, C. and Allison, R. 168, 177
Kotter, J.P. 180, 189
Kraft, M.A. and Grace, S. 134, 139
Krathwohl, D.R., Bloom, B.S., and Masia, B.B. 49, 59

Lamb, P., Lane, K. and Aldous, D. 7, 15
Lawrence, G., Kingston, K. and Gottward, V. 112, 114-115
Lawrence, J. 36, 41, 107, 115
Lawson, H. 175, 177
Lee, A. 142, 151
Leirhaug, P.E., MacPhail, A. and Annerstedt, C. 53, 56-57, 59
Lemov, D. 92, 95, 98
Lewin, K. 180, 182, 189
Lewis, K. 133, 136, 139
Littlefair, D., Jopling, M. and Kelly, N. 61, 67, 72
López-Pastor, V.M., Kirk, D., Lorente-Catalán, E., MacPhail, A. and Macdonald, D. 42, 59, 173, 177
Low, K. 133, 136, 139
Lundy, L. 7, 15
Lynch, S.: and Curtner-Smith, M. 160, 162; and Norley, J. 43, 49, 59
Lyra, O., Koullapi, K. and Kalogeropoulou, E. 149, 151

MacConville, R. 146, 151
MacPhail, A. 170, 177
Maher, A. 9, 15; and Macbeth, J. 9, 15
Marks, B.A. 150-151
Marmeleira, J., Folgado, H., Martinez Guardado, I. and Batalha, N. 52, 59
Marsh, C. J. 107, 109, 116
Marshall, S.J. and Welk, G.J. 165, 177
Marzano, R.J. and Pickering, D.J. 92, 96, 98
Mascret, N., Elliot, A.J., and Cury, F. 100, 105-106, 116
McGill, M.R. 88, 95, 99
McLennan, N. and Thompson, J. 134, 139
Metzler, M.W. 110, 116
Ministry of Education Singapore 31, 41
Mitchell, F., Gray, S. and Inchley, J. 73-74, 83, 170, 177
Moral-Garcia, J.E., Jiménez, A., Cabaco, A.S. and Jiménez-Eguizabal, A. 130, 136-137, 139
Mordal Moen, K., Westlie, K., Gerdin, G., Smith, W., Linnér, S., Philpot, R., Schenker, K. and Larsson, L. 160, 162

Morgan, B. 7, 15
Morgan, K. 75-76, 83; and Sproule, J. 73, 83, 110, 116
Morgan, N. and Ellis, G. 93, 97, 99
Mosston, M. and Ashworth, S. 35, 39, 41, 82-83, 110, 116, 134, 139
Muijs, D. and Bokhove, C. 22, 26
Murdoch, E. and Whitehead, M. 34, 41

Nair, J. 43, 57, 59
National Deaf Children's Society (NDCS) 143, 147, 151
Nicholls, J.G. 105, 116
Ní Chróinín, D., Fletcher, T. and O'Sullivan, M. 104, 116
Nind, M., Flewitt, R. and Payler, J. 150-151

Oak National Academy 38, 41
O'Donovan, T., Sandford, R. and Kirk., D. 156, 162
Ofsted (Office for Standards in Education, Children's Services and Skills) 31-32, 35-38, 41-42, 48, 50-53, 56-61, 64, 68-72, 89, 117-119, 128, 166, 171, 173-175, 177
ONS (Office for National Statistics) 177

Parry, W. 170-171, 177
Paseka, A. and Schwab, S. 8, 15
Pastore, S. 56-57, 60
Patterson, J.T. and Lee, T.D. 105, 111, 116
Pekrun, R., Goetz, T., Titz, W. and Perry, R.P. 134, 139
Penney, D. 134, 137, 139; Brooker, R., Hay, P. and Gillespie, L. 104, 106-107, 116; and Harris, J. 166, 170, 177
Persson, M., Espedalen, L.E., Stefansen, K. and Strandbu, Å. 174, 177
Piaget, J. 119, 128, 130, 139
Placek, J. 63, 69, 72
Pritchard, A. 17, 26
Purdue, K. 150-151

Quarmby, T.: Sandford, R. and Elliot, E. 156, 162; Sandford, R., Green, R., Hooper, O. and Avery, J. 155-157, 159-161, 163; Sandford, R., Hooper, O. and Gray, S. 156, 159-161, 163
Quigley, A., Muijs, D. and Stringer, E. 21-22, 26
Qunito Romani, A. 168, 177

Ramires, V.V., Dos Santos, P.C., Barbosa Filho, V.C., da Silva Bandeira, A., Tenório, M.C.M., de Camargo, E.M., de Paula Ravagnani, F.C., Sandreschi, P., de Oliveira, V.J.M., Hallal, P.C. and Silva, K.S. 134, 139
Rindler, V., Luiggi, M. and Griffet, J. 168, 177
Ritchhart, R.: and Church, M. 120, 127-128; Church, M. and Morrison, K. 120, 128
Roberts, K. 167-168, 171, 177; and Brodie, D. 167-168, 177; Kovacheva, S. and Kabaivanov, S. 168, 174, 177
Roffey, S. 93, 95-96, 99
Rogers, B. 88, 95-96, 99
Rosenshine, B. 18, 20, 26, 107, 110, 116, 121-122, 128, 185, 189

SAMHSA (Substance Abuse and Mental Health Services Administration) 155, 163
Sandford, R.: Quarmby, T. and Hooper, O. 155, 163; Quarmby, T., Hooper, O. and Duncombe, R. 155, 163
Schindler, A.W. 23, 26
Scott, S.H. 111, 114, 116
Scottish Government 155, 163
Shea, J.B. and Morgan, R.L. 111, 116
Sherrington, T. 179, 189
Shoffner, M. 7, 15
Shropshire Deaf and Hard of Hearing Forum 143, 152
Shulman, L. 61, 72
Shute, V.J. 64, 72
Siah, P.C., Tan, C.S., Lee, W.Y. and Lee, M.N. 143, 152
Siedentop, D. 31-32, 34, 41
Signature 147, 152
Simmons, J. and MacLean, J. 51, 60
Simonton, K.L., Garn, A.C. and Mercier, K.J. 134, 140
Smith, A. 172, 177
Smith, D.C. and Neale, D.C. 66, 70, 72
Smith, M. 154, 163
Spackman, L. 53, 57, 60, 64, 66, 68-70, 72
Sperka, L. and Enright, E. 172, 178
Sport and Recreation Alliance 165, 178
Sport England 165, 167, 175, 178
Sprake, A. and Walker, S. 165, 178
Stenhouse, L. 107, 116
Stevenson, P. 143, 152
Stidder, G. 173, 178; and Blair, R. 104, 116
Stolz, S.A. and Kirk, D. 166, 178

Strandbu, A., Bakken, A. and Stefansen, K. 168, 178
Strickland, S. 92, 99
Stride, A., Brazier, R., Piggott, S., Staples, M. and Flintoff, A. 165, 178
Sutherland, S. and Parker, M. 160, 163
Sweller, J. 21-23, 26, 122, 128

Tan, S.H. 117, 129
Thorburn, M. 42, 60
Thorpe, R.D., Bunker, D. and Almond, L. 126, 129
Tod, J. and Powell, S. 94, 99

UK Sport and Sport England 167, 178
UN (United Nations) 7, 15
UNESCO (United Nations, Educational, Scientific and Cultural Organization) 28, 30-31, 41, 134, 155, 163

Van Manen, M. 82-83
Vaughan, J., Mallett, C.J., Potrac, P., López-Felip, M.A. and Davids, K. 109, 116
Veal, M.L. 42, 60
Venugopalan, A. and Reghunadhan, R. 147, 152
Vygotsky, L. 121, 129

Wakefield, J. and Lawrence, J. 21, 23, 26
Walters, W., MacLaughlin, V. and Deakin, A. 50, 60
Warwick, P., Vrikki, M., Mette, A., Karlsen, F., Dudley, P. and Vermunt, J.D. 7, 15
Weare, K. 94, 99
Wheeler, S. and Green, K. 168, 172, 178
Whipp, P., Taggart, A. and Jackson, B. 9, 15
Whitehead, M. 34-35, 41, 73, 76, 83, 100, 104-105, 110, 116
Whitehouse, K. 88, 99; Barber, L. and Pepperell, R. 91, 99, 107, 116
Wiggins, G. and McTighe, J. 51, 60
Williams, A. and Cliffe, J. 42, 57, 60
Wood, D., Bruner, J.S. and Ross, G. 121, 129
Wood, S., Ford, K., Hardcastle, K., Hopkins, J., Hughes, K. and Bellis, M. 155, 163
World Federation of the Deaf 150, 152
World Health Organization 73, 83

YST (Youth Sport Trust) 165, 170, 175, 178

Zhang, J. and Zhang, C. 8, 15
Ziehe, T. 104, 109, 116
Zimmerman, B.J. 135, 140

SUBJECT INDEX

ability(ies) 1, 6, 16, 29, 54, 61, 75, 77, 80-82, 92, 106, 120, 128, 133, 166, 183; grouping 16, 135; lower 106; to think 32, 117-118, 120, 127
ableism 144
abuse 156; emotional neglect 154; physical 90, 154, 156; sexual 154; verbal 154
academic 101, 132, 156, 173, 180, 183, 188; content 120, 179, 183; excellence 131; journal 81; performance 134, 148, 154; qualification 179-180; year 13, 16, 36, 50, 74, 184
accountability 52, 108, 138, 183
achievement 16, 53, 58, 65; goal theory 105-106; *see also* goals
active 9, 13, 16, 31-34, 63-64, 71, 75, 100-101, 104, 107, 109, 112, 119-120, 130, 136, 142, 171, 174-175; learning 16-17; *see also* learning
activity: area 8, 165, 169; /task for learning 1, 53, 71, 121; *see also* task
adaptation (of curriculum and/or teaching) *see* differentiation
ADKAR model (Hiatt) 180, 182
adult: other than teacher (AOTT) 121; trusted 155, 160
adverse childhood experiences (ACEs) 154-155
affective domain 19, 22, 49, 130-132, 134-138; *see also* cognitive, domain; domains of learning; holistic; physical, competence; physical, domain; social-emotional
agency 51, 88, 95, 101-102, 114, 133, 158, 176; agents 101, 110, 176
aim 19, 164-165, 188; of curriculum 27, 30-31, 34-35, 38, 107-108, 136; of department 108-110; of physical education 34, 50, 101, 156, 165; pupils 16, 38, 68, 77, 126, 144-145; of teachers 3, 5, 27, 70, 75, 79, 83, 136; *see also* curriculum; learning outcome; objective; physical education
analysis 8, 19, 58, 74, 86, 96, 101, 119, 126, 182
anger 155
anxiety(ies) 155-156; *see also* trauma
application (Bloom) 119, 126
assessment 3, 16, 18, 27, 31, 42-43, 47-53, 56-58, 76, 81, 100-114, 120, 133, 135-138, 173-174, 182-183, 187-188; aims of 51, 53, 56; criteria for 46, 48, 52, 57, 113; data 1, 51, 53; for learning 2, 42, 48, 51, 53, 56, 58, 61, 64, 76; of learning 1, 42-43, 48, 51, 56-58, 64, 135; literacy 56-57; of outcomes 42, 52; peer 13, 63-64, 113, 135; policy 42-44, 47-51, 56-58; of process 28, 42, 48, 52, 119, 135; self 13, 107, 113; *see also* formative assessment; peer and self-assessment; relationship, between curriculum, pedagogy and assessment
athletics 5, 29, 31, 34, 91; track 87, 90
attainment 42, 46, 49, 52, 56-58, 91, 160
attendance 180, 186
attention deficit hyperactivity disorder (ADHD) 154-155
attitude 19, 28, 49, 54, 71, 74-75, 97, 130, 132, 135, 137, 138
authority 76-78, 80, 81, 134
autonomy 77, 80-81, 106, 112, 132-134, 136-138

badminton 17, 62-63, 66, 69, 70, 88, 166-167, 169-170
barriers to participation 87, 174
basketball 29, 34, 66, 77, 85, 95, 165, 169, 170

Subject Index

behaviour 1, 16-17, 22, 25, 83, 86-98, 100, 106, 110-111, 114, 132, 155-157, 183, 186-187; good 84, 86, 88-90, 93, 95, 97; for learning 3, 22-23, 84, 92-94, 97; management 84-85, 87, 89-90, 92-94, 96-97, 155; policy 84, 89-92, 96-97; positive 88, 91-93, 97; 3 Rs 91; *see also* behavioural; behaviours; misbehaviour
behavioural 17, 85-87, 92, 156
behaviours 19, 21-22, 25, 35, 73, 83, 88, 90-93, 95, 109, 112, 135, 138, 156-157, 181
belief(s) 3, 19, 22, 83, 108-109, 132, 160, 169; *see also* self-belief; value; values
biking 169
biomechanics 111, 114
blading 169
Bloom's Taxonomy 19, 24, 49, 119-120, 123, 126, 130
boarding 169
body image 102, 156
boxercise 169
brain 111, 114, 155, 187
British Sign Language (BSL) 142, 145, 147, 149-150
BTEC in sport 143, 173; *see also* examinations in physical education
bullying 87, 90

captain 78, 80, 157-158
central nervous system 111
change 179-190; *see also* models of change
changing 86, 158-159; body shape 102; conditions 34; curricular 42; rooms 85-87, 91, 96, 102, 126, 156; teacher 110; time 25
child development 154
choice 77, 81, 87, 93, 100, 103-104, 109, 141; of physical activity 77, 80, 100, 133, 137-138, 170, 173; *see also* options in physical education
class 1-2, 6, 16, 28, 30, 36, 39, 44-46, 51, 62-63, 66, 68, 75, 78-80, 82, 85-88, 90, 93, 95-96, 102-103, 111-112, 124-125, 142, 145, 147, 153, 157-161, 172, 185; arrangements 88; ethos 91; management 47-48, 84-86; routines/rules 88, 91-92; teacher 39, 79, 87, 103, 105, 172
classroom 9, 88-90, 105, 158, 183, 188; assistant 5-6, 8-10, 12-14, 121; environment 84; *see also* inclusive, learning environment; learning environment; teaching, assistant
climbing 33-34, 101
cognitive 19, 21, 43, 49, 117-119, 122, 125-128, 130, 132, 136-138, 148, 157, 187; development 119, 123, 127; domain 19, 21, 49, 117-119, 125-127; load theory 21, 23; processes 19, 124, 126-127, 177; *see also* affective domain; domains of learning; holistic; knowledge; physical domain; thinking
cold calling 124-126
collaboration/ive 11, 33, 58, 64, 74, 80, 132, 170, 186, 188
communication 8, 38, 50, 54, 61, 67, 71, 93-94, 97, 103, 108-110, 134, 142, 150; styles 142, 145
community 30, 75, 90, 101-102, 142, 153-154; deaf 142-143, 145, 147; hearing 142-143
compassion 159; *see also* empathy; sensitive(ity)
competence 23, 32, 38, 68, 71, 73, 75, 77, 100-114, 117, 119, 132-133, 135, 170
competition 29, 34, 76, 101, 134, 156, 166, 170, 172, 174
concentration 148; fatigue 148
concept 11, 19, 22-23, 31-32, 35-36, 38, 43, 66, 117-118, 121-122, 127, 160, 164-165, 176
confidence: pupil 25, 27, 33, 73, 81-82, 88, 97, 102, 104-105, 107, 113-114, 137, 148, 186; teacher 2, 13, 36, 88, 148, 182
consistency (of teachers, teaching) 51, 89-90, 97, 103, 106, 185
Consortium for Research in Deaf Education 141
constructivist theories of learning 110
content 1, 4, 8-9, 16, 18, 21, 27-32, 34-38, 40, 43, 47-48, 50, 52-53, 58, 61, 66, 93, 104, 107, 113-114, 120-121, 149, 155, 164, 166, 168-174, 179, 183, 186; *see also* curriculum
context: of physical education 14, 16-18, 21, 23-24, 117, 126-127, 155-157; in which working 1, 3-4, 6-7, 14, 16-18, 20, 22-24, 29, 34, 37, 39, 50, 71, 79, 82, 89, 93, 100-103, 105-106, 108-112, 119-121, 124, 127, 141, 143, 153-155, 161, 173-175, 179, 181, 185, 187-188; *see also* physical education
continuing professional development (CPD) 6, 8-9, 13-14, 56-57, 70, 143, 147, 149-150, 179, 181, 184; *see also* professional development
continuity 28, 36, 40, 53, 114, 166, 172, 186; in the curriculum 3, 23, 27-28, 30, 36-37, 39-40, 166, 169; *see also* progression
coping 34, 155; mechanisms 156
core physical education 142-143, 166, 170
cover supervisor 102
CPD *see* continuing professional development (CPD)
creation 39, 89, 119, 123, 126, 181

Subject Index   199

creative 34, 81, 119, 169
cricket 29
culture 75, 88-91, 94, 135-136, 142-143, 170, 186; see also ethos
curriculum 2-3, 5, 8, 12-14, 17, 23-24, 27-31, 33-39, 43-44, 51-52, 57, 77-78, 81, 87, 89, 91, 93-94, 100-101, 103-110, 113-114, 120, 133, 135-136, 143, 147, 150, 155, 165, 169, 171-173; breadth, depth and balance 12, 14, 31-32, 34, 38, 107, 165; definition 27; design 8, 16, 27-28, 30-31, 37-38, 40, 104, 136; diversity 38; flexibility 30; map 6, 38, 102; multi-activity 30, 33; planning 6, 8, 28, 32, 81, 103, 106-107, 110; policy 28; rationale 31, 35, 38; review 8, 10, 12-13, 30-31, 38; revising 39, 136; see also aim, of curriculum; plan; planning; relationship, between curriculum, pedagogy and assessment

dance 29, 34, 39, 86-87, 96, 165-166, 169, 171; studio 87
deaf 141-144, 148, 150; aware 142-145, 147-149; community 142, 145, 147; deafness 141-142, 144, 150; identity 142, 145, 148-149; see also hearing; special school; surdophobia
deaflympics 145, 147-148
decision 8-9, 20, 22, 30, 33, 52-53, 56, 80, 82, 103-104, 107, 109-110, 132-133, 138; -making 9, 76, 103, 126, 132, 135-136, 160
definition 27-28, 104, 106, 132, 165
demonstrate(ion) 16, 18, 22-25, 30-31, 33, 43, 51-54, 56, 78, 85, 88, 91, 96, 101, 106, 108, 117-118, 123, 126-128, 135, 137, 145, 159, 161, 173, 181, 186; demonstrate progress 144; by pupils 29; by the teacher 29, 62-63, 69-70, 146, 160; see also model; modelling
depth of processing 20-21; see also information processing
dialogue 42, 56, 62, 81-82, 108, 142
differentiation (of curriculum and/or teaching) 9-10, 14, 18, 29, 35, 76-77, 113; strategy for 9
disability 9, 56, 90-91, 141, 150
discrimination 90, 143
discussion 11, 77-79, 103, 109, 136, 149, 158
disease, chronic 155, 175
domains of learning 19, 22-25, 49, 57, 117; see also affective domain; cognitive domain; holistic; physical domain
dual coding 23; see also information processing

ecological dynamics 109-110
educational research 187
Education Endowment Foundation (EEF) 179, 181-182, 184-185, 188
Education Health Care Plan (EHCP) 142
education policy 138
effort: decline in 131; pupils 19, 44, 76, 79, 82, 92, 106, 134, 160; teachers 10, 18, 37, 93, 159, 189
emotion 19, 22, 49, 130, 132, 134-135, 138, 156, 158-159
emotional: intelligence 94; resilience 133-134; see also social-emotional
empathy 132, 134, 137, 159-160; see also compassion; sensitive(ity)
empower(ment) 88, 133-134, 145, 148
encourage(ment) 102, 121, 158-159, 173, 187; pupils 50, 76, 90, 131, 145, 168-169; schools 89; teachers 4, 14
engagement 6, 8-11, 13, 18, 20-22, 27, 43, 56-57, 74, 77-78, 81-82, 85, 94-97, 110, 119-120, 130-131, 133-138, 156, 160, 164, 170, 173, 179-180, 183, 186-188; see also participation in physical activity
enjoy 11-12, 29, 31, 33, 39, 63, 69, 71, 80-81, 87, 101, 148, 171
enjoyment 52, 73, 77-78, 131, 137, 165, 168, 170-171, 173, 175
enthusiasm 131, 175; of pupils in lessons 95, 131, 133, 135-136; teacher 91-92
epistemological 108; see also ontological
equipment 6, 10, 28, 77-78, 87, 90-91, 95-97, 142-143, 158, 168; see also resources
ethos 87-88, 91; see also culture
evaluation: pupil 7, 33, 65, 68, 119, 126, 135; teaching 14, 51, 76, 81, 92, 106, 111, 131, 134, 137, 182
evidence: -based 2, 88; -informed 157-158
Evidence Based Education (EBE) 179
examinations in physical education 23, 74, 142, 173; see also BTEC in sport; GCSE
extra-curricular activities 1, 5, 13-14, 29, 94, 103, 164, 166, 170-175

facts 28, 117-118; see also knowledge
feedback 1, 3, 6-8, 11-14, 18-19, 24, 29, 47-48, 52-53, 61-71, 78-79, 82, 102, 106, 109-113, 118, 122, 127, 133, 135, 137, 143-144, 149, 158, 182, 185, 187; correction after 69-71; peer 13, 22, 25, 61,

63, 68, 70-71, 127; self 68; verbal 61-62; *see also* self and peer, feedback
feelings 19, 49, 56, 102, 130, 132-136, 156, 159-160
fitness 34, 157, 166-167, 169-170
football 5, 29, 85, 95, 101, 148, 165-167, 169-170, 179, 183; Gaelic 13
formative assessment 107-108, 112, 120, 135, 173; *see also* assessment, for learning
fresh start approach 29, 37; *see also* transition, from primary to secondary school
futsal 169-170

games 12, 29-30, 33, 77-78, 109, 127, 158, 165-167, 169-170, 172; competitive 166-167, 170; games-based 25, 109, 134; individual 165; invasion 5, 77-78; team 11, 29-30, 165-167, 169-172, 175

games for understanding 126
GCSE 49, 74, 86, 96-97, 100, 102, 143, 148, 166, 173; *see also* examinations in physical education
gender-stereotypical curricula 165
gesture 79, 145, 147
goals 34-35, 52-53, 76-77, 79-80, 88, 106, 111-112, 121, 147, 169, 173, 185; collective 132, 164-165; mastery 105-106; performance 106; setting 81, 133; *see also* achievement, goal theory; mastery
golf 167, 169
government 42, 51, 89, 147-148, 165, 174-175
The Great Teaching Toolkit (Coe, et al) 35, 121
gymnasium 87, 90
gymnastics 5, 29, 34, 39, 43, 45, 48, 54, 57, 86, 91, 95, 156

head, heart and hands 43-44, 48-49, 57
head of: department 5, 43, 48, 50-51, 56-57, 171; of physical education 89, 136; of year 97; *see also* physical education department
headteacher 89, 172
health 34, 73, 91, 101, 154, 165, 167-168, 170, 175, 183; -related 165, 168-169, 175; and safety 91, 183; and well-being 101, 130, 154, 168; *see also* mental health; safety; well-being
healthy lifestyles 133, 136
hearing 141-143, 146, 150; aids 143, 149; community 142-143; hard of hearing (HoH) 141-150; loss 141-142; world 142, 144, 150; *see also* deaf
hockey 29, 34, 77, 165-166

holistic 8, 19, 43, 49-50, 57, 117, 130-131, 134, 136, 138; *see also* affective domain; cognitive domain; domains of learning; physical domain
homeschooled 141
hook activities 126
household dysfunction 154

ideal: ideal-typical school 165; -type 165
inclusion 3, 9, 12-13, 134, 141, 144; frameworks 143; spectrum 143
inclusive 6, 8-9, 14, 56, 75, 136; curriculum and delivery 143; learning environment 134; *see also* classroom, environment; learning environment
inclusivity 131, 137
inequalities 171
information processing 20, 23; *see also* depth of processing; dual coding; schema
instructional: decisions 53; designs 134; video 158
instructions 17, 87, 143, 146; teachers 25, 62, 70, 85-86, 92, 95-96; verbal 68, 121, 146
intended learning outcome *see* learning outcome
intent, implementation, impact (Ofsted) 31-32
interact(ing) 76, 79, 84, 90-91, 93, 97, 106, 110, 120-122, 135, 137, 155-156
inter-school sporting competition 170
intervention 43, 64, 76, 79, 88, 90-91, 97-98, 134, 143-150, 172, 175; culture 135
iPad 158
isolation 66, 95, 114, 127, 147

javelin 31, 34

kabaddi 169
key stage: -3 33; -4 33, 39, 43-44, 49, 133
kit 85, 88, 90-91, 154
knowledge 9, 16-17, 19-20, 22-24, 27-32, 36, 39, 43, 48-54, 56-58, 61, 73, 89, 94, 97-98, 101, 103-104, 107-110, 112-113, 117-127, 130, 132, 135, 144, 147, 149, 157, 165, 168, 173, 180-181, 184-186; declarative 19-20, 28, 30, 117-119, 127-128; definition 27; metacognitive 117-118, 122; prior 20, 22-23, 28, 53, 113, 119-120, 122-123, 126-127; procedural 19-20, 28, 30-31; retrieve 20, 22-23, 119-120, 122, 126; skill and understanding 16-17, 20, 22, 24, 27-28, 36, 43, 48, 50, 52, 56, 98, 120, 126, 132, 165, 168; *see also* facts; subject knowledge of teachers
kwik-cricket 169

language 48, 67, 90, 125-126, 142, 147, 150; body 91, 93; *see also* British Sign Language (BSL)
learner 17, 19, 21-22, 30, 35, 74, 93, 109, 111, 121, 130; independent 16, 21; unique 16, 19; *see also* principles of learning, responsibility for own
learning: challenge in 3, 106; deep 120; definition 17; effective 17-18, 28, 61, 135, 186; journey 35, 38-39; process 3, 16-17, 20, 25, 35, 121, 124-125, 156, 187; pupil ownership of 25, 64, 69, 81, 133; theory 16, 103; *see also* active learning; constructivist theories of learning; principles of learning
learning environment 9, 84, 86, 89-98, 107, 110, 124, 131, 136, 186; *see also* classroom, environment; inclusive, learning environment
learning outcome 18, 24, 42, 50, 52-53, 61-62, 64-69, 71, 85, 87, 92, 96, 108, 111, 113, 122-123, 126-127, 131, 133, 136-137, 179, 184, 188; *see also* aim; objective; success criteria
learning point 53-55, 57, 63, 66, 68-69, 71; *see also* teaching point
learning support 24, 35, 110, 112, 132, 185; team 154
leisure activity 168
lifelong participation in PA and sport 73, 164-165, 167-169, 173-174
lip: pattern 145; read 142, 150
low socioeconomic status 154; *see also* social class

mainstream 141-142
martial arts 167
mastery 19, 38, 43-44, 47-48, 51-52, 54, 57, 75-76, 78-80, 82-83, 105-106, 134; *see also* achievement, goal theory; goals
memory 20-23, 47, 111, 118, 120, 155
mental health 130, 133, 155; *see also* health
metabolic rate 165
middle leader 89
misbehaviour 84-90, 92, 95, 97; *see also* behaviour
misconceptions in learning 19, 48, 53, 61, 63, 66, 70, 92; *see also* learning
mixed ability groups 16-17, 24, 77, 79-80, 137; *see also* ability, grouping
model 18, 24, 122, 185, 187; behaviour 93; good practice 79; perfect 63, 68; performers 161; role 79; skill 82; *see also* demonstrate(ion)
modelling 82, 187; by teacher 79, 93-94, 122, 185; *see also* demonstrate(ion)
models of change 179-181; *see also* change
mood 91, 158; board 157, 159-160
moral 28, 43, 130
motivation 3, 11, 22-23, 28, 31, 33, 56, 73-84, 87, 101, 104-107, 112, 120, 130, 132-135, 138, 185; intrinsic 133, 138; *see also* motivational; self-determination theory
motivational 82; climate 73, 75, 77-80, 83, 136; learning environment 134; theory 73, 75-76, 82; *see also* learning environment
motivator for human behaviour 100
motor competence 32, 38, 119
movement 32, 34, 37, 49, 53, 66-67, 78, 91, 109-111, 113, 119, 145, 157, 165; form 34, 38-39; pattern 31-34, 38-39, 105, 110-111, 113-114; *see also* patterns of movement
multi academy trust 141, 149
musculoskeletal system 111

National Curriculum for Physical Education (NCPE) 28, 31-33, 36, 38, 43, 107, 120, 165-166, 169, 171, 174-175
National Deaf Children's Society (NDCS) 143, 147, 151
netball 29, 78, 165-166, 170

objective 24-25, 42, 48, 50, 52-53, 56-58, 65, 73, 108, 120, 123, 157-158; *see also* aim; learning outcome
observation 11-13, 61, 64, 67, 71, 79, 118, 135, 172, 188; *see also* observe(d); observer
observe(d) 7-8, 11, 13, 22, 24, 43, 48, 58, 61-62, 67, 69-70, 73, 76, 83, 112-113, 135, 147, 185-186; *see also* observation; observer
observer 46-48, 62-64, 69, 71; *see also* observation; observe(d)
ofsted 31-32, 35-38, 42, 48, 50-53, 56-58, 61, 64, 68-71, 89, 117-119, 166, 171, 173-175
ontological 108; *see also* epistemological
options in physical education curriculum 39, 133, 136; *see also* choice
outstanding physical education lesson 44, 64, 135
overload 21, 122, 184; cognitive 23, 122, 187; sensory 149

parent/guardian 6, 8, 14, 51, 94, 97, 107, 182, 186
parkour 171

participation in physical activity 3, 73, 119, 165; see also engagement
patterns of movement 105, 110; see also movement
pedagogical 6, 9-10, 64, 76, 81-82, 108; approach(es) 5, 8, 75-76, 81, 104, 110, 112, 114, 126, 170; decisions 8, 52; see also teaching, approach
pedagogy 12, 43, 101-114, 161; see also relationship, between curriculum, pedagogy and assessment
peer 11, 13, 42, 61, 68, 82, 88, 91-92, 97, 121, 133, 137, 154, 156, 160-161, 173, 176; evaluation 76; group 143; pressure 124; see also feedback, peer
peer and self-assessment 13, 63-64, 107, 113, 135; see also assessment
peer review (teacher) 7, 11-12
personal growth 131, 137, 142
physical: competence 73, 100-117; domain 24, 30, 33, 100-116, 130, 135-137; see also affective domain; cognitive domain; domains of learning; holistic
physical activity (PA) 33, 73, 75, 80, 100-102, 104, 119, 130-131, 133, 135, 137, 164-178; participation outside lessons/throughout life 3, 27, 33, 119, 130-131, 164-178
physical education: aims of 34, 50, 101, 156, 165; meaning 104; value of 3, 19, 50, 104, 108-109, 137, 172; see also context, of physical education
physical education and school sport premium 36
physical education curriculum see curriculum, physical education
physical education department 3-14, 16-17, 24, 29-31, 37-38, 40, 42-43, 47-53, 56-58, 74, 89-90, 92, 97, 103-104, 106-109, 112, 114, 131, 136-137, 141, 143-144, 146, 148-149, 165-174, 181, 185, 188; see also head of, department; head of, physical education
physical inactivity 100, 166
physical literacy (PL) 73, 104-105, 110, 176
pillars of progress (Ofsted) 32, 38, 119
pitch (sports) 90
plan 2, 10, 12-13, 111, 118, 145, 181, 183-187; curriculum 27, 32, 37, 103-104; lesson 77, 183-185; for teaching 10, 22, 53, 56, 66, 68, 88, 104, 184-185; see also curriculum; planning

planning 4-5, 8, 10, 13-14, 18, 22, 27, 35, 47, 53, 56-57, 65, 68, 78, 80, 88, 90-93, 95-97, 103, 106-107, 111, 114, 117-119, 123, 127; curriculum 39, 68, 106-107, 110, 171; see also curriculum; plan
prejudice 143
primary academy/physical education/school 29, 32, 36-38, 43, 141, 168, 170-174; see also transition, from primary to secondary school
principles for facilitating and enhancing learning (Capel, Whitehead and Lawrence) 1-4, 7, 16, 19-21, 25, 73, 104, 143-144, 159-160, 169, 171, 182
principles of instruction (Rosenshine) 18, 20, 110
principles of learning: building from previous 25, 29, 38, 117; prior 18, 20, 22-23, 25, 35, 39, 61, 110, 119, 122, 124; responsibility for own 19, 21, 36, 39, 93, 98, 120, 128, 133; see also learning
principles of movement 67, 119
professional development 6, 9, 24, 39, 57, 70-71, 81, 136, 143, 149, 179, 181, 184-186, 188; see also continuing professional development
progression 3, 27-41, 47, 64, 68-69, 105; definition 28; see also continuity
psychological 104-106, 134, 155; needs 106, 132, 134
public nature of physical education participation/ setting 87, 102, 143, 156
punishment 94; see also sanctions
pupil: autonomy 77, 80-81, 106, 112, 132-134, 136-138; concerns 75, 77, 102, 144, 146, 149, 156; culture 134, 136, 142-143, 175; engagement 20-22, 27, 43, 56, 74, 77-78, 81-82, 85, 94-97, 110, 119-120, 130-131, 133-137, 156, 160, 164, 170, 173, 179-180, 183, 186-188; perspective/voice 7-8, 10-11, 13-14, 24, 75, 81, 96, 100, 133, 135-136, 146, 150, 159-160
Putting Evidence to Work (Education Endowment Foundation) 181

QR code 158
qualified teacher of the deaf (ToD) 142, 144, 146, 148
quality (e.g. assessment/curriculum/feedback/ learning/lessons/teaching) 17-18, 22, 24-25, 35, 37, 42, 50, 53, 88, 92, 96, 109-110, 122, 126; high-quality physical education 39, 73, 107, 134, 143, 165, 174
questioning/questions asked of pupils 19, 21, 24, 38, 63-64, 70, 78, 87, 112, 117-119, 121-125, 128

readiness to learn 23
reasoning 95, 120, 130, 155
recall (by pupils) 18, 118-120, 122-123, 125-127
record(ing) assessment 51, 53, 56, 112
recreational 164, 166-167, 169-171, 174-175
reflect(ion) 2-15, 17, 20, 22, 24, 35, 43, 52, 57, 74-75, 79, 82-83, 95, 97-98, 100, 112, 114, 135, 149-150, 157, 159, 161, 181, 185, 188
reflective practice *see* reflect(ion)
relationship 8, 105-106, 117, 132, 135, 137, 155-156, 159, 175; between curriculum pedagogy and assessment 95, 101, 103-106, 109-110, 113-114; pupil-pupil 80, 88, 93-94, 96-97, 137; skills 132, 135; teacher-parent 94, 97; teacher-pupil 63, 71, 76-77, 79, 81-82, 87, 91-95, 97-98, 105-110, 112, 114, 132, 146, 148-149, 157, 159, 160; *see also* assessment; curriculum; pedagogy; social-emotional
remember(ing) 56, 120, 126
resources 6, 87, 104, 106-108, 113, 168, 183, 185; *see also* equipment
respect 88, 90-92, 134, 142, 155
retention rates 21, 111, 180, 186
review of learning 13, 24-25; *see also* learning
rewards 88, 90-92, 96, 161; *see also* sanctions
routine(s) 2, 6, 25, 36, 43, 88, 90-91, 95-97, 120, 125, 127, 158-160; *see also* rules
rowing 101
rugby 29, 91, 165-167, 169-170
rules 32, 38, 77, 84, 88, 90-92, 96-97, 118-119, 130, 156; *see also* routine(s)

safe space 146, 157
safety 87-88, 91, 110, 159-160, 183; *see also* health, and safety
sanctions 88, 90, 97; *see also* punishment; rewards
scaffold 18, 120-122, 124
schema (use in learning) 20-23; *see also* information processing
self and peer: assessment/evaluation 76, 113; feedback 61, 68, 71; *see also* assessment, peer; feedback, peer; peer and self assessment
self-awareness 132, 135, 157, 160; *see also* social-emotional
self-belief 159-161; *see also* belief(s)
self-confidence 93; *see also* confidence

self-determination theory (Deci and Ryan) 75, 105-106, 131-133, 137-138; *see also* motivation
self-efficacy 22, 160
self-esteem 49, 81, 97, 133, 160
self-management 132, 135; *see also* social-emotional
SENCO *see* special educational needs co-ordinator
SEND *see* special educational needs and disabilities
sense of belonging 137, 159-160
sensitive(ity) 91, 159; *see also* compassion; empathy
shout(ing) 96, 144, 146
sign language 142, 147, 149-150
skill(s) 9, 16-17, 19-24, 27-29, 31, 36-37, 43, 48-54, 56-57, 63, 66-67, 69, 71, 75, 77-78, 82, 87, 89, 93, 98, 107, 110-111, 113, 120, 122, 124, 126-127, 132, 134-138, 142-143, 147-148, 157, 160-161, 165, 168-169, 171-174, 181, 186; *see also* knowledge
social: awareness 132, 135; capital 154; cohesion 16; comparisons 133; dynamics 131, 175; phenomena or process 165; *see also* social-emotional
social and emotional literacy 94
social class 96, 175
social-emotional 22, 49, 94, 130-132, 134-138; *see also* affective domain; social, awareness
socialising 170
social work 154
soft start (to the lesson) 158-160
special educational needs and disabilities (SEND) 5, 56, 141-153
special Educational Needs Coordinator (SENCO) 8-9, 142
specialist equipment (for hard of hearing pupils) 142
special school 141; *see also* deaf
specifically resourced provision (SRP) 141-142, 147-148
spectrum of teaching styles (Mosston and Ashworth) 35, 110, 134
spinning 169
sport 5, 9, 14, 29, 32, 36, 75, 78, 81, 101, 103, 108-109, 119, 134, 143, 145, 147-148, 164-175, 183, 188; conceptualised 164; participation in 167
Sport Education 78, 81, 134

Sport England 165, 167, 175
sporting capital 168, 172
sports: careers 167-168, 174, 176; coaching 109, 172; hall 62, 90, 126
staffing 103, 107, 112, 114, 172
STEP principle (Space, Task, Equipment, People) 143
strategy 32, 38, 93, 106, 117-119, 124, 126, 156, 158-161, 179, 182-184; assessment 120; behaviour 93-94; cognitive 19; grouping 79-80; intervention 43, 98; learning 16, 18, 21-23, 25, 64, 66, 76, 121, 136
stress 154-155, 159; positive 154; toxic 154-155
strict 92, 95
structure(ed) 24, 153, 180, 184; assessment 43, 50, 105-106; learning 18, 20, 79, 104, 106, 133, 159, 184; lesson 21, 35, 78, 93, 127; of schools 9, 103; and sequence of activities 91, 121-122, 159; TARGET 76-83; thinking 120; see also assessment; learning; TARGET
subject knowledge of teachers 10, 39, 48, 61, 63, 66-68, 71, 186; see also knowledge
success criteria 18, 64-66, 71, 111-113; see also learning outcome
support 2-3, 7, 9-10, 16-22, 24-25, 27-28, 30, 35-36, 38-39, 43, 48, 50, 53-54, 58, 61, 69, 71, 76, 88-90, 93-94, 102, 104, 106-107, 109-114, 117-118, 120-122, 124-128, 132, 134, 136, 142-144, 149-150, 153-155, 157, 159-161, 179-188
surdophobia 143; see also deaf
sustainability 187-188
swimming 5, 34, 66, 90, 101-103, 105-107, 109-114; pool 90, 102, 105, 113
synthesis 119, 126

table tennis 157-158, 169
tactics 22, 32, 38, 67, 78, 126, 134
talent 9, 145
TARGET (Ames, 1992) 76, 80-83, 134
task 9-10, 13, 18, 29-30, 53, 61, 63, 65-67, 71, 76-77, 79-81, 91, 96, 110-111, 121, 133-134, 143, 149, 158, 170; see also activity, /task for learning
taught 1, 2, 8, 10, 12, 16, 24, 27, 30-32, 34-36, 40, 43, 46-48, 50-53, 57-58, 61, 65, 67-68, 84, 89-91, 96-97, 104, 106

teacher agency 88
teacher education 2-5, 65
teacher presence 95, 97
teacher-pupil relationship 63, 71, 76, 79-80, 91-98, 105-110, 112, 114, 132, 134, 146, 148-149, 157, 160
teaching: approach 16-17, 20, 35, 39, 71, 82, 92, 126, 131, 134, 136-137, 184-185; assistant (TA) 42, 148; didactic 29, 126, 134; effective 84, 131; point 126, 143; see also learning point; pedagogical
teamwork 49, 78, 134, 136-137
tennis 17, 22, 29, 34
termly reflections 137
test 111, 173
thinking 49, 117-120; activities 126; government 174; hard 121-122, 124; pupils 20, 35, 121-128; routines 120, 125; skills 19; teacher 2, 12, 21, 29, 67, 184; see also cognitive domain; knowledge
think, pair, share 121-122
3 B's (brain, biomechanics and behaviour) 111
three-step model for making change 180
time 2, 8, 16, 36, 38, 42, 47, 52, 68, 73, 76-77, 81, 86, 88, 91-93, 108, 114, 123-124, 127, 134, 147, 149-150, 153, 157, 159, 161, 164, 168-170, 172-174, 188; changing 25, 87, 158; feedback 68, 70-71, 158; learning 1, 19, 24, 29-30, 32-35, 38-39, 76, 85, 87, 104, 113, 122, 188; leisure 100, 167; spare 101; on task 18-19, 91, 127, 149; teacher planning 6, 10, 13, 35, 67, 70, 77, 92, 103, 111, 113, 145, 147, 172, 181-182, 184-188; of year 103, 149
timetable(ing) 103, 142, 174
traditional 5-6, 11, 13, 29, 30, 77-78, 160, 166-167, 169
traffic light cards/system 158-160
transition: between activities/lessons 71, 80, 88, 95; from primary to secondary school 27, 36, 38-40, 168, 174; see also fresh start approach; primary
transport 183
trauma 153-156, 159-161; -affected pupils 153, 156-157, 159, 161; -aware lens 156-157; -aware pedagogies 153, 157-158, 161; see also anxiety(ies)
trust: pupils 11, 94, 160; teachers 7

understanding *see* knowledge, skill and understanding
unit of work 8-9, 17, 24, 29-31, 33, 36, 39, 42-43, 47-52, 54, 56-58, 65, 80, 104-105, 107-108, 127, 147, 169; *see also* objective

value 50, 57, 79, 93, 101, 108-109, 114, 120, 125, 131, 133, 136-137, 142, 146, 150, 159, 172, 185; *see also* physical education
values 3, 9, 28, 31, 89, 103-104, 108-109, 132; *see also* belief(s)
verbal(ly) 7, 18-20, 23, 53, 61-62, 65, 87, 91, 93, 117, 121-122, 135, 154
video 150, 158
visual 20, 23, 65, 113, 145; nature of physical education 61, 68, 133; and verbal clues 19-20, 23, 93, 121

voice 7, 24, 96, 145, 182; pupil 7-8, 10-11, 13-14, 24, 75, 77, 81, 133, 146, 150, 159-160, 182
volleyball 34

walking 169
walkthru 179
warm strict approach (Lemov) 92, 95
warm-up 24-25, 28, 62, 69, 85-86, 95, 122
weather 87, 143, 149
well-being 101, 130, 133, 137, 154-155, 159, 168; *see also* health
workload 184

yoga 166, 169, 171
Youth Sport Trust (YST) 165, 170

zone of proximal development (Vygotsky) 121

For Product Safety Concerns and Information please contact our EU
representative GPSR@taylorandfrancis.com
Taylor & Francis Verlag GmbH, Kaufingerstraße 24, 80331 München, Germany

www.ingramcontent.com/pod-product-compliance
Lightning Source LLC
Chambersburg PA
CBHW060300240426
43661CB00060B/2843